LETTERS OF
RICHARD FOX
1486–1527

OXFORD UNIVERSITY PRESS
AMEN HOUSE, E.C. 4
LONDON EDINBURGH GLASGOW
LEIPZIG NEW YORK TORONTO
MELBOURNE CAPETOWN BOMBAY
CALCUTTA MADRAS SHANGHAI
HUMPHREY MILFORD
PUBLISHER TO THE
UNIVERSITY

RICHARD FOX
Bishop of Durham
From the portrait at Lambeth
By permission of the Archbishop of Canterbury

LETTERS OF
RICHARD FOX
1486–1527

Edited by
P. S. *and* H. M. ALLEN

OXFORD
AT THE CLARENDON PRESS
1929

PRINTED IN GREAT BRITAIN

FVNDATORI NOSTRO

PREFACE

ON 5 October 1528 died Richard Fox, bishop of Winchester, founder of Corpus Christi College in Oxford. For the observance of the centenary this collection of letters has been put together under pressure. There has not been time to work up its contents, and we cannot hope that it is complete. Formal acts and deeds have been set aside, though it has not always been easy to draw a line between them and letters; so too the letters which Fox wrote and received jointly with others. His letters to and from the Popes of his time have also been excluded, on the ground of their formality.

Our principal endeavour has been to arrange the letters in due order and to produce a correct text. In all cases but two (nos. 3 and 10) we have reached contemporary sources; either original MSS. or official copies, or else printed books. Except for one letter (no. 3) the whole book has been corrected in proof either with the originals or with rotographs.

When we began in February, we hoped that the volume might be completed by the 5th of October. But though the Printer and his staff wrought wonders, we could not do our part; and it seemed better to delay the book rather than let it lack that careful revision which is only possible in proof. Even so we are conscious of many shortcomings. But the observance of a centenary has its value, and a book which appears long *post festum* loses readers.

Our purpose in this undertaking has been, by means of his own words, to allow later generations to know more fully the Founder to whom under God this College owes its being and well-being. It may serve too, we hope, to supplement the full and interesting biography prefixed by Mr E. C. Batten in 1889 to his edition of Fox's Register for Bath and Wells; and further, to illustrate the life and occupations of an English bishop at that important period.

The part which Fox played in the history of England is not well known and evident, for a material reason. It is not without cause that the great series of State Papers begins with the reign of Henry VIII. Before that date 'note-paper' was not cheap nor abundant. Communication was no doubt largely oral; and apart from official and legal documents which needed the permanence of vellum, not much was committed to record. Hence Fox has to reply (nos. 57 and 81) that he has no books nor writing of what he had done at Calais or on the Border twenty or thirty years before. Even when letter-writing becomes usual and ample, it needed the genius of Wolsey to perceive the importance of preserving letters; and it is his correspondence which forms the basis of the State Papers in their opening volumes.

The early letters in this collection are drawn largely from official records, at Oxford and Cambridge, at York and Wells and Durham. The more interesting part of the book comes when—thanks to Wolsey and in a lesser degree to Claymond—Fox begins to speak for himself, vigorously personal and human. The Lambeth portrait by an unknown artist, which we are permitted to reproduce, shows him in his Durham days; his face careworn but his natural force still unabated.

In access to sources so widely scattered we have known many kind helpers: the Dean and the Town-Clerk of Wells, the Librarian at Lambeth, the Chapter-Clerk at Durham, the Masters of St. John's and Pembroke Colleges at Cambridge; at the Public Record Office Mr Hilary Jenkinson and Mr C. S. B. Buckland; at the British Museum Mr E. G. Millar, himself one of Fox's *filii*. Many of the letters from Corpus sources have been discovered by Dr and Mrs J. G. Milne, the former an *alumnus* of both Oldham and Fox; in the course of labours by which they are steadily reducing the College archives to order. Three undergraduates of Corpus also have taken part in copying the letters and verifying the proofs, Mr R. I. James, Mr J. A. C. Cruikshank, and Mr R. B. Melland. Thus has our task been made light.

P. S. A.   H. M. A.

C.C.C.

Crastino Animarum 1928

RICHARD FOX

THE Founder's life may be divided into three periods. Until he is forty hardly anything is known of him. Tradition ascribes his education to Boston grammar-school and to both Universities; but there is no documentary evidence in support. Sir Edmund Chambers suggests that he may be the 'Ricardus Fox, gramatice magister ac eciam baccularius' who was admitted into the gild of Holy Cross at Stratford on Avon in 1477–8; but apart from this there is nothing surely known of him till 1484–5, when Richard III sought to forbid his institution to the country vicarage of Stepney because he was abroad with 'our rebel, Henry ap Tudder'.

After Bosworth Fox rose rapidly to be one of Henry VII's most trusted advisers; bringing peace to England torn and exhausted with civil war, harassed by continual threats from without. Almost beyond hope it must have seemed at first: had Zimri peace who slew his master? Yet with wisdom and courage and patience the task was accomplished; and after thirty years of service he could lay it down.

Then he turned again to his spiritual calling. As minister of the Crown he had been fed from the King's bishoprics. Four sees he had ruled, Exeter, Bath and Wells, Durham, Winchester; but only the two last had known him. He had never sat under Stapeldon's soaring canopy at Exeter nor looked up at Bubwyth's kneeling figure on his beautiful tower at Wells. Thinking of all the souls 'whereof I never see the bodies', he obtained leave to withdraw from Court to his diocese; and spent his last twelve years in active promotion of godliness and good learning.

When these letters begin, the first period is over and its

mists dispelled. 'One thing had hit out aright'; the master with whom he had jeoparded his head, 'the King that was my maker', had taken the crown by force of arms from its hated holder, and Ropsley could no longer serve Mr Secretary 'for his kitchen'. But his affection for his Lincolnshire village has been discerned in a south porch built on to the church in 1486—no doubt his first thank-offering.

The two first letters show him as a target for aspirants to favour and bounty, and thereafter this frequently recurs; since largess could then be claimed from a bishop almost as much as the hospitality for stint of which Ayscough of Salisbury had been slain in 1450 on the downs above Edingdon. In 1492 Fox is sent by the King to Calais; where, while concluding peace with France, he makes good cheer with the captains and improves the harbour. At Wells the absent Bishop stands for his rights, on behalf of his church and his successors; though wishing to deal justly with the citizens. Durham he was obliged to see, for the Prince-bishop governing Norham Castle was in close touch with the Warden of the eastern marches at Berwick; and as a result perhaps of his fortnight's siege at Norham in 1497, he improved the water-supply of that strong hold, by pools and conduits which the Office of Works has lately exposed again to light amid lovely lawns. His grants to his mighty men involved him in discussions with the Durham Prior.

As his power grew, the Universities made claims upon him. At Cambridge he was elected Chancellor. Then Pembroke persuaded him to be its Master; as an executor of the Lady Margaret he could not but take interest in Fisher's work at St. John's; at King's he designed glass for the chapel windows. In Oxford he was officially Visitor to the Colleges of Wykeham and Waynflete; and to Balliol, at their request, he gave new statutes. But his principal service continued to the State, a merciful man, ensuing peace, far-sighted into the future. Peace abroad, with France, with Flanders, with the Scots, painfully forged in long negotiations; and at home peace, goodwill towards men, turning the hearts of the disobedient to the loyalty of the just, by trusting them.

When Henry's eighteen-year-old son succeeded, men wondered what the Lord Privy Seal would do 'to rule the King's grace'. Fox went on his way, keeping in the background, steadily serving the Crown; ready at need to equip transports and go with the army to France, to still riots or collect subsidies. A modern bishop would wonder to be called to such tasks. Before long Wolsey emerged, able, untiring, intensely efficient; and with one accord Warham and Fox retired before him, the former rejoicing like a prisoner to lose the chains of office, the latter pleading passionately for permission to put away worldly things.

The familiar portrait of Fox by Joannes Corvus shows a grim, gaunt old man, almost blind, leaning upon the top of his staff; one, seemingly, who has done with this world, and who, weary and austere, treads the common road to the gate of death. What an astonishing contrast is the man whom these vigorous letters reveal, their vigour almost increasing with the years! At 70, when men count their work mostly done, Fox retired from State service only to throw himself into new activities elsewhere. In his diocese he wrestles with the 'enormities of wicked men', and teaches his religious in their mother tongue, 'common, plain, round English, easy and ready to be understood'. Embracing the new classical education, he founds first a College in one of the Universities; then schools on his manor at Taunton and in his own home town of Grantham—this last but three days before his death.

His College in Oxford was to help men up the ladder that leadeth to heaven. At first it was to be for the young monks of St. Swithun's at Winchester, studying at the University; but Bishop Oldham of Exeter persuaded him that monkery had done its work, and that the future would need larger freedom in a world which was offering new opportunities for learning. With all his power he carried through the changed scheme; acquiring the site, ordering the building, choosing a President and approving Fellows (his poor kinsman to be the first), endowing them with lands in the counties round, sending their kitchen stuff from London by river, while yet they 'live upon his purse'; collecting splendid books for their library, reading their verses, anxious for their health 'if the death increase'.

In these letters he is seen in many lights. With political sagacity he knows the importance of commanding the seas if Calais is to hold; his warning that 'our manner is never to prepare for the war till our enemies be light at our doors' has often been heard since. In home affairs his influence is for mercy and moderation; and how great was his part in the government is shown in the appeals to him to return to Court, 'for all great matters be deferred to your coming'. His wisdom appears too in his readiness to learn from others. The purpose of his College is changed at the suggestion of a friend; how readily he had adopted the new ideas may be seen by comparing the medieval books at Auckland with those of the classical revival which he gathered for Corpus. For his first Fellows he accepts the advice of Claymond, and even gets round his own Statutes to accommodate his friend's choice already made.

The dignity of his relations with Wolsey is impressive. The future Cardinal makes his entry here at the age of 36, Fox's 'assured chaplain', full of 'humble commendations' to his 'singular good lord', 'half afraid that ye be displeased' and 'trusting that ye will take my doing in good part'; and Fox replies as a 'loving brother', careful for his friend's health in his 'outrageous charge and labour'. In a few years Wolsey has bounded up the ecclesiastical ladder, and soon as Legate wields authority supreme. Fox at once adopts the proper forms towards one whom he had lately commanded, and becomes the 'humble orator' of his 'very loving spiritual father'; but the good feeling between them is not changed, though the elder man sees the younger preferred before him. His solicitude continues. 'Never none had less help in his intolerable labours' than Wolsey; who is advised to lay apart all business from six o'clock in the evening, in order to secure needed rest. To give Wolsey a summer holiday Fox gladly places 'the poor lodging of Esher' at his disposal, bidding him 'use it always . . . right as your own'. When Wolsey writes him a letter with his own hand, Fox 'marvels when ye could find the time to write it yourself. . . . I will keep it and some time look upon it for my comfort'.

In their educational plans they co-operate. Wolsey sends lecturers to the University, and Fox has a College ready to receive them: hence the lustrous names of Clement and Lupset and Hervet, of Kratzer and Vives, are associated with Corpus, though they were never Fellows. Over Wolsey's successful 'Treaty of Universal Peace' Fox rejoices without reserve: 'None Englishman gladder than I. . . . It shall be the best deed that ever was done for the realm of England'.

Even when Wolsey, intoxicated with power, was riding the Church to its fall, Fox continues his old manner without a trace of resentment; his petitions against oppressive action still couched in the due forms of respect, as a 'daily bedeman' from his 'poor house at Marwell'. Nowhere does there appear any sign of that ill-will between them which is embodied in certain stories, and which needed no ingenuity to imagine.

Talis erat dum vixit. We who still live upon his purse may wonder with what trenchant thoughts that old man whom Corvus saw, with the dim eyes and 'as deaf as a stock', yet thinks of the house he builded so strong for the *filii non minus quam si vos genuissem, nobis charissimi*; and in his Chapel, where his prayer must have been *lucrari animas*, we may ask ourselves what use we are making of the opportunities he has given.

NOTE

THE Latin letters are printed on the principles we have adopted elsewhere; the English letters are more difficult. In Fox's day spelling was still unfixed; writing was the possession of a few, and even these wrote without either certainty or consistency. In consequence words often end with flourishes which should have significance, but which are so irregular as to give the impression that the writer intended nothing more by them than ornament; and they would, if accepted, create such grotesque forms that they must be neglected. Every letter of the alphabet which is clearly written we have tried to reproduce faithfully; those, too, which are represented by recognized signs. Abbreviations about which there is no doubt are given at length; in doubtful cases the letters added are shown in italics. In contractions where there might be doubt, e.g. between *ar* and *er* in *marvel*, the uncertain letter is printed in italic. The form w^t is printed as *with*, o^r and yor as *our* and *your*, M as Mr; in such words as *info^{r}m*, *hono^r* we have followed modern use. Final ę is shown as *is*, in italics. In the headings BM = British Museum, RO = Record Office.

It will be noticed that we have not followed Dr Fowler's preference for Foxe as the Founder's name. In the letters printed here his name never occurs; nor is it easy to find elsewhere. In his Winchester Registers both forms are found, Fox more commonly. In the contemporary inscriptions for the books, very numerous, presented by the Founder to the College Library, the name is always Fox: so too in the grant of arms to the Founder's kinsman, John Fox of Ropsley, in 1521.

Of the 91 letters in this collection, 37 are printed for the first time: nos. 1, 2, 10, 13, 15, 16, 22, 23, 25, 26, 29–34, 36, 46, 48, 51, 53, 54, 56, 60–63, 68, 69, 72, 74–78, 84, 91.

A further 27 hitherto have only appeared in epitome: nos. 38–45, 47, 49, 50, 52, 57–59, 65, 66, 71, 79–82, 85–87, 89, 90.

SOME DATES OF FOX'S LIFE

c. 1446–7.	Born at Ropsley, Lincs.
1484–5.	Vicar of Stepney. Richard III complains of the appointment in a letter of 22 Jan. 148⅘, because Fox is 'nunc et ad tunc existens cum magno rebelle nostro Henrico ap Tudder, nuncupato Comite Richmond'.
22 Aug. 1485.	Present at battle of Bosworth.
1485.	Royal Secretary.
24 Feb. 1487.	Keeper of the Privy Seal.
Feb. 1487.	Bishop of Exeter.
May 1492.	Bishop of Bath and Wells.
3 Nov. 1492.	Negotiates Peace of Étaples with the French.
1492–3.	Makes sluices for Calais harbour.
May 1494.	Bishop of Durham.
1496.	Concludes *Intercursus magnus* with the Flemings.
Aug. 1497.	Besieged in Norham Castle.
Nov. 1498.	Embassy to James IV at Melrose.
1499–1500.	Chancellor of Cambridge University.
Oct. 1501.	Bishop of Winchester.
1507.	Master of Pembroke College, Cambridge: till 1518.
May 1516.	Resigns Privy Seal.
5 March 1517.	Foundation of C.C.C.
1522.	Foundation of Taunton School.
2 Oct. 1528.	Foundation of Grantham School.
5 Oct. 1528.	Dies.

TABLE OF LETTERS

** Autograph throughout.   * By a secretary, autograph signature.
‡ Autograph rough-draft.   ‖ Contemporary copy.

Letters indented are written to Fox.

‖1. Gigli. Carmelianus..	⟨1486	London?⟩
‖2. Gigli. Cepi..	⟨1486	London?⟩
‖3. W. Todde. I comaunde..	31 March ⟨1487⟩	York
‖4. Oxford Univ^y. Etsi..	⟨c. 22 Aug. 1488	Oxford⟩
‖5. Gunthorp. I recommaunde..	5 Sept. ⟨1489⟩	Windsor
‖6. Wells Corp^n. We recommaunde..	22 April ⟨1493⟩	Wells
‖7. Wells Corp^n. Where as by..	27 April ⟨1493⟩	Warwick
*8. Darcy. I commaunde..	10 May ⟨1495⟩	London
**9. Darcy. I commaunde..	⟨1497?⟩	Norham
‖10. Dorrell. In my..	⟨1497?⟩	London
*11. Darcy. I commaunde..	29 July ⟨1500⟩	Isleworth
‡12. Darcy. After all..	24 Aug. ⟨1500⟩	Berwick
‖13. Castell. With all..	2 Jan. ⟨1501⟩	Durham
‖14. Castell. After my..	31 Jan. ⟨1501⟩	Coventry
‖15. Castell. In my..	14 Aug. ⟨1501⟩	Durham
‖16. Castell. As hertly..	6 Sept. ⟨1501⟩	Richmond
‖17. Oxford Univ^y. Tanta..	20 March ⟨1503	Oxford⟩
‖18. Oxford Univ^y. Studuimus..	⟨1503?	Oxford⟩
‖19. Frost. Please it..	14 Oct. ⟨1505⟩	?
‖20. Wells Chapter. In our..	4 Nov. ⟨1505⟩	Wells
21. Erasmus. E priscorum..	1 Jan. 1506	London
**22. Claymond. I haue..	21 July ⟨1506?⟩	Richmond
**23. Claymond. I commaunde..	24 Dec. ⟨1506?⟩	Southwark
‖24. Wells Chapter. In moost..	19 Jan. ⟨1507⟩	Wells
‖25. Pembroke Coll. Nemo est..	7 Aug. 1507	Cambridge
**26. Collingwood. Quum..	⟨1508?⟩	?
27. Albericus. Quum..	8 Aug. 1508	Paris
28. Albericus. Et hac spe..	1 Jan. 1509	Paris
‡29. Darcy. Thes novellis	⟨Aug. 1509	Craven⟩
‖30. Pembroke Coll. Quanquam..	24 Dec. 1509	Cambridge
‖31. Pembroke Coll. In our..	9 Feb. ⟨1510?⟩	Cambridge
‖32. Pembroke Coll. We po$u$r..	9 April ⟨1510?⟩	Cambridge

B

***33. Claymond. I thank..	19 Aug. ⟨1511⟩	Nottingham
***34. Commissary to Claymond. I wryt..	⟨1511	Oxford⟩
***35. Wolsey. Aftyr moste..	30 Sept. ⟨1511⟩	Windsor
‖36. Oxford Univᵞ. Oxoniensium..	21 Dec. ⟨1511⟩	Oxford
***37. Wolsey. Aftyr moste..	26 Aug. ⟨1512⟩	Farnham
***38. Dawtrey. Please it..	5 May ⟨1513	Southampton⟩
***39. Wolsey. Yistredaye..	11 May ⟨1513⟩	Portsmouth
***40. Wolsey. I am preuye..	15 May ⟨1513⟩	Southampton
***41. Wolsey. This afternone..	16 May ⟨1513⟩	Southampton
***42. Henry viii. This selve..	19 May ⟨1513⟩	Southampton
***43. Wolsey. This daye..	19 May ⟨1513⟩	Southampton
***44. Wolsey. Hidder be..	21 May ⟨1513⟩	Southampton
***45. Wolsey. Yistre night..	4 June ⟨1513⟩	Southampton
***46. Wolsey. I haue great..	8 June ⟨1513⟩	Southampton
***47. Wolsey. ..my departing..	17 April ⟨1514⟩	Esher
‡48. Darcy. After most..	18 May ⟨1514?⟩	Templehurst
*49. West. Humble..	6 April ⟨1515⟩	Paris
***50. Wolsey. After my..	20 July ⟨1515⟩	Esher
***51. Rawlyns. Aftur dew..	⟨1515–16?	Oxford⟩
***52. Wolsey. In my most..	23 April ⟨1516⟩	Winchester
***53. Barker. In the moste..	22 Dec. ⟨1516⟩	?
‡54. Claymond to I. Braynton. After..	17 Jan. ⟨1517⟩	Oxford
55. The Reader. For asmoche..	22 Jan. 1517	Winchester
*56. Claymond. I haue..	25 Feb. ⟨1517⟩	Esher
*57. Wolsey. After my..	30 April ⟨1517⟩	Winchester
*58. Wolsey. After my..	10 May ⟨1517⟩	St. Cross
*59. Wolsey. In my..	12 June ⟨1517⟩	St. Cross
‖60. C.C.C. Quum nos..	22 June 1517	Winchester
*61. Claymond. I commaund..	17 July ⟨1517⟩	Winchester
*62. Claymond. After hertie..	18 Aug. ⟨1517⟩	St. Cross
*63. Claymond. I commaunde..	25 Aug. ⟨1517⟩	St. Cross
***64. Linacre. Cum tu..	⟨c. Sept.　1517	London⟩
*65. Wolsey. In my moste..	15 Feb. ⟨1518⟩	St. Cross
*66. Wolsey. In my moste..	30 Oct. ⟨1518⟩	Marwell
*67. Wolsey. Ingentem..	2 Jan. ⟨1519⟩	Marwell
*68. Fitzjames. After..	12 Jan. ⟨1519⟩	Redlynch
*69. Bere. Bothe I..	13 Jan. ⟨1519⟩	Glastonbury
70. Erasmus. Reuerendissime..	25 May 1519	Antwerp
***71. Wolsey. After my..	14 Aug. ⟨1519⟩	Southwick
‖72. Oxford Univᵞ. Quod homines..	⟨1520	Oxford⟩

APPENDIXES

LIST OF PLATES

fo. A². At the deuoute and dylygent request of the ryght reuerende fader in God and lorde Rycharde, bysshop of Dureham and lorde pryueseall of Englonde, this lytell boke named Contemplacion of Synners is compyled and fynysshed.

The sayd blessyd fader in God, desyrynge gretly all vertue to encreace and vyce to be exyled, hath caused this booke to be enprynted, to the entente that oft redynge this booke may surely serche and truely knowe the state of his conscyence.

[Sum domini Richardi Smythe et amicorum : emptus anno 1501, precium vi^d. Liber septimus in Registro. Numerus 7, fol. 1.
Presented to the College by Nath. Ellison, Fellow, 1708 : Δ. 15. 13.]

[Presented to the College by Thomas Tanner, bp. of St. Asaph 1732–5 : Δ. 16. 7.]

The Contemplacion of Synners, 10 July 1499, title-page

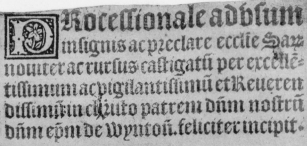

Processionale, 1508, title-page

‖ 1. FROM JOHN GIGLI

BM. Harl. MS. 336, f. 1 v⁰.   ⟨London?⟩
                                               ⟨Autumn 1486.⟩

[John de Giglis (†1498) was a native of Lucca who came to England in
Papal service. Already he was prebendary of Lincoln, and archdeacon of
London; and he made his way at Court so successfully as to receive a canonry
at Salisbury and, just before his death, the see of Worcester.

Early in the reign of Henry VII he addressed to John Russell, bishop of
Lincoln (1480–†1494) and Keeper of the Privy Seal, a short treatise *De
obseruantia quadragesimali*, discussing the question whether it were permissible
to take food more than once a day during Lent. Fox, now about 40, was
coming to the front: a man to be courted. Gigli employed another Italian
as intermediary to show him the treatise, in ms., and having secured the
inevitable compliment, presented an illuminated copy to Mr. Secretary;
according to the custom of the time (cf. no. 64) using the same book to catch
two patrons.

This brief letter is attached at the beginning, on a leaf of which the recto
is blank; and the offering was enlarged by the addition of some compli-
mentary verses composed by Gigli for the King's marriage, 18 Jan., and the
birth of Prince Arthur, 20 Sept. 1486. The preface to this second part (no. 2)
emphasizes Gigli's obligations to Fox. As the latter had not yet received the
privy seal (24 Feb. 1487), the presentation of the little volume, now in the
British Museum, can be dated with some precision.]

DOMINO RICARDO, REGIO SECRETARIO, IOHANNES DE GIGLIS,
   APOSTOLICVS SVBDIACONVS ET COLLECTOR, SALVTEM
   PLVRIMAM DICIT

Carmelianus¹ noster questiunculas quas iam dudum hortante
reueren⟨do⟩ in Christo patre, domino Episcopo Lincolniensi
De obseruatione quadragesimali scripseram, a te michi
remissas reddidit; tuoque nomine retulit te cupere vt
transcriptas alio volumine eas tibi restituerem. Feci igitur
quod iussisti, libellumque ad te mitto; munus certe pro tuis
erga me meritis exiguum, sed optimo ac beniuolentissimo
animo tibi donatum. Quod cum tanti faciendum erit quanti
pro summa doctrina ac sapiencia tua iudicaueris, vtcunque
censueris, animum, queso, non rem ipsam, diiudices, que,
vt dixi, exigua est.

¹ A native of Brescia, who came to England under Edward IV and
ensconced himself in the Court, as secretary and chaplain to Henry VII,
'luter' to Henry VIII, †1527.

Sed qui dat quod habet, satis dedisse videtur. Ergo tu litteras, cum nichil aliud possideam, qualescunque in me sint, tantum a me expectato. Ego autem, si me, vt facis, amaueris, plurimum te michi prestitisse fatebor. Vale et indies dignitate atque auctoritate augeare.

‖ 2. FROM GIGLI

BM. Harl. MS. 336, f. 67 vᵒ.   ⟨London?⟩
⟨1486.⟩

VENERANDO DOCTORI DOMINO RICARDO, SERENISSIMI DOMINI
     REGIS SECRETARIO, IO. DE GIGLIS, APOSTOLICVS SVB-
     DIACONVS ET COLLECTOR, S.P.D.

Cepi iamdudum scribere Epithalamium de nuptiis serenissimi Regis nostri: quod aduersa valitudine, que studia mea interea sepius interrupit, non tam cito vt cupiebam ac iustum erat, perficere potui. Accesserunt etiam indies occurrentia negotia quamplurima; quibus inpedientibus necesse fuit vt vltra quam voluerim ac debuerim, inceptum opus differrem. Quod ⟨cum⟩ tandem, prout otium nactus sum (neque enim id continuum fuit, sed frequentissime aut rei familiaris aut aliarum cura interpolatum) perfecerim, statui id tibi, cui omnia debeo, dicare. Ea est namque tuorum erga me meritorum vis, vt nisi ingratus esse velim, te et colere et diligere maxime debeam; tuque ea virtute ac doctrina etiam preditus es vt inter maximas ocupationes tuas, que te a latere clarissimi atque optimi Regis vix decedere sinunt, et litteris plurimum delecteris et litteratos atque ingeniosos homines summa beniuolentia complectaris: quo certe nichil potest esse magno viro preclarius, estque eo excellentius quo in summe fortune hominibus rarius id contingere videamus.

     Ea enim est temporum nostrorum infelicitas vt non solum indocti sed etiam hii qui se doctos appellari volunt, cum ad summos euecti sunt honores, litteras quarum[1] suffragio ad

---

¹ quorum *MS.*

eos peruenerunt, plurimi eorum aut respuunt penitus aut
certe parui facere incipiunt: satiricum[2] illud comprobantes,

> Didicit iam diues auarus
> Tantum admirari, tantum laudare disertos,
> Vt pueri Iunonis auem.

Non fecerunt sic summi illi atque immortales viri, quorum
memoriam post tot secula ad nos delatam summa veneratione
et admiratione colimus. Illi profecto quamuis summos
honores ac dignitates consecuti essent, ita tamen litteras
coluerunt vt earum[3] cognitione se nobiliores illustrioresque
crederent, maximumque ornamentum honorum suorum in
his consistere putarent. Nam vt Marcum Catonem consu-
larem et omnibus honoribus in Romana republica functum,
qui in vltima senectute Grecas litteras didicit, pretermittam,
atque etiam reliquos quamplurimos qui in summis honoribus
maximam operam ac studium litteris impenderunt; qualis
M. Cycero qui libera aduc ciuitate pater patrie est appellatus,
qualis Cesar, qualis Augustus fuere, summi imperatores et
orbis terrarum victores (in quibus an maior fuerit litterarum
aut rei militaris, an vero inperandi gloria, non facile quisquam
iudicauerit): Alexandrum Macedonem tacere non possum,
qui cum Darium potentissimum regem victoriis et armis
premeret, audiuissetque Aristotelem libros quosdam disci-
pline sue in publicum exhibuisse, litteris ad eum missis
factum reprehendit; intercetera inquiens, 'Quomodo ego
ceteris prestare potero, si que a te didici, ceteros etiam scire
contingat. Malo enim doctrina quam copiis, quibus omnis
supero reges, prestare'. Hic idem aliquando dixisse fertur
se plus Aristoteli quam Philippo patri debere; 'nam hic'
inquit 'vitam dedit et regnum, ille doctrina et moribus me
instruxit'. Idem ipse Alexander prelio ingenti cum Dario
commisso, cum victor euasisset atque inter predam omnium
Darii rerum pretiosissimam capsulam inuenisset, consuleret-
que quidnam in illa reponendum esset, aliis pecuniam, aliis
aurum, aliis gemmas, aliis pretiosissima queque ex regia

---

[2] Juv. 7. 30–32.   [3] eorum *MS*.

supellectile respondentibus, ille inquit, 'Nil horum, sed
tam pretiosa custodia solos Omeri libros dignos esse reor'.

Nostros quoque recensere iuuat. Anne Dauid rex electus
Dei litteras aut nesciuit aut contempsit? qui versu lirico
Psalterium illud, quo nichil suauius, nichil sanctius, nichil
eruditius excogitari potest, dicitur scripsisse. Anne filius
eius Salomon, sapientissimus et gloriosissimus rex, indoctus
fuit? qui Sapiencie Exclesiasten et Cantica Canticorum,
libros doctrine et sentenciarum grauitate plenos, quos
quotidie ferme in manibus habemus, summa cum elegantia
conscriptos reliquit. Quid denique sancti Apostoli ac reliqui
Christiani nominis principes? Cyprianum dico, Ambrosium,
Hyeronimum, Aurelium Augustinum, Hylarium Pictauen-
sem, Gregorium Ro. pontificem, alterum etiam Gregorium
Nasanzenum, Basilium, Ioannem Chrisostomum et similes:
qui non solum litteris claruerunt, sed etiam docuerunt
neminem sacerdotali fastigio dignum censendum nisi
doctum et litteris eruditum.

Tibi igitur, qui tua virtute ab optimo Principe [4] (apud
quem non minus auctoritate quam fide polles, et a quo pro
tuis meritis magna consecutus es, maioraque indies con-
sequeris) horum quos iam commemoraui immitatori, hos
versiculos nostros, a quibus non putamus te abhorrere,
dicauimus, precipue cum serenissimi Regis laudes plurimum
contineant: quibus non parum te delectari nequaquam
dubitauerim, eoque maxime quod in hiis nichil nisi Chri-
stianum, nichil a me fictum leges, ita vt preter metrum
poeticum nil esse censeas. Quare etiam minus curare
debeo eos qui poetica leuia atque indigna que a grauibus
viris scribantur, iudicare solent. Quid enim interest si
verum versu aut soluta oratione scribatur? Possem ego
grauissimos ac doctissimos viros, tam ex nostris quam ex
gentilitate, qui versu quamplura scripserunt, in medium
afferre: quorum auctoritate ineptias atque rusticitatem
istorum quorum ingenia nil suaue aut elegans contingere
possunt, facile contunderem.[5]

---

[4] This clause is unfinished.   [5] contonderem MS.

Sed cum his michi nunc non est contencio. 'At' inquient 'non decet ecclesiasticum hominem hymenea canere, nuptiarum pompas delitiasque describere: secularium potius quam ecclesiasticorum hanc curam esse.' Sane quasi matrimonia sancta prophana sint, et inter ecclesiastica sacramenta fides catholica ea non connumeret. Cum certe rectius meminisse deberent Saluatorem ac magistrum nostrum D. Ihesum nuptiarum in Cana Galilee conuiuio atque celebritati interfuisse, neque ea exorruisse, et presentia sua corporali non modo sed etiam admirabili diuinitatis potencia aqua in vinum versa decorasse. Reprehendent forte quod hec a nobis versu sint conscripta. Reprehendant igitur et sanctum Dauid, qui, vt paulo ante diximus, non heroico sed lirico, quod infimum est genus carminis, res diuinas scripsit. Cur denique, queso, non liceat ecclesiastico homini, in communi omnium gaudio, de ea re a qua populorum salus tantique regni tranquillitas ac quies sempiterna dependeat, gratulari? Iniquus certe est qui hoc non fecerit, sed longe iniquior qui ne fiat prohibere voluerit.

Tibi autem si hec nostra placebunt, non videbor michi frustra laborasse. Sane arbitrii tui erit, an regiis auribus, vel qui inpublicum exeat, dignum hunc nostrum laborem iudicaueris. Vale et me, vt facis, ama.

‖ 3. FROM WILLIAM TODDE

York City MS.   York.
                                                    31 March ⟨1487⟩.

[A contemporary copy among the archives of the City of York: printed by R. Davies in the *Proceedings of the Archaeological Institute* for 1846. Fox is now Bishop of Exeter and Keeper of the Privy Seal. On 31 March the town-council of York received report of a confession made by one James Taite, about the Earl of Lincoln's flight on 19 March to join the rebellion of Lambert Simnel. News of such moment is sent on at once to the King, through his secretary.

As we have not seen the MS., we reproduce Davies' text.]

TO THE RIGHT REVEREND FADER IN GOD AND MY RIGHT
    ESPECIALL AND SINGLER GOOD LORD THE BISSHOP OF
    EXCESTRE, THE KINGES SECRETARY

Right reverend fader in God and my right especiall and singler good lord,

I comaunde me unto you with hertly thaunkes for your good lordship shewed unto this poore Citie at all tymes, moost specially at such tymes as Maister John Haryngton hath be with you in mateirs of the same: for the which we have bondon us to your continuall service.

Sir, after certain reportes maid unto me concernyng langage shewed to be uttred by oone James Taite of this Citie, I calling unto me certain of my brether and othre of the Counsaill of this Citie have examined the matier this day, as apperith more at large in a bill herin cloused; be-suching you to shew the same unto the Kinges grace, and therupon undrestand furthre his pleasure therin (which and all othre I shal be glad and redye to accomplisshe to the uttermast of my powre during my life by Goddes grace), and that ye woll geve credence therin furthre unto this berer. And our Lord God preserve you, right reverend and my right especiall and singler good Lord in felicitie.

From York the last day of the month of Marche.

Youre moost humble servant and bedeman
William Todde,
maier of the citie of York.

‖ 4. FROM THE UNIVERSITY OF OXFORD

Register F, f. 158 vº. ⟨Oxford.⟩
Anstey p. 537. ⟨c. 22 August 1488.⟩

[From the University Letter-book, Register F, in the University Archives: printed by H. Anstey, *Epistolae Academicae Oxon.* ii, OHS, xxxvi, 1898. It follows letters to the Bishops of Ely and Winchester ⟨Alcock and Courtenay⟩ and others, also asking help for the restoration of the University Church, one dated 22 August; and it immediately precedes a document of 12 December, 4 Henry VII ⟨1488⟩.]

EPISCOPO EXONIENSI

Etsi nullo vnquam tempore nostra in te merita tanta fuerunt aut esse potuerunt, dignissime Presul, vt tua item in nos beneficia iure aliquo nostri superioris meriti vendicare possemus; in tua tamen benignitate atque humanitate magis quam in nostris meritis fisi,[1] non veremur aliquid abs tua paternitate exposcere; hoc ante omnia rogantes, vt hec nostra causa, vel petitio potius, grata tibi esse possit. Quam vt paucis nos expediamus, hanc esse scito.

Ecclesia beate Marie in Oxonia—ad quam non pauci totius orbisterrarum viri sepenumero accedunt, cum ad nonnullas omnium facultatum admissiones videndas, tum ad magistrorum inceptiones, que ibi honoratissime nostrorum maiorum instituto hactenus celebrate sunt—tanta temporis longitudine inueterata est, vt de ruina citissime futura (quod absit) multum suspecta esse videatur, idque in tempestatum turbinibus que ecclesiam illam instabilem vacillantemque reddunt. Quocirca nos hec nostra damna imminentia preuenire amouereque cupientes, nostrarum insuper facultatum[2] mediocritatem nobiscum considerantes, rogamus tuam paternitatem etiam atque etiam vt aliquid nobis tantam edificii curam subeuntibus tanto patre dignum concedatur. Nichil ad tui nominis immortalitatem nostreque Vniuersitatis decorem magis conducere posse arbitrabimur. Id volumus tibi persuadeas, dignissime Presul, qualiacunque tua in nos beneficia erunt, nos omnes tue prestantissime paternitatis amantissimos semper fore.

[1] sisi *MS.*   [2] facultatē *MS.*

‖ 5. TO JOHN GUNTHORP

Liber Ruber, Wells, ii. 26 v°.   Windsor.
Baildon p. 116.   5 September ⟨1489⟩.

[The second part of the Wells Chapter Minute-book known as *Liber Ruber*
contains contemporary copies of letters to and from Fox on matters in which
the Dean and Chapter were concerned: see also nos. 19, 20, 24. They have
been printed by W. P. Baildon in a report of the Historical MSS. Commission, 1914.

Gunthorp, well-known as a scholar, was Dean of Wells 1472–1498. He
had been Keeper of the Privy Seal to Richard iii in 1483, but was pardoned
by Henry vii. Like Fox he was often at Court, and was much employed
in diplomacy.]

Maister Dean,

I recommaunde me vnto you. And for such besinesse as
I haue now in hand about thies ambassadour*is*[1] and other
maters, I may not at this tyme write vnto you my mynde
at large in all maters.

Wherfore I hertly pray you that in suche thinges as I haue
commaunded my welbeloued seruaunt Edmunde Mill,[2]
this berer, to shew vnto you on my behalue, ye wille yeue
vnto hym therin asmoche feith and credence as if I spake
personally with you my selve.

And here after at better leiser I shal write vnto you my
selve. And thus I committe you vnto our Lord.

Writen at Windesore the v^te day of Septembre.

                                    your lovyng broder
                                    R. Exoniensis.

---

[1] from France, including the famous scholar Gaguin. They were now
returning: see W. Campbell, *Materials for the reign of Henry VII*, ii (1877),
p. 505.

[2] husband of Fox's niece, Anne. See no. 24.

‖ 6. FROM THE CORPORATION OF WELLS

Corporation Acts i, p. 180.   Wells.
                                    22 April ⟨1493⟩.

[Nos. 6, 7 are preserved in the Acts of the Corporation of Wells; copied in officially among the proceedings of 11 June 1493. Fox, translated to Bath and Wells in May 1492, had sent the Burgesses a 'bylle' with the following 'articles to be shewed to the Maister of the Towne and his brethern by the commaundemente of the Lorde of Bathe:

   fyrste, they holde theyme for the Kyng*is* burgeiss*is* and not myne;
   secundely, they vsurpe the makynge and amovynge of burgeyss*is*, where the auctoryte theroffe perteyneth oonly to me;
   thirdely, where my baylyf by myn auctoryte makith a burgeys, he can not be so accepted amonge the burgeiss*is*, vnto he eftesones be made by theym;
   fourthly, where by my customaryes whiche I haue seyne, the burgeiss*is* by custome of my maner shulde sewe vnto my mylles, the saide burgeiss*is* vsen strange mylles.' (Acts i, p. 178.)
They replied with a 'bille of ansuere' accompanied by this letter. Fox's rejoinder (no. 7) is moderate and conciliatory.]

LITTERA MISSA DOMINO EPISCOPO PER CIVITATEM WELLEN

Righte reuerende fader in God and our alther[1] synguler good lorde,

We recommaunde vs vnto your good lordeshipp in as humble wyse as we can or may suffice; mekely bysechynge your good lordeshipp not to yeue hasty credence to eny synystre informacion yeuen ayenste your saide Cyte. For vnfeynyngely ye shall fynde your saide Cyte of as good and feythfull disposicion toward your saide lordeship after ther power as they can thenke to be. For they thenke in ther mynd*is* that they haue as grete a treso*u*r of your lordeshipp as your saide Cyte had of eny lorde Bysshop at eny tyme sith your honorable see biganne there, your noble excellente wysedome and high discrecion remembred.

And, good lorde, we haue made ansuere, vnder your correccion accordynge to your commaundemente, vnto your bylle mynystred vnto vs in your bihalf by our good maister the Deane of Welles,[2] as symple wytted men withoute lernynge, praynge your good lordeship to accepte it with fauour and to take our entent*is*.

   [1] of all; also alder, aller.   [2] Gunthorp; see no. 5.

And, good lorde, we thenke in our mynd*is* that oon of
your articles concernyth the amovynge of Roberte Broke
from our company of burgeiss*is*. We sende you with our
bille of ansuere the copy of the acte made ayenste hym in
that bihalf. By whiche it apperith, yf he wolde haue payde
the summe of his dutye, he nedyd not to haue be amoved;
for he had receyued the saide money and xx^s more, as it was
sufficiently proued afore vs. And we deme that he sterith3
your lordeshipp for the mylles also, sayenge that he can not
bere the ferme in lesse than your burgeiss*is* be compelled &c.
Good lorde, if he and his felawe wull leve the mylles, we
shall fynde ij other to take it at the same rente, and fynde
good sufficiente suertees withoute suche maner of trowble.

Nomore, but almyghty Jhesu euer preserue your righte
honorable astate with encrece. From your Cite of Welles
the xxiith day of Apryll.

‖ 7. TO THE CORPORATION OF WELLS

Corporation Acts i, p. 180.   Warwick
                                         27 April ⟨1493⟩.

LITTERA DOMINI EPISCOPI DIRECTA AD CIVITATEM WELLEN

Where as by your writinge sente and delyuerd vnto me by
your comburgeys, this berer, ye desyre me to yeue non hasty
credence ayenste you, affermynge your disposicion vnto me
as good as ye can thynke: neighbours, I haue yeue you no
cause to thenke that I am lighte of credence, for I neyther
haue condempned ne sued nor vexed you vpon eny mater
that I haue not firste caused you to be spoke with and herde
at lengthe, nor yet at this tyme am I so disposed to do. How
be it ye make me suche answere vpon my firste article that
ye yeue me righte good cause to sue you; and as for your
good disposicion towarde me, I haue yeue you non other
cause, nor shall do withoute your grete deseruynge. I knowe
it is my dutye to loue and cherysshe you, and so wull I do, as
ferre as I may withoute doynge my churche and successours

3 moves, persuades to act.

wronge. I thenke also it shall be your wysedome to owe me
your good hert*is*; for I thanke God and the Kynge it lith
in my power to do you good and pleso*u*r: as so suerly I was
determyned to haue do, and namely in suche thyng*is* as
some of you haue sued in tyme passed.

I pray you, neighbours, sette aparte all wylfulnesse and
haultesse and be contente to lyve vnder the righte of the
Churche accordynge to your dutye; and or ye appoynte to
stryve with the same, loke vppon your neyghbours how
they haue spedde in case lyke. Loth wolde I be that all the
londe shulde mokke bothe you and me to stryve for your
name: how be it that it toucheth me moche nere than it
doth you, seynge that it cowde not be litull preiudice to me,
stondynge your lorde and lorde of the burgh, to suffre you
to calle yourselfe the Kyng*is* burgeiss*is*. Whiche claymeth
no thynge on you more then the dutye of your allegeaunce;
nor noughte ye haue nor holde of hym within that burgh,
nor of non of hys predecessours, excepte ye wull byde by
the graunte of Kynge John: whiche I trowe at lengthe ye
wull refuse.

Neighbours, your ansueres, specially vppon this article,
accordith to no lawe nor reason: nor they be not those
wherwith ye shulde desyre me to holde me contented, for
thei be neyther clere, certeyne, ne resonable. And therfore,
as ye wull that this matier take an ende bitwixte vs a parte,
by mutuell communicacion withoute fallynge to the sute in
the lawe, I pray you sende me assone as ye goodely may,
oon of the beste of your comburgeisses, and a man lerned
in the lawe, furnysshed with suche euydenc*is* as ye haue.
And or they departe fro me, I truste either partie shall better
knowe the righte of the other: wherwith of reason he
shulde holde hym contente. As so ye shall be sure I wull
furthwith do, when I shall be enfourmed that your righte is
better than myne; trustynge to fynde semblable disposicion
in you for your partye. And thus fare ye well.

At Warrewyke the xxvii[ti] day of Aprill.

* 8. TO THOMAS DARCY

RO. Anc^t. Corresp. 51, no. 169.   London.
Gairdner ii, p. 57.   10 May ⟨1495⟩.

[This group of letters, 8 to 14, is concerned with Fox's administration of the Border, as Prince-bishop of Durham: to which see he had been translated in May 1494. They were printed by J. Gairdner, *Letters and Papers of Richard III and Henry VII*, vol. ii, 1863 (Rolls Series). Gairdner supplies the year-date by supposing that the jousts mentioned were those held at the installation of Prince Henry as Knight of the Garter, 17 May 1495.

Thomas Darcy (1467–1537) was appointed Captain of Berwick in 1498 and was created a baron by Henry VII in 1505. But in the next reign he lost his head for treason after the Pilgrimage of Grace.]

Mastre Darcy,

I commaunde me hertely to you. And right sorie I amme that for suche desease as I haue had, I myght not be at the Courte now at the beynge thare of your seruaunte, to haue holpen hym forthward in suche matiers as ye had to doo thare aboute the Kinge at this tyme. How be yt I vndrestonde by hym he hath spedde right well therein. And thereof I amme verray gladde.

Asfor the matier of the Bordurs, I had rydded yt my selve ere he came hydre. And as for the oder matier concernynge the justes, my mynde ys, and so I will, for many consideracions whiche I shall shew vnto you at our next communicacion togedres, advise you and hertely requyre you that ye no thinge mynde that matier ne entende yourselve therevnto in eny wise; for I assure you neither my selve ne noone oder frende of yours here thinke that yt can be eny matier fittynge¹ or conuenyente for you. And therefore I thinke veraly yt shalbe beste that thare be as litle communicacion thereof for your partie as can in eny wise. And whan I shall next speke with the Kinge is grace, I doubte not soo for to ordre that matier toward*is* hym as he shalbe right well contented with the same way.

And thus hertely fare ye well at London the xth day of May.

                        Assuredly yours
To Mastre Darcy.   Ri. Duresme.

¹ sittynge *MS*.

** 9. TO DARCY

RO. Anc^t. Corresp. 51, no. 170.   Norham.
Gairdner ii, p. 74.   ⟨1497?⟩

[Contrary to his predecessors' custom Fox retained in his own hands the governorship of Norham Castle. During this period he improved the defences by constructing an inner moat; which has recently been laid bare by the Office of Works. Gairdner conjecturally assigns this letter to the year in which he was besieged there by James IV and successfully conducted the defence.]

Maistre Darcye,

I commaunde me to you. And wher ye write to me that ye haue receyved my lettres of different sentence, I wold the clerke that soo interpreted them to you, coude shewe me that difference. Ye be not the gentilman that I woll stond in termys with, but what soo euer ye write or saye to me, I shall take yt for the best, and as ye soo menyd; and soo I praye you doo myn.

And as I wrote byfor, your Vndreconstable stondeth accursed by cause he hathe not obeyde my monicion; and that shold he vndrestond, wer not for your sake. Neuerthelesse for the well of hys saule he can noo lesse doo then sue for absolucion; and I praye you cause hym forthwith to deliuer the goods at Bukton to the p*u*rser, whiche ys ther redye to receyve them and shall paye the bryn⟨ge⟩rs for theyr labours. I doubt not ye remembre that ye promised me at Twedmouthe that they shold forthwith haue be sent thyder.

And thus hertely fare ye well at Norham this Fridaye.

Assuredly yours
Ri. Duresme.

To Maistre Darcy.

D

‖ 10. FROM W. DORRELL

Corpus MS.   London.

⟨1497?⟩

[A xviie. copy in the 'Bursary Transcripts', vol. xxx, f. 69. The original is no doubt somewhere in the College Archives, but has not yet been found. Only a conjectural date is possible; seemingly at some time when Fox was in the North.]

My singular good lord,

In my hartiest manner I recomend me to your good lordship, and I send you in this boxe the acquittance sealed and enclosed by Mr Bray[1] and by me.

My lord, forget not my Lady of Clyfford.[2] Yesternight I had a letter from her to giue you thankes for hyr. I haue broken nowe the matter to the Kinges grace for hyr, and to my Ladyes grace; that nowe with your help I trust she shall come vp and attend vppon my Lady. And therefore sleight her not, for she sligteth nat you. Our Lord prosper you, and I shall euery day pray to our Lord God.

From Lundon this Saturday, redy to horse to ryde Northward.

Your chaplen

W. Dorrell.

To my singular good lord, my lord of Duresme.

---

[1] Possibly a kinsman of Sir Reginald Bray, who had been in the service of the Lady Margaret.

[2] Perhaps Anne St. John, who before 1493 married Henry Clifford (c. 1454–1523), the 'Shepherd Lord', from Bolton and Skipton in Yorkshire. She was a cousin of the King, and niece to the Lady Margaret; upon whom she was now to attend.

*11. TO DARCY

RO. Anc^t. Corresp. 51, no. 171.   Isleworth.
Gairdner ii, p. 84.   29 July ⟨1500⟩.

[On 6 July 1500 (not 1499, as Rymer) Darcy and Cholmeley were appointed, with others, commissioners for settlement of disputes upon the Border: see J. Bain, *Calendar of Documents relating to Scotland*, iv, 1888, p. 334. In 1501 Fox laid down the governance of Norham Castle, and with the King's consent made Cholmeley keeper.]

Maistre Darcie,

I commaunde me hertely to you. So yt is, sens your departure the Kinge hath seene the indenture of Sir Richarde Cholmeley, and at the sight thereof he hath founde dyuers and many thinges therein that he hath caused to be amended, booth in his indenture and yours. And after the forme that he hathe now caused theyme to be devised and made, I sende you with this berar the oone parte assigned with the Kinge is honde and sealed with his privey seale, and the oder parte therof to be in likewise assigned with your honde and sealed with your seale; and so assigned and sealed with your seale to sende yt vp hidre to me as shortely as ye can, and therewith also the oder indenture that ye had assigned and sealed with the privey seale byfore your departure: whereof I pray you faile not in any wise.

Yt hath plaised the Kinge is grace to ordeyne and make by his patente a Mastre Carpentar for that towne of Berwik; and to haue a seruaunte vnder hym in the rowme of a souldear at x marcs wagies and xx^{ti}s. rewarde. The maistre carpentar wilbe with you at Michaelmas or soone therevpon. I assure you he is righte cunnynge and diligente in his werkes; and whan so euer ye shall haue any werkes of your owne, if ye take his advise therein, he shall advauntage you large monee in the buldynge thereof, aswell in the devisinge as in the wirkenge of yt. His seruaunte alsoo ys a right gode werkeman; and yf ye thinke ye will in honde with your werkes shortely, ye may by thadvise of the said seruaunte make your provisione of tymbre and stoone now this somer. And thenne at the commynge of the saide maistre carpentar ye may goo in honde with your werkes assoone as ye will at your plais*ure*. I pray you hertely be gode maistre to theyme boothe for my sake; and that the seru*au*nte may haue his wagies withoute any appechemente sens the date of the said patente. And I doubte not they shall booth doo you that seruice in your werkes, that ye shalbe contente to be their gode maistre: thoughe I had not desired you therfor, yit neuertheles I pray you eftsoones be the better maistre to theyme for my sake.

And thus hertely fare ye well at Istelworthe the xxix^th day of July.

Assuredly yours
To Maistre Darcie.   Ri. Duresme.

‡ 12. FROM DARCY

RO. Anc^t. Corresp. 51, no. 155.   Berwick.
Gairdner ii, p. 283.   24 August ⟨1500⟩.

Right reuerent fadir in Gode and my syngler goyd lord,

After all dew recomendacions, plesethe your lordschip to be aduerticyd. Os I cam in Yorkschir taward*is* Berwike the most party of gentilmen of the same, os Sir John Hastyng*is* &c, held me cumpany, and so I taryd in huntyng with tham a fortnyght. My lord of Carlell*is* folk*is*, os thay sayd, wass warned I schold hav no game in the forest of Galtrice,[1] and so I spared for the tym, havyng specyall tr*u*st oppon your lordschip in that matter. And forther, off newes her at Berwike, os I can concev, the Scott*is* hath moch off theyr desire, and sewre I am thay make soich avant.[2] And os for owre parte, haithe os yit very smale redress. Os all at large I am sewre the Kyng*is* grace and your lordschip schalle knaw herafter, when the day off diot takethe eynd: wich I dem wolle not be this moneth, foryit ther is mone matter*is* far owet of frame.

---

[1] outside the walls of York, and stretching northwards 15 ms.
[2] such a vaunt.

At my cumynge hom into Yorkschir I send Sir Rich*ard*
Chomlay the Kyng*is* letter, wich was derected to hym and
me for the sendyng vp of the hayr of Fenwik*is*; and a letter
fro me to knaw wait tym wher best to sit oppon comission
for the said Fenwik etc. And he oppon the same, withowte
knawlege to me, rode from Berwike to Newcastell, and in
his way hom toke the said Fenwike with hym: noo knawlege
giffyn to Roger Fenwike, wich I thinke me wold at first hav
deliuerd hym˙assewred to hym or me, os I wen, at the first
request. Bo⟨t⟩ Sir Rich*ard* did this for his thank, os I suppos.

Bot verely, my lord, I met Roger at Morpethe the most
sore man that myght be, feryng that your lordschip hade be
set any thyng aganste hym or preve to this matter; bot he
wass the most glad man that I hade seyn, after I schewed
hym of a seuerte the contrare, and ho⟨w / ye weyr his
speciall goyd lord and myn bothe.

M⟨y / lord, both I and my lady wass in all your new
wark*is*[3] at Doresme, and veryly thay are of the most goyd⟨ly
and best cast that I hav seyn, after my poyr m⟨ynd; / and
in especyall your kechyn passethe all oth⟨er⟩. / We hade
huntyd ther with Mr Chancler ⟨and / Mr Tres*u*rer, bot in
goyde faithe we and owr serua⟨unt*is* / and dog*is* wass soo
were, we myght not. And therfor I was⟨s / so bold oppon
your lordschip that I had of your veneson bothe with me
and sen⟨t / to Berwike.

At my cumyng to Berwike I offerd to ⟨Mr / Doctor to go
with hym and help to eynd all matt⟨er*is* / concernyg the
comission. His answer wass that Sir Rich*ard* Chomlay and
he with otherst schold eynd that t⟨hey / had begoyn, and
for caws that Sir Rich*ard* and I m⟨yght / not both be forthe,
I was best content to tare. My lord, os your lordschip
semethe best, helpe now Roger Fenwike; for of faithe all
the con⟨tre / saith this matter lithe moch oppon his well,
and in my mynd ye can not hav a trewer serua*u*nt.

A litill matter of vnkyndnes happed betwixst my cossyn

---

3 Darcy wrote first *logyngis*. Fox's buttery hatch in Durham Castle is
dated 1499.

Gray and me, off wich your lordschip schall hav the certante
with my serua⟨n⟩t: bot not os no complaynt of hym, for
I feyr ye schall hav enowe. Howbeit I trust your goyd
auertisment*is* schall do hym goyd, and cawse the Kynge to
⟨be⟩ better served with hym.

And after os my mynd and service / i⟩s and schalbe to
your lordschip, so I beseich yow to be my goyd lord; and
I schall besech the Trenete to preserve your lordschip frome
all aduersites.

My lord, the debites calle vere sore oppon me for ther
feys. I beseich your lordschip be meyn therin (and for
Galtrice specially),[4] os ye seme goyd, and tak no disples*ure*
that I pot yow to so moch payn.

Writtyn at Berwike the xxiiij^{the} day of Awgost.

‖ 13. FROM THOMAS CASTELL

Durham Register, f. 123.   Durham.
                                    2 January ⟨1501⟩.

[Nos. 13 to 16 are consecutive in the small Register of the Priors of Durham,
now in the Library of the Dean and Chapter. We are indebted to Mr K. C.
Bayley, Chapter Clerk, for the information that they come between documents
of Sept. 1500 and April 1502: so that the year-date can be assigned with
certainty.

Thomas Castell was prior of Durham from 1494 to 1519. The grants to
which he demurs in this letter were made by Fox on 19 Aug. 1498 to Thomas
Garth and John Hamerton for their strenuous defence of Norham during
the siege a year before.]

My moste especiall and singler goode lord,

With all dew reuerance and obedience I recomend me
vnto your good lordship. And where your lordshyp hath
here to fore, like as your lordship hath done in your last
letters, wryttyn to me and desyryd diuers and, as my
brethern and I thynk*is*, veray many confirmacions made and
to be maide vpon your grauntez, and sum that your lordship*is* predecessors, as ferr as I can fynd, hath nozt before
grauntid, I beseche you, my lord, to be so good and
graciouse lord to my brethern and me, as to spare and be

---

4 Interlined, but struck out.

content that the confirmacions your lordship lately wrote
fore, procede noght, bod that your seruauntz may be content onely with your lordship*is* awne graunt*is*; and allso
that ye will be so good to vs as to spare desire of any mo
confirmacions here after. And thus doyng your lordshypp
byndith my brethern and me, besid*is* all our dewtye, to aw[1]
and offyr vp for your lordship our speciall prayers to
almyghty God: to whos blissid kepyng I euer commend
your gode lordshyp.

At Durham the secund day of Januarye.

> By your humble chapeleyn and orator
> Thomas prior of Duresme.

|| 14. TO CASTELL

Durham Register, f. 123.   Coventry.
Raine p. 289.   31 January ⟨1501⟩.

[Printed by J. Raine, *History* .. *of North Durham*, 1852: 'a mild, gentlemanly
letter', he calls it.]

Entierly welbelovyd broder,

After my hertye recommendacion, wher as I have writtyn
to yow diuers tymez and many for the confirmacion vnder
your covent seal of certeyn grauntz that I have maid to my
seruauntz, for such seruice as thei have doo to me and that
my chirche, as well in werr as in pease, and specialy in the
Castell of Norham, as well in the tyme of the siege[1] as before
and after, als long as the werre endured; I have vnderstond
that ye make greate stoppage and difficulte with long delayes
in the said confirmacyon making. Wher of I can nozt a
littell marveill, seyng that I make nozt theis grauntz bod for
good and resonable causes and great seruice, done more for
the defence of the land of my chirch then to me. Allso I
make no grauntz bod old and vsuell, and such as my predecessors have made byfore me in their dayes.

And I am nozt yhit goyng fro yow. Ye do me great
wrong thus to ymagyn vpon my departyng fro yow. Itt is

---

[1] owe.   [1] in Aug. 1497.

a tokyn that ye holde yow wery of me; wher of your selve to wittnesse I neuer gave yow causes. I think I have be as kynde and lovyng to yow and yours as euer was bysshop of that see to any of your predecessours, and veraly ye have be the same to me; and therfor I marveil greatly where of thys estraungesnes growith. I pray yow eftsones make no difficulties in the confirmacions of any of the grauntz that I have made or her after shall make, as ye wol the continuaunce of my old love and fauour to yow.

Att Couentre the last day of Januarye.

Your loving broder
Ri. Duresme.

|| 15. FROM CASTELL

Durham Register, f. 123 v⁰.   Durham.

14 August ⟨1501⟩.

My especialest good lorde,

In my moste humbly and dew maner I recommend me vnto your good lordship. And wher as your lordship wrote vnto me lately for the confirmacion of the bailifwike of Derlyngton vnto William Bettis, my lord, ther is ane office passid afore vnto maister Hadoke of the office of Derlyngton. And, my lorde, I have made serche within our recordez of the same office, and I can find no precedent ther of that euer your myter was chargid with eny suche fee. And, my lord, I have att your formare commaundmentt confermyd your graunt both of Gatesheued and Aukland, wher as I can nozt perceve that euer eny such grauntz was made aforetyme, either be your recordez or ours.

My lord, I am right well content to perform your commandment or pleasour in euery behalf to the vttermast of my power. And zhit, my lord, please itt your good lordship to call vn to your remembraunce what your lordship wold lay and say vn to me in case like, if I shuld charge your myter with such fee as neuer was afore in your recordez nor in ours. Your lordship myght be myscontent with all.

My lord, how your successor wol lay suche mater vn to my
bretherne charge and myne, my lord, I knaw not; bod ay,
my lorde, I dowt the worst. And, my lorde, secular people
will say that, and if your beidmen, my brethern, and I con-
ferm office or thing that your lordship or your successor is
nozt content with ilk, then, my lord, the party wol say that
thei woll assh[1] there fee of me and my brethern: which is
agayns all ryght and good conscience. My lord, I fere not,
ne yhit my brethern neythir, thys wanton sayng; for, my
lord, itt stondith neither with law ne conscience.

My lord, I besech your lordship to take with me no dis-
pleasour, thof[2] I shew your lordship my poore mynd; for,
my lord, in tyme of neide or cause of compleyntt I have
none othir comforth of refuge and counsell bod onely in
your good lordship. And I besech the same so to vse me
and take me, and euyr, my lord, to shew your good mynde
and lordship, that wol help in trobill or besynes in tyme of
neid. And thus to the blissid Trinites kepyng I euer comend
your good lordship.

Fro Duresme the xiiij[th] day of August with the hand of
your humblest chapeleyn and oratour

Thomas prior of Duresme.

‖ 16. TO CASTELL

Durham Register, f. 124.   Richmond.
                                6 September ⟨1501⟩.

Ryght intierly welbelovid broder,

As hertly as I can I commaund me to yow. And well
I remembre that emonges oder I wrote vn to yow for the
confirmacion of William Bettis patente of the bailifwik of
Derlyngton. And be your last writing vnto me I conceve
ye make a difficultie ther in for two causes. One is that my
seruaunt Thomas Haidok hath one office of Dernton; the
secund is that ye can nozt in your registre fynd eny grauntz
of the said office with such a fee. Trouth itt is Thomas

---

[1] ask.   [2] though.

E

Haidok hath a graunt; bod that is of the custodye of the maner and nozt of the bailifwik. And where the burghes have bene commonly, and for the moste partie befor my tyme, latten to ferme, which was thoccasion of evil justice and moch extorcion and hinderaunce of the lord*is* proufit*is* both at Derlyngton, Aukland and Gatisheued, I have in my tyme caused all the said burghes to be occupied by way of approumente. And so I have graunted this office of Derlyngton to William Bett*is* by way of emproument: which, I make yow soore, hath bene to me, and shall be to my successor, moche more proufitable then to lett or putt them to ferme. Doubte yow not, broder, I shall no thyng desyre you to doo that shall be hurt or preiudice to the mitre of that my churche. And therefore eftsones, I pray yow as hertely as I can, latt the said William have my said graunt of thoffice of Derlington confermyd.

I have written to my Chaunceler to spede the p*a*rdon that ye desire. Call vpon hym for the spede ther of. And as for any money for your oder graunt, if the money shal come owt of your purs, surely I woll none, though itt wer worth a M[1] li. And therfor care ye nozt for that mater.

Send me a copy of the confirmacion that ye wold have for the custodie of such landez as be holden of you by knyghte seruice, and I shall look vpon itt. I wold full fayn do for you in all maters nozt hurtfull to my successors. I have euer doubtid of that mater, and so I doo yhitt. Ye can not clame the custodie of any landez bod such as be holden of you by knyghte seruice. For of the other neither yow nor I can have the custodie, except thei come by meynes of oder that be holden by knyghte seruice as by the prerogayve. Send me the said copie, and I shall see itt, and therupon doo that I may lawfully. And as for new eleccion, ye shall nozt nede to send this quarter of a yere. And thus hertely fare ye right as I wold do my selve.

Att Richemount the sext day of Septembre.

With the hand of your loving broder

Ri. Duresme.

|| 17. FROM THE UNIVERSITY OF OXFORD

Register F, f. 189.   ⟨Oxford.⟩
Anstey p. 683.   20 March ⟨150⅔⟩.

[From the same Register as no. 4. Following a series of letters, to the Lady
Margaret, the King, and the Bishops of London and Rochester ⟨Warham
and Fitzjames⟩, all concerned with gifts to the University and all with the
same month-date. From the sequence of the Register the year-date can be
assigned with certainty. Fox had been translated to Winchester in the
autumn of 1501.]

AD DOMINVM RICARDVM WINTONIENSEM EPISCOPVM.
REVERENDO IN CHRISTO PATRI, ETC.

Tanta nostram in rempublicam tua semper fuere merita, tot
sudores, colendissime Pater, vt nisi tua singularis natura satis
supraque satis nobis spectata foret, nichil vnquam amplius
petere contenderemus quod tantam sanctitatem tuam ad
nouos vsquam inuitaret labores. Sed liberale tuum ingenium, cunctis prodesse semper vigilantissimum, non mediocriter suadet et hortatur, in hiis presertim que publice vtilitati
et saluti inseruiunt, tam reuerendum Patrem feliciter pulsare.

Duo igitur sunt, sanctissime Pater, que vehementius obsecramus: primum vt inuictissimo Principi nostro, apud quem
primus et coniunctissimus merito euasisti, significes nos suis
votis maximo cum gratiarum cumilo libentissime applau-
sisse, suaque exemplaria tuam per dignitatem ad nos trans-
missa nostro publico in senatu vnanimi omnium consensu
iam comprobata esse.

Id vero est quod secundo in loco obnixius imploramus;
vt tua dignitas, in qua plurimum spei semper collocauimus,
serenissimam maiestatem regiam Oxoniensibus mansuetis-
simam semper conserues.

Age igitur, clementissime Pater, vt quam nobis de te
expectationem huc loci egregie concitasti, hanc in hiis per-
pulchris huius nostri gymnasii agendis negociis non minori
diligentia confirmes et ostendas. Qua in re non tam vtilitati
nostre quam glorie tue consuluisse[1] videberis. Interim preces

---

[1] consiluisse MS.

nostras² et officia reuerendissime paternitati tue perpetuo
pollicemur et vouemus. Et ita in Christo valeas, colendissime Presul, bonarum artium fons vberrime.

Dat*um* Marcii die xx°.

‖ 18. FROM THE UNIVERSITY OF OXFORD

Register F, f. 189 v°.   ⟨Oxford.⟩
Anstey p. 686.   ⟨1503?⟩

[From the same Register as nos. 4, 17: the last item in the book, following
a document dated 11 May, 18 Henry VII ⟨1503⟩.]

REVERENDO IN CHRISTO PATRI DOMINO RICARDO
DEI GRATIA WINTONIENSI EPISCOPO ETC.

Studuimus non mediocriter, clementissime Presul, et semper
maxime optauimus, nos illum videre diem quo tuam dignitatem ad ocia potius quam labores, ad requiem magis quam
turbam, aliquando inuitaremus. Verum (quod sine dolore
non referimus) fortune mutabilitas id non patitur, presertim
hiis in diebus, quibus nostra Vniuersitas illud in periculum
pene adducta est, cui si non dabitur frenum, plane aperte
videre licet quod non paruam inde est reportatura iacturam.

Omni igitur spe salutis penitus orbata foret nostra respub-
lica, si eum te patronum sepissime experta non fuisset, qui
suas res cum priuatas tum publicas diligentius semper cura-
uerat. Nam Oxoniensis Achademia, que bonis litteris,
magna gloria, preclaris virtutibus olim floruerat, acerbis
cladibus iam plena, sic credimus, funditus deperiisset, si
cumilatus ille tue beneuolentie ardor quem in eandem semper gessisti, mox tuis cum litteris non occurrisset. Quibus
reuera nihil mandaueras, quod pro viribus huc loci non
aggressi sumus. Creberrimis namque instamus contionibus,
vt hii tam infesti pacis perturbatores dignas aliquando dent
in corpore penas: quorum vero quosdam vinctos in carceri-
bus coniecimus. Quosdam enim exules nostraque a priuata
patria pulsos esse promulgauimus; sed, quod dolenter scri-
bimus, in finitimis iuxta nos opudulis latitant, licentiusque

² nr̄a *MS.*

quam par est sua temeraria vtentes audatia, Oxoniensibus
stomachantur, senatorum sanguini, vt accepimus, se auden-
tius insultaturos comminantur, et mala malis superaddere
nituntur.

Quare te maxime obtestamur per prudentiam qua nulli
cedis, per charitatem qua cunctos exuperas, perque illum
amorem quem tum re tum consilio nostre Vniuersitati
semper sanctissime professus es, vt modum tecum excogites,
quo eorum tam nefarii conatus tandem opprimantur, no-
strisque a confiniis longius propulsentur; profitemurque
omnes nihil hic loci esse quod tue a nobis tam benemerite
clementie dedicatum paratissimumque non sit.

Vale.

‖ 19. FROM WILLIAM FROST

Liber Ruber, Wells, ii. 120.   ?
Baildon p. 188.   14 October ⟨1505⟩.

[Nos. 19, 20, 24 come, like No. 5, from the Chapter minute-book at Wells.
They are about a mill erected by the Chapter on the Tone at Ham, in their
manor of North Curry; which, though profitable to them, caused floods and
hindered navigation between Taunton and Bridgwater. The Prior of Monta-
cute also was concerned, because he had erected a 'bay of stone'. Fox's
intervention was on behalf of his tenants in the manor of Taunton Dean.

Frost was the steward of his bishopric, 'a sadde, substanciall, feithfull man,
and well lerned in the lawe' (no. 66); upon whom he relied. At his death,
between 6 and 30 July 1529, Frost left the manor of Owslebury, near
Marwell, to increase the endowment of his master's College. His name is still
commemorated among its principal benefactors.

In 1507 as the result of a commission the Chapter was obliged to remove
its buildings.]

Please it your good lordship to vnderstand that accordyng
to your commaundement Maistre Thesaurer, Mr Mylle[1] and
I, at our late beyng at Tanton, mette with my lord Tinens,[2]
Mr Symound*is* and Doctor Tomyowe of the churche of
Wellys, and the Stuard of the Prior of Mountacu at Ham-
mylle. And ther was with vs of your towne of Taunton Sir

[1] See no. 5.
[2] Thos. Cornish, suffragan bp. of Bath and Wells, with title from the
island of Tenos in the Aegean.

Thomas Greynefeld, Maister Newton and meny of the moost honest merchaunt*is* and tenaunt*is* of your[3] towne and lordship of Taunton; and also diuerse of the Abbot of Glastonbury tenaunt*is*, of the forsaid Prior of Mountacu tenaunt*is*, which be sore greved and annoyed by occasion of the saide mylle: as your lordship may perceyue by the copyes of the bill*is* of complaynte above said, which were putt vnto vs before we mette at the said myll.

All which parties complaynaunt*is* were ther with vs and shewed vnto theym of Well*is* there greves as appereth in ther said bill*is*, and offered theym self to be sworne vpon a boke that there complaynt*is* were true &c. Wherupon we viewede the grounde, the water and the floode yat*is* and bay[4] of stone rered by the said Prior, which be the cause of the said nusanz. And the forsaid persounes of Wellys cowde not denye but that your tenaunt*is* of Taunton can haue no passage with bot*is* by that myll to Brigewater as they ought to haue, nor in maner denye but by the makyng of the said bay of stone and floode yat*is*, the water, when flood*is* bee, ouer flowen the grounde adioynyng.

And after long communicacion betwene vs of the premisses hadd, they of the churche of Well*is* appoynted with vs to commen with me of their company, and before Alhalowetyde to send writyng vnto your lordshipp what direccion they will take for reformacion of the nusanses forsaid: which wilbe, as in your mynd*is*, full hard to doo, oonlesse the said baye and floode yat*is* be vtterly take awaye and amoued from the growne[5] of the water. And if by the meanes of your good lordship it may be soo doon, ye shalnot oonly doo grete good to your owne tenaunt*is* but also vnto meny other, and haue their prayers for euer. For vndoubtedly, and this be not reformed, ye shal haue grete losse in Ruysshton[6]: for their bee nowe dyuerse tenement*is* liyng in your haund*is*, and no man will fyne[7] for theym &c.

---

3 As bp. of Winchester, Fox was lord of the manor of Taunton Dean.
4 dam.   5 groyne.
6 between Ham and Taunton.   7 pay rent.

And also euer sithe this Hammyll was made, ye haue lost
ij^s rent of a were that ye hadde ther &c.

And as touchyng the manor of Stanelynche[8] in the lordship of Dounton, which was Henry Higons, my lord, at our
beyng ther ther was Elisabeth that was the said Higons wyfe,
and shewed vnto vs a dede endented,[9] beryng date the vth
yer of King Edward the iiijth: by the which Richard bisshop
of Sarum, John Swynforde[10] clerk, and other, lett the said
manor and other landis vnto Sir Roger Tocotis for terme
of vij yeres, the remandre therof after the saide terme vnto
Henry Higons and to Elisabeth his wyfe and to the heyres
of the body of the said Henry &c.

She shewed no dede of feoffment by the which the forsaid
Bisshop of Sarum and other were enfeoffed in the said
manor, nor she shewed no lettre of attorney that the said
Bisshop and his coofeoffees, shuld make to delyuer season of
the said manor to the said Sir Roger Tocotis &c. But she
shewed a lettre of attorney that Sir Roger Tocotis made to
oon Gregory Thornton and Thomas Thornton to receyue
for hym season of the said manor &c. I haue the copy of
the said dede and lettre of attorney, and also I haue in
writyng the sayng of suche witnesses as she brought befor
maystre Tresourer and me to testifie of the lyuerey and
season of the said manor: which prove not directly the
lyuerey and season therof, as your lordship shal more
playnly see at my commyng to your good lordship, which
I truste shalbe sone after Alholowtyde.

I haue apoyntede with Maistres Higons that if she haue
eny other writyng concernyng the premisses, she to send it
to London to hir counsayll, and they to awayte vpon your
lordshipp to shewe it. And as ⟨for⟩[11] the occupacion of the
said manor, I haue taken a direccion betwen Maister Wod-
shawe and the fermor therin, as your lordship writte vnto
me to doo.

And as for eny other grete matiers, we hadde not yet

---

[8] Standlinch, s. of Salisbury, near Downton.   [9] entented MS.
[10] Suyfor??e MS.   [11] the line of the MS. ends at as.

hidderto, as knoweth our lord God: who preserue your good lordship in body and helth long to endure.

Scribeled the xiiijth day of Octobre with the hande of your seruaunt

William Frost.

‖ 20. FROM THE CHAPTER OF WELLS

Liber Ruber, Wells, ii. 114 v°.   Wells.
Baildon p. 185.   4 November ⟨1505⟩.

Right reuerende fader in God and to vs moste singuler gode lord,

In our mooste humble wyse we recommennde vs. Please it the same to vnderstande howe that dyuerse of the brethern of our Chapitre werr with your officers at our myll of North-cory, and ther hard the greves and complayntis which your tenauntis made. And wher as it is thought by theym that our said myll shuldbe the occasion of the grete floodis and drownyng of the medews, which in our myndis is not thought possible to be, neuerthelesse to haue you good lord vnto vs as ye haue euer been, and also to cesse theyr clamours, we shalbe contented to lese a quarter rent, and for that tyme to cause the floodyatis of our said myll to be pulled vp, so that the water shal haue his full course: wherby it shal apper herafter whether that our myll be the occasion of eny suche flodis and drownyng of the medews.

And as for bote passage, your said officers knowe right well that in all the somer season the water is so lowe, and so meny shelpes[1] and bayes in the ryver betwene our myll and Taunton that it is not possible to convey eny bote that way. And in the wynter season the medewes be so filled and replenysshed with water that the bootis may go ouer at euery place, so that they shal not be lett by the myll.

My lord, these thyngis considered, we truste that ye wull contynue as good lord nowe vnto vs as ye haue been beforn

---

[1] sandbanks.

tyme. And thus the holy Trinite contynue you accordyng
to your noble desires.

From Well*is* iiijth day of Nouembre
By your dayly orators
the brethern of the Chapitre of Well*is*.
To the right reuerend fader in God and our singuler good
lord, my lord of Wynchestre.

21. FROM ERASMUS

Luciani Opuscula, 1506, tit. v^o.　　　　　London.
Erasmus, Ep. 187.　　　　　　　　　1 January 1506.

[The preface to a translation from Lucian, presented to Fox, no doubt in ms.,
to provoke his bounty: first printed in Paris by Badius, 13 Nov. 1506.

In 1506 Erasmus was still little more than 'vng religieux de l'ordre de
Saint Augustin', of no reputation. He was on his second visit to England,
and was just completing under Colet's patronage at St. Paul's the first great
work of his life, a new translation of the New Testament into Latin; tran-
scribed 1506–9, but not printed till 1516. Maintenance was necessary, to give
him leisure.

In Oct. 1511 he again courted Fox with a letter, not extant. Ammonius,
who presented it, reported favourably: 'Wintoniensis te accusare videtur
quod exterum secum agas nec vnquam ad se accedas. Respondi, vt in buccam
tunc venit, subrustica quadam verecundia te id agere.' Ten days later he
reported again: 'Wintoniensis . . putabat sacerdotium te habere. Respondi
spem quidem sacerdotii tibi datam, sed sacerdotium nondum datum: ille
subridens interrogauit num illa spes alere te posset. Subrisi vicissim: "Atqui"
inquam "auri et temporis dispendio hanc spem Erasmus emit". Tunc ille
iussit me de hac re secum alias commodius loqui.' But though Erasmus had
now proved his right to leisure, nothing came of it (cf. no. 70); for Fox was
'ita his rerum turbinibus occupatus vt aegre rebus aliis vacare queat'. In
March 1512 the desired benefice came from another patron, Abp. Warham.

Fox's appreciation of Erasmus appears in a letter of Thomas More, 15 Dec.
1516, after the publication of the New Testament: 'Wintoniensis Episcopus,
vir vt scis prudentissimus, in celeberrimo cetu magnatum quum de te ac
tuis lucubrationibus incidisset sermo, testatus est omnibus approbantibus
versionem tuam Noui Testamenti vice esse sibi commentariorum decem,
tantum afferre lucis: eadem ademptis figuris Graecis Latine dici, etiam si
nihil aliud in editione Vulgata fuisset mendae quod mutaretur.']

REVERENDO PATRI DOMINO RICARDO EPISCOPO WINTONIENSI
ERASMVS ROTERODAMVS SALVTEM PLVRIMAM DICIT

E priscorum vsque saeculis mos hic in haec nostra tempora
deductus est, amplissime pater, vt Calendis Ianuariis, principe ineuntis anni die, munuscula quaepiam missitentur;

F

quae nescio quid laetioris ominis afferre creduntur, tum iis
ad quos abeunt, tum illis ad quos redeunt. Itaque quum ego
dispicerem ecquid tandem muneris a nobis iret ad tantum
patronum, ad tam potentem amicum, neque quicquam in
mea reperirem supellectile praeter meras chartulas, profecto
chartaceam strenam mittere sum coactus: quanquam quid
aliud potius mitti conueniebat ab homine studioso ad Prae-
sulem omnibus quidem fortunae muneribus magnificentis-
sime cumulatum, sed qui virtutem virtutisque comites
honestas litteras infinitis calculis anteponat, quique tanquam
contemptim poeneque dixerim inuitus fortunae dona admit-
tat, contra animi bonis quum sit opulentissimus, tamen
semper magis ac magis cupiat ditescere?

Porro nostrum hoc munusculum, si nulla alia licet, saltem
Terentiani Parmenonis exemplo hoc nomine commendabimus; quod non ex Aethiopia, verum e Samosata vsque
Graeciae vrbe sit profectum. Est autem dialogus Luciani,
cui titulus Toxaris siue de amicitia, quem nos paucis his
diebus Latinum fecimus. Qui quidem (vti spero) non omnino futurus est ingratus tuae excellentiae, vel ob id quod
amicitiam praedicat, rem adeo sanctam vt barbarissimis
etiam nationibus olim fuerit veneranda. Nunc Christianis
vsqueadeo in desuetudinem abiit, vt non dicam vestigia,
sed ne nomen quidem ipsum extet: quum nihil aliud sit
Christianismus quam vera perfectaque amicitia, quam com-
mori Christo, quam viuere in Christo, quam vnum corpus,
vna anima esse cum Christo; hominum inter ipsos talis
quaedam communio qualis est membrorum inter se corporis.
Neque minus tamen iucundus quam frugifer futurus est, si
quis modo decorum obseruet, quod in personis situm est.
Nam Mnesippi Graeci sermo quam totus Graecanicum quiddam sapit! comis, facetus, festiuus. Contra, Toxaridis
Scythae oratio quam tota Scythicum quiddam spirat! sim-
plex, incondita, aspera, sedula, seria, fortis. Quin etiam
dictionis discrimen quasique diuersum filum a Luciano de
industria affectatum pro nostra virili referre curauimus.

Hanc igitur qualemcunque clientuli tui strenulam, amplis-

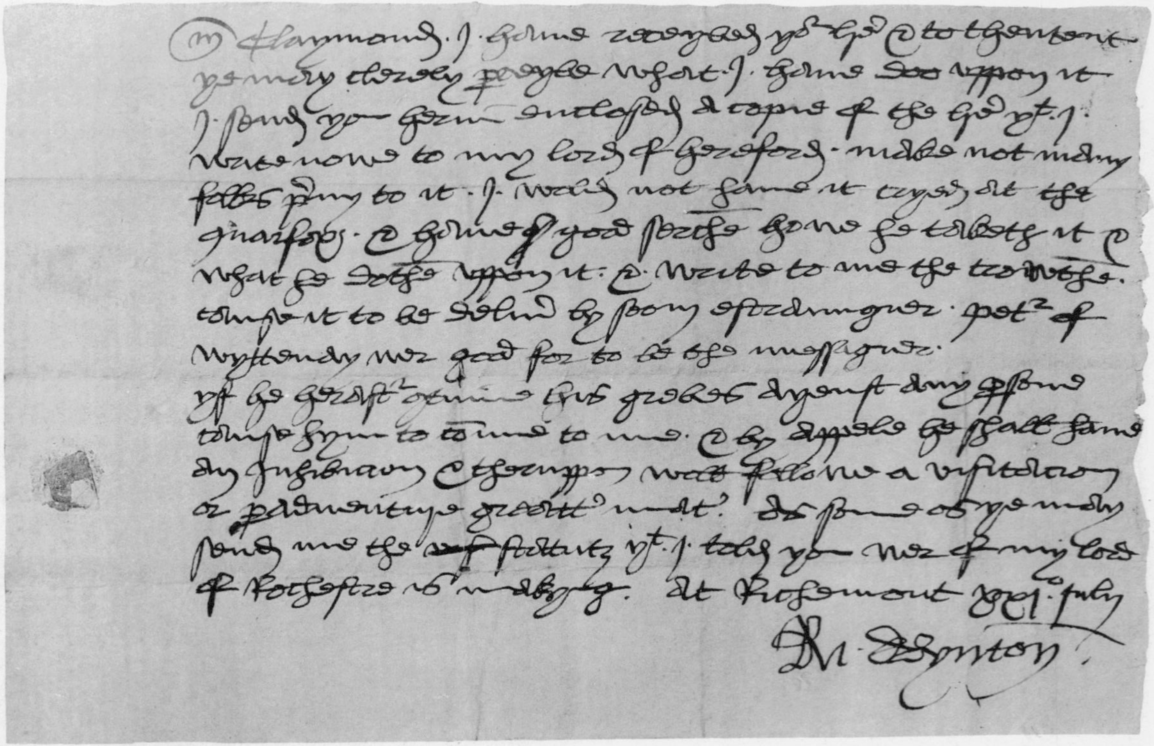

Autograph letter of Fox, 21 July 1506: No. 22

sime Praesul, felicibus auspiciis accipe; et Erasmum, sicuti iampridem facis, amare, ornare, iuuare perge.

Vale Londini Calendis Ianuariis.MDVI.

** 22. TO CLAYMOND

Corpus MS.   Richmond.
                                                21 July ⟨1506?⟩

[As Bishop of Winchester Fox was Visitor of Magdalen College, Oxford. In 1504 Richard Mayew, who had been President of Magdalen since 1480, was appointed Bishop of Hereford—a see which he held till his death in 1516. His diocese drew him away from his College, and his absence caused such complaint among the Fellows that Fox decided to remove him at Christmas 1506. Thus a year-date may be conjectured with probability.

It appears that Fox was consulting the new Statutes made for Christ's College, Cambridge, by Fisher, bishop of Rochester, on behalf of the Lady Margaret. They have been edited by H. Rackham, 1927.

John Claymond (c. 29 Sept. 1468–19 Nov. 1537) was Fox's trusted friend; their intimacy dating from about 1486. A Lincolnshire boy, he came to Magdalen College School, and then passed into the College: Demy 1484, Fellow 1488, President 1507 (see no. 23 introd.). Fox appointed him to a school in Durham, and in 1505 to the mastership of St. Cross at Winchester (no. 58n); and finally persuaded him to migrate to preside over his new college. Claymond is notable as a scholar; as witness the MSS. and books, the latter throughly read, which he presented to the Corpus Library. Among them are about 25 Greek MSS. which he bought from Grocin (†1519).]

Maistre Claymond,

I haue receyved your lettre, and to thentent ye may clerely perceyve what I haue doo vppon it, I send you herin enclosed a copie of the lettre that I write nowe to my lord of Hereford. Make not many folks preuy to it. I wold not haue it cryed at the Quarfox.[1] And haue good serche howe he taketh it and what he dothe vppon it, and write to me the trowthe. Cause it to be deliuer by soom estraungier. Peter of Wyttenay wer good for to be the messagier.

Yf he herafter continue his greves ayenst any persone, cause hym to comme to me, and by appele he shall haue an inhibicion, and theruppon woll followe a visitacion or per-aduenture greatter mater. As sone as ye may, send me the

---

[1] now Carfax: the centre of Oxford, where the two great roads cross.

statut₃ that I told you wer of my lord of Rochestre is makyng. At Richemont² xxj° July

Ri. Wynton.

To Maistre Claymond.

** 23. TO CLAYMOND

Corpus MS.   Southwark.
                                   24 December ⟨1506?⟩

[On 20 Jan. 1507 a Visitation of Magdalen College, Oxford, was held under Fox's direction. It lasted ten days, and in the course of it many complaints and quarrels among the Fellows were brought up. One of them was about the mode of electing a Vice-President. This office was then held by John Stokesley (no. 69n); but the President (clearly Mayew) and eight senior Fellows had elected one, John Gold, to take his place.

It seems almost inevitable to connect this letter with the troubled time before the Visitation: under such conditions Fox might well think it urgent to rise before dawn in midwinter and write to his faithful friend. He was in the north of his diocese about this time in 1506: for on 19 December he gave orders at Esher.

From the preservation of this among other letters to Claymond he clearly is the President addressed. Mayew remained President till Christmas, and Claymond was not elected till January. Possibly Fox was giving him the title in anticipation; but a letter of 1510–11 (see p. 161) suggests a later date.]

Broder maistre President,

I commaunde me hertely to you, and haue receyved your lettre, and seen the mater wheruppon is resyn the variance amongs your compaignye, and thinterpretacion remitted to me. And albe it I hade small laysure to attende to such maters, sens theyr commyng to me, yit haue I hard theyr opinions and other mens of my counsell also. And full sorye am I to vndrestand such sinistre construccion amongs them, that wher ther is noo resonable occasion whye they shuld make any such doubtes or questions vppon thestatut₃, they can or woll fall soo lightly therto. Yt is a full evill signe of goode disposicion. It commeth of pride and wilfulnesse which wold be repressed, and ellys it shall retourne to the great dishonour and hurt of the place. I praye God, I heer noo moo such variances amongs them.

---

² The palace at Shene on the Thames above London, which Henry vii built, and named after Richmond Castle in Yorkshire, which he loved. Cf. no. 71.

Asfor my interpretacion in that behalue, ye shall shortely haue it vnder my seale formally in writeng. And by cause what inconuenient may fall in the moyne time, I write to you at this tyme what my saide interpretacion shalbe. Wherunto I woll ye and all the compaignye and euery of them stond and obeye as if it wer in writeng vnder my seale. My saide interpretacion is and shalbe this: *quod ille aliquis in quem octo poterunt circa eleccionem Vicepresidentis consentire, non debet esse aliquis de illo octo. Sed debet esse omnino alia et distincta persona ab ipsis octo, videlicet nona persona.* The raisons why I thus interpretat the Statute for lak of laisure can not be writen at this tyme, nor I am not bounden to shewe them by my writeng. But thus I doo interpretat it *ex pura et sana conscientia et secundum mentem Fundatoris, quatenus potui eam colligere ex verbis Statutorum.* And to this as a boue I woll that bothe you and your compaigny condescend and agree them *sub pena periurii.*

And thus fare ye all well at Saynt Mare Ouerey[1] in great hast *in vigilia natiuitatis Domini ante horam quintam in Aurora mannu propria*

Ri. Wynton.

And I woll that this interpretacion in theleccion of the Vicepresident serue and be extended to like cases in theleccions of all other officers, and to be obeyed and kepen *sub dicta pena periurii.*

To my welbeloved broder the President of Magdalene College in Oxford.

|| 24. FROM THE CHAPTER OF WELLS

Liber Ruber, Wells, ii. 140. Wells.
Baildon p. 200. 19 January ⟨1507⟩.

Right reuerend fader in God and to vs moste singuler good lord,

In moost humbliest wyse we recommend vs vnto your good lordshipp. And where as we vnderstand that by the

[1] A priory of Austin canons, founded in 1106 in Southwark, s. of London Bridge.

meanes of your kynde and lovyng nece Maistresse Mylle and hyr husband ye arr esspeciall good lord vnto vs towchynge the matier of our mylles of Cory: in the beste maner that we can, we thannke your good lordship in the same, besechyng you of contynuaunce, and that it will please you to yeve credence vnto our ryght trusty and welbeloued brother Maister Thomas Harryes in suche thyng*is* as he shal move your saide lordshipp towchyng the same matier. And thus the Holy Trinite preserue you.

Written at Well*is* the xix^th daye of Januarye.

By your orators the Subdeane and Chapitre of the Cath*edral* churche of Well*is*.

To the right reuerend fader in God and their singuler good lord, my lord of Wynchestre.

|| 25. FROM THE FELLOWS OF PEMBROKE COLLEGE, CAMBRIDGE

Pembroke Register, 9. 17.   Cambridge.
                                                    7 August 1507.

[The College invites Fox to become its Master, in succession to Roger Leyburn, bishop of Carlisle, †c. 17 July 1507. Fox accepted the slight burden (tantillum oneris) and held office till 1518. See also nos. 30–32.

His interest in the College is shown by a gift of £50, 2 Oct. 1502, for two 'sacerdotes theologie' to say masses for John Dawyson, late Dean of Salisbury (†12 Oct. 1485), to whose prebend of Brownswood in St. Paul's Cathedral Fox had succeeded, 'et pro bono et felice statu Ric^l. Wynton': each to receive £4 a year till all spent (Reg. 3. 26).]

REVERENDISSIMO IN CHRISTO PATRI ET DOMINO, DOMINO RICHARDO WYNTONIENSI, PRESVLI MERITISSIMO ET CHRISTIANI GREGIS PASTORI VIGILANTISSIMO, SCOLASTICI[1] IN AVLA PENBROCHIE CANTABRIGIE GRATIAM ET PACEM.

Nemo est mortalium, dignissime Antistes, rem secum tacitus considerans, qui triste et lamentabile fatum nobis iamdudum obtigisse non diceret, qui nedum nostri Collegii patrono et alumno verum diligentissimo Custode ac piissimo in nos patre Rogero Carliolensi Episcopo orbati sumus. Que res

---

[1] SCOLATISCI *MS.*

tanta nos afficit molestia, tam animos suspensos reddit, quod iure perpetuis futuris temporibus (quum ipsius reminiscimur) casum ipsum inopinatum deflere compellimur. Sed quum viam vniuerse carnis transiit, atque in supernam Iherusalem deuotam eius animam, quod et omnes optamus, susceptam esse pie credendum est, hinc omnia modestius ferenda iubet ratio: quod et mesticiam nostram in parte tollit.

Nobis tamen orphanis atque orbatis, considerantibus ad quem potissimum confugiemus aut a quo consolacionem perditam integre recuperare mereamur, nemo hominum preter te, dignissime Presul, occurrit, qui nos mestos atque desolatos nostra sentencia consolari queat. Tuam igitur paternitatem oramus et obsecramus in Domino Ihesu vt nostrum omnium patronus et Collegii nostri Custos (ad quod vnanimes te eligimus) esse digneris. Qua in re pro-culdubio honesta, non minus rem gratam Deo et mortalibus iucundam nostra opinione effeceris,[1] quam si nouum aliquod Collegium funditus erigere et perficere curaueris. Nam vt vulgo dici solet, non minoris probitatis esse existimatur rem partam tueri et conseruare, quam quippiam nouum magna cum diligentia adipisci conari. Audi, imo exaudi, nos, colen-dissime pater, et noli vota nostra atque suspiria postponere: sed ad memoriam reuoca quam pium et sanctum opus est nostram fidem (que Christiane religionis fundamentum est) defendere et propugnare; ac etiam quam pium et sanctum est eos regere suaque tueri, qui sacris litteris operam dant vitamque in eis consumunt, ea condicione atque animo vt que ad veram vitam pertineant, imperito vulgo euangelizent. In qua re nostrum Collegium aule Penbrochie (ad laudem Dei dicimus) non parum omni tempore vigilantissimis Custodibus floruit et profecit.

Te igitur obsecramus, benignissime pater, tantillum oneris subire ne recuses; vt sub te tanto patre nostra studia floreant atque vita nostra studiose regatur. Quod si feceris, nos sedecim presbiteros sacre theologie deditos posterosque no-stros pro tua dominacione indies ad Deum oraturos non

---

[1] efficeris *MS*.

absre obligas. Et vt animos nostros in hoc nostro negocio exploratius habeas, nostris confratribus Thome Patenson, sacre theologie bach*alaure*o, et Iohanni Hostebe, in artibus magistro, fidem prebeas, obsecramus. Vale, dignissime Antistes, et Aule Pe*n*brochie electe Custos.

Ex Cantabrigia vij idus Augustas 1507.

Reuerendissimo in Christo patri et domino domino Richardo Wyntoniensi, presuli meritissimo et Christiani gregis pastori vigilantissimo.

** 26. FROM ROGER COLLINGWOOD

Corpus MS. 102, f. 1 v°.   ?

⟨1508?⟩

[The preface to a mathematical treatise, *Rogeri Carbonis in ligno Arithmetrica experimentalis*: probably autograph. The MS. did not come to the College Library from Fox, but was presented in 1617.

  Collingwood was Fellow of Queens' College, Cambridge, in 1497; and in 1498–9 received payments from the University for teaching mathematics. He was M.A. in 1499, and dean of Queens' in 1504. On 16 Sept. 1507 he received leave to go abroad for four years to study canon law; and, evidently through 'mutacio et patrie et studii', left this work incomplete. His name disappears from the College books in 1509–10; but he returned again to Cambridge and was proctor in 1513.]

COLENDISSIMO IN CHRISTO PATRI AC DOMINO, DOMINO
    RICARDO, DEI PROVIDENCIA WINTONIENSI EPISCOPO, SVVS
    SCOLARIS ROGERVS COLLINGWOOD SALVTEM PLVRIMAM
    DICIT.

Quum nonnullos annos mihi, licet indigno, Vniuersitas Cantebrigie, mater nostra, onus docendi iuuenes quadriuiales sciencias imposuisset—quarum Arithme*tri*cam ceteris antiquiorem, veluti fundamentum sine quo alie esse nequeunt, pre omnibus honorandam amplexandamque semper estimaui—, quumque omnium rerum numerorum naturam maxime stupendam esse facile posse ostendi non dubitassem; mecum tunc statui nonnulla de numerorum natura, que mihi satis admiranda videbantur, opusculo quodam colligere. Verum inceptum opus mutacio et patrie et studii imperfectum relinquere nos coegit; necdum ocium nacti sumus vt perficiamus.

Quamobrem, vt reliquimus, incompletum opus ex parte, sed artem ipsam completam, ad te mittimus: quod tuo nomini dedicari, si dignum foret, non modice desidero. Te autem tocius regni negocia rempublicamque curante, que te vnum fere hiis temporibus nouit habere amicum, circa istec parua vacare non posse scimus. Quare cui opusculum hoc recognoscendum committes, liberum esse correctorem sed peritum cupimus; ne ignorancia contempnere suadeat, et non intellectum abiiciat quod intelligens non paruipendendum forsan esse iudicaret.

Vale atque valeas semper Deum oro.

27. FROM PHILIP ALBERICUS

Coena, 1508, tit. v°.

Paris.
8 August 1508.

[The preface to *Coena saluberrima Baptistae Fiaerae Mantuani, medici et peritissimi et litteratissimi, lautius ab ipso nuper instructa et multo sale condita*, Paris, Badius, 13 Aug. 1508: a series of descriptions, in elegiacs, of various articles of food, of their value to the human body, and of methods of cooking them. The approach to Fox was part of Albericus' strenuous efforts to enter royal service. In addition to no. 28 he also addressed himself to the King with a translation of Cebes' *Tabula*, presumably into Latin, and some poems: one *ad Henricum regem de honore per eum allato studiosis Cantabrigiensibus*, perhaps an allusion to the royal visit of April 1506 for the opening of Christ's; others *de mortis effectibus ex hyeme et nocte descriptis* (Norfolk MS. 306, in Bernard ii. 3204: kindly pointed out to me by Mr F. Madan).]

FRATER PHILIPPVS ALBERICVS MANTVANVS REVERENDISSIMO
IN CHRISTO PATRI ET DOMINO, DOMINO ROBERTO EPISCOPO
WINTONIENSI, REGII APVD ANGLOS SIGILLI CVSTODI, S.D.

Quum superiore estate me amor vestri in istas oras appulisset, accidit vt mihi cum excellenti Regis protomedico Io. Baptista Boario[1] de re litteraria sermo fieret; qui (vt solent omnes que callent extollere) carminis ac rerum nature scientiam in eodem commode componi asserebat. Visa est mihi

---

[1] A Genoese, whose sons Erasmus accompanied to Italy in 1506 as supervisor of their studies.

sano sententia hec iudicio digna; idque in Arato, Lucretio, Mallio Ausonioque laudatum est. Adde quod et vtriusque, poeseos scilicet ac medicine, repertor idem Apollo dictus est.

Quum autem hoc a plerisque conciuibus meis obseruari retulissem, plurimum gauisus est et etati nostre gratulatus; Mantue imprimis, quod alumnos habeat antiquam poesim ad Deum et Dei opus naturam referentes. Veluti est insignis poeta Baptista Carmelita theologus, talis in templo qualis in bello Virgilius; necnon et phisici ambo, Baptista Fiera Ludouicusque Galbaneus. Is siquidem, vt per etatem licuit, festiua, alioqui salibus referta scripsit poemata; alter autem ingenio et doctrina priscam illam fragrantiam redolens, calamo vberiore plurima tum soluta tum pedestri oratione complexus est. Iocundum profecto quippiam ei referre visus sum; quia et, vt plerique, aliene non inuidet Minerue, et quod ambo iam commilitones Papie sub eodem duce stipendia litteraria emeriti sunt. Eius etiam summopere ingenium ad omnia facile mihi collaudauit; iniungens vt operam darem quo ex eius officina aliquid habere posset.

Quamobrem quum nuper Mantue agerem, ex multis que is mihi legenda concessit, Cenam (hoc enim nomine libellum vocat) adinueni: non illam que furto olim sublata mihi manus pererrabat, sed elegantiorem decoctioremque. Rogaui eum, et sub affinitatis que michi cum eo est vinculo perstrinxi, vt opusculum illud mihi non denegaret, quo protomedici vestri votis morem gerere possem. Quod quum assequutus sim, volui vt prius tue quam medici mense cena hec afferretur. Non enim oblitus sum quanti me haud merentem facias, quantaque abs te susceperim, qui Regis seruitio tot iam pollicitationibus me addicere nitebaris. Verum non mea hec causa acta sunt, sed tue virtutis magnanimitatisque: tu enim ille es (vt breui cuncta perstringam) in cuius animo non ab re regii pectoris archana collocantur. Vale.

Parrhisiis. Sexto Idus Aug. M.D. viii.

28. FROM PHILIP ALBERICUS

De casu animae.   Paris.
                                                  1 January 1509.

[A second dedication to Fox, perhaps in mitigation of the mistake about his name in no. 27. The book, a treatise by Albericus *De casu animae*, has disappeared; but Wood (*Hist. Vniu. Oxon.*, 1674, ii. 229) preserves the title and gives this extract from the preface with the date. For source he cites 'MS. in bib. Barloviano'; so that the book was probably never printed.]

Et hac spe semper operatus sum, vt tibi patrono meo studiorum meorum labores quantuloscunque offerrem. Videbor enim mihi ingrate egisse, nisi meam in te venerationem literario munere ostenderim, qui elapsis temporibus potentissimum Regem, cuius consilia in te vno conquiescunt, cuius arcanorum solus es conscius, tam propitium habes. Nouit enim quanto sis ingenio et prudentia Praesul, et te veluti fidum Achatem sibi nunquam seiungendum adiunxit.

‡ 29. FROM DARCY

RO. S. P. 1: 229, f. 8.   ⟨Craven.⟩
Brewer i. 157.   ⟨August 1509⟩.

[Fox clearly was regarded as having been the principal minister under the late King, and his position in the new reign was being much discussed. Darcy had been created a baron in 1505.]

Thes novell*is* haithe ben her sethe the Kyng is coronacion.[1] Firste sent to me by Sir Edward Ratcliff and others, shewyng that it was said by my lord of Northumberland is serua*untis* that my lord of Bukyngham[2] sholde be protector of Ingland and that ther m*aiste*r sholde rewlle all frome Trent northe and haue Berwic and the Marches, and that such grantes as I hade of offices was befor the Kyng was crowned and of noyn effecte.

Item by the said lord*is* serua*untis* cumyng into Craven from London, ther sayng*is* was that if ther lord hade nott rowmes in the northe as his fader hade, it shold not long

1 24 June 1509.
2 Edward Stafford (1478-1521); executed later on a charge of treason.

be well. This Richard Tempest squier herd of and shewde me, with other gret bostes and common brewtt*is*, wich wer to long to write.

Item vppon Saynt Lawrence daye[3] William Feherre, a poyre gentilman, cam from London, and he shewde and confessed that Gilson, Ratclif and onne Typpyng, serua*unt*t*is* to my said lord in Saynt M*a*rtynes in London ny his plasse, shewde to hym that Sir Risse ap Thomas[4] was gonne to the see, fled furthe of his cuntrey.

Item I truste to gett sum of the bryngers vp of thes talles and others mo in my hand*is*. They be but amongst knaff*is* and craft*is* men and begger*is*.

Item the common sayng withe euere m*a*rkett man that cumes frome London, is that the Lord Pr*e*veye Sealle, seyng of his owen crafte and police he canne not bryng hym self too rewlle the Kyng is grace, and put owt of faffour therle of Surrey,[5] therle of Shrosbere, the Busshop of Dorisme,[6] M*r* M*e*rnye, M*r* Brandon[7] and the lord Darcy, now he woille prove a nother waye; wich is too bryng in and bolster hym self to rewlle all with the Duke of Bukyngham and therlle of Northumbre. And dowbtles faste they cursse and speke evill of my Lord Pr*e*vey Sealle beyond messewr.

My lord, goyd it is to haue a goyde eey. Thoss much be bot sayng*is*: as I her, I woill warnne yow, my lord of Dorisme and Mr Mernye, wilst I lif. Therfor shew this, as ye thre semes goyd, to the Kyng is grace or otherwis. Feeherre I haue taken, and kepis hym to I haue worde frome yow: and by that tyme, if I canne trye the begynyng of the talles, I shalle haue moo, and lett for no man, I warrant yow.

---

[3] 10 Aug. 1509.   [4] Sheriff of Pembrokeshire.

[5] Thomas Howard (1443–1524), earl of Surrey 1483, victor of Flodden 1513, lord-treasurer 1501–22, duke of Norfolk 1514. In 1497 he raised the siege of Norham and released Fox.

[6] Thomas Ruthall, secretary to Henry VII and by him appointed to Durham 1509: †1523.

[7] See no. 39.

|| 30. FROM THE FELLOWS OF PEMBROKE COLLEGE, CAMBRIDGE

Pembroke Register, 9. 20.   Cambridge.
                                          24 December 1509.

[The College will testify its gratitude for the Master's vigilant care, perhaps in connexion with the new reign, by definite obligations to pray for him.]

REVERENDISSIMO IN CHRISTO PATRI ET DOMINO, DOMINO
    RICARDO DIVINA GRATIA WINTONIENSI PRESVLI DIGNIS-
    SIMO, ET AVLE PENBROCHIE CANTABRIGIE CVSTODI BENE-
    MERITO, SVI HVMILES ORATORES IPSIVS COLLEGII
    STVDENTES GRATIAM ET PACEM.

Quanquam omne beneficium pergratum esse debet, pater clementissime, illud tamen multo gracius longeque iucundius videri solet, quod quis nullis suasionibus, nullis precibus, nullis denique officiis in alium contulerit. Et quoniam id in te ex tua vetere beniuolentia vigilantissimoque tuo animo erga tuum nostrumque Collegium, in nostris negociis pertractandis perficiendisque exploratum habemus, non possumus non quotidie maiore in te vnum non obseruancia modo, sed etiam pietate quadam accendi atque inflammari. Itaque dies atque noctes cogitauimus quidnam egregium possimus de nobis prestare, quo aliqua tandem ex parte tantum tuum erga nos patrocinium, si minus re ipsa, voluntate saltem dissoluere incipiamus. Quare cum etiam atque etiam huiusmodi nostros cogitatus animis volutaremus nostris, inuenimus denique nullum a nobis tibi referri conuenientius posse officium, quam apud gloriosissimum Deum pro tua dominacione supplices effundere preces, quo hic gratia et in futuro gloria perfruaris eterna.

Hinc est, dignissime Antistes, quod nobiscum nos decreuimus pro nobis posterioribusque[1] nostris, quod preter id quod in nostris publicis ad populum declamacionibus, praeter id etiam quod in quotidianis nostris missis memoriam tui semper facimus, adiicimus et hec munuscula, vidilicet vt quater in anno, vt puta primo die mensis Marcii, vigesimo

----
[1] posteriembus que MS.

quarto die mensis Maii, vicesimo sexto die mensis Iulii, et
vicesimo quinto die mensis Nouembris, aut postridie, singulis annis missa *Salus populi* in nostra capella per omnes et
singulos nostros collegiatos, dum in humanis agis vitam,
pro incolumitate bonoque statu tuo solenniter celebretur; et
posteaquam ab hac vita excesseris, quamcitius ad nostram
peruenerit noticiam, solennes exequie cum missa in crastino
cum aliis xxx^ta peculiaribus missis pro anima tua tuorumque
benefactorum animabus, quam maturius fieri poterunt, per
nos celebrentur.

Et vt hec presens nostra concessio sigillo nostro communi signata firmiter et inuiolab⟨il⟩iter obseruetur, volumus
quod hec et in nostro registro atque inter ceteras nostre
Domus ordinaciones inseratur, atque in quolibet termino
cum eisdem nobis coram legatur: ad quam rem etiam obser-
uandam singuli Socii ad nostrum Collegium in posterum
recipiendi iuramento astringantur.

Datum Cantib^e. in Aula predicta, nono Kl. Ianuarias Anno
a natali Christiano millesimo quigentesimo nono.

‖ 31. FROM THE FELLOWS OF PEMBROKE
COLLEGE, CAMBRIDGE

Pembroke Register, 3. 9.   Cambridge.
                                            9 February ⟨1510?⟩

[Closely connected with no. 32. It seems as though Hudson had been
removed by Fox, with the provision of a chantry for his maintenance; and
had tried to return to Pembroke and the enjoyment of his Fellowship on the
pretext that the provision was inadequate. From no. 32 it appears that Fox
had been so indignant at the support given to Hudson by the Fellows that
he had threatened to resign the 'tantillum oneris' of being Master.

A date may be conjectured from the disappearance of Hudson's name from
the College 'Rationarium' in 1510.]

Most reuerend fadre in God, our singlar good lord and
Master,

In our most humble wyse we recommend vs to your good
lordshipe, besechyng you to be good lorde vn to this berer,
your Scolare, our Feloo, master William Hudson[1]: which

---

[1] From the diocese of Durham; Fellow 1498, M.A. 1502.

of latt hath commyn to your Colege, trustyng ther to enioy hys felyshipe, certefying vs that the chauntre which your good lordshipe assygned vn to hym is no perpetuite. Wher for, if that be of trowth, we your orator*is* and scolars with on assent and consent be contentyd to take and accept hym as Feloo in your Colege accordyng to the Statutes of your Colege. Whiche we truste shalbe to the pleaso*u*r of God, thonour of your Colege and the great preferment of lernyng both in the Vniuersite and in your Colege.

For it is seen to vs that noon of your scolars in your Colege is mor able nor lyke to content better in the Vniuersite than is he, in reddyng the lecto*u*r of diuinite fundyd in your Colege for a Feloo, aftir the departyng of master Robert Shorton,[2] which is now reder therof. Wherin (thes premysses tendrely consideryd) we besech your good lordshipe to be good lord vn to the said Mr William Hudson and to vs, and to accepe hym as Feloo in your Colege accordyng to our Statutes. And we shall pray for your prosperite and welfair vn to allmyghty Gode: whom we besech to preserue your lordeshype in long lyve to endure to his plesure.

Yevyn in your Colege Penbrukhall in Cambryge vnder the seale *Ad causas*, by the holl and singlar consent of your orator*is* and scolars, the nombre of xiiij[th], the ix[th] day of Februarij.

Your humble scolars and daly orator*is*
the student in your Colege Penbrukehall.

To the most reuerent fadre in Gode, our singlar good lorde and Master, my lord of Wynchester good lordeshipe.

---

[2] M.A. from Jesus Coll. 1503; Fellow of Pembroke 1505; first Master of St. John's 1511–16; Master of Pembroke 1518–1534; †17 Oct. 1535.

‖ 32. FROM THE FELLOWS OF PEMBROKE
COLLEGE, CAMBRIDGE

Pembroke Register, 3. 16.   Cambridge.
                                          9 April ⟨1510?⟩

Ryght reuerent fader in God, and our most singler good
lord and *Master*,

    We po*ur* scolers and daylye orators with dew reuerence
and submissyon recomend vs to your good lordshype.

    It is so, we resayvyd your lordshipeis most kynd and
louyng letters by Mr Lambert, your depute and president;
wherin we persayve your lordship shuld not be contentyd
with vs in diuers causis and varianc*is* concernyng your
Colege and certen of the Felaws of the sam: for the which
discontentacion we be ryght sory and hevy. And mych more
be cawse that on of your Scolars & Felaw of your Colege,
Mr Robert Cronkar, late with your lordship at London,
browght vnto hus hevy tidyng*is*, if it shuld so be your
⟨will⟩[1] to be so hevy lord to forsake vs, to the vtter disco*m*-
fort of vs all and gret hurt and damage vnto your Colege
so doyng, and specyally that myght insew therby: the wich
God forbed, or any such gret mysfortune shuld cum to vs
and to your said Colege.

    Wherfor we all with on assent and ych on of vs your said
scolars and faithfull orators mekely besech your good lordship to continue good lord and *Master* to vs all your Scolars
and your said Colege, and to give credence in the maters
concernyng your Colege to the brynghers of thes our lettres,
your said depute Mr William Lambert and Mr John Hoste-
bye, Felaws of your College; and with God*is* grace we shall
so indevyr vs hensforthe to ordre our self so that it shall
be to the contentacyon of your good lordship and to the
encrese of studye and vertue.

    Also we mekely besechyng your lordship to loke vpon
the Statut*is* and laudable costomys of your College; to the

---

[1] Some such word must be supplied.

which and to your good and vertuose mynd and conscience
as meke disciples and scolars with on assent submitt vs and
ich on of vs, to stand and be rewlyd in all cawsis and maters
of your sayd College sithyn your lordshipis days. And therupon your daily orator Mr William Hudson is come mekely
to submitt hym selfe to your good lordship: to whom we all
and ich on of vs mekely beseche your lordship to be good
lord and beneficiall. We trust veryly to the pleasure of God
and also to the conforthe of vs all, as he knowith best: who
myght long continue your good lordship in prosperite and
helth to hys pleasure.

Wrytyn and subscribyd with our hand*is* accordyng to
your lordshipis commawndment, and also seallyd with the
comyne seale of your said College the ix day of Aprile in
Cambrige.

Your said scolars and orators of Penbrokehall.

> per me Willelmum Lambert
> per me Robertum Cronckar
> per me Robertum Shorton
> per me Guilielmum Lwyud
> per me Georgium Thomson
> per me Iohannem Fewterar[2]
> per me Christoforum Chenyson
> per me Robertum Falyat
> per me Iohannem Adison
> per me Rolandum Bolron
> per me Richardum Sotheby
> per me Richardum Peppyr
> per me Cuthbertum Marschiall.

[2] Later a monk at Syon, and a benefactor to the Library there.

H

** 33. TO CLAYMOND

Corpus MS.

Nottingham.
19 August ⟨1511⟩.

[The year-date can be supplied from the King's movements. The identity of the godson who was causing Fox such anxiety by unruly conduct at the University we have not been able to discover. He appears again in no. 34.]

Maistre Claymond,

I thank you for your goode and kynde lettre towcheng the owtrageuxe demeanor of my godsoon: wherof I am full sorye, and daily shall praye God that it may amend. I haue of late vndrestond that it commeth to hym of kynde and woll take hym by seasons till he comme to a greatter age.

Yt is to me noo small displaisure: God knoweth what I entended tawards hym. I hade the moynys to haue got hym fayre lyvelod, as sone as I cowde haue gotten a dispensacion for hym. And now I am at my wyttis end.

I can not be soo sone with you in thoes parties as I supposed. I can not depart fro the Kyngis grace, and it wolbe thexaltacion of the Crosse[1] byfor he can be with you. In the moyen tyme I praye you take soom pacience with hym. The weder is soom what colder then it was, and euery daye shalbe colder; which shall soom what abate the disposicion of hym.

Ye may be sure that as sone as the Kyng commeth to Wodstok I shall see you. And thus fare ye well at Notyngham the xix daye of August.

Ri. Wynton.

To Maystre Claymond at Kytlyngton besids Oxford.

[1] 14 Sept.

** 34. FROM THE COMMISSARY TO CLAYMOND
Corpus MS.   ⟨Oxford.⟩
                                              ⟨1511.⟩

[Evidently in conjunction with no. 33. Fox's 'jentyll wrytyng' does not survive. As the office of commissary was rotatory, the holder of it at this time cannot be determined without a definite date.]

Mastyr Cleymude,

I wryt on to ʒu be cause I wold neythyr my lord nor ʒu shall take labour to cum on to me. ʒe know my lorde Chawnceler commawndede me to execute the Statut*is* a cordyng to the mynde of my lord of Wynchestyr: the wych wyllyd me, as euer I myth do hym plesure, to execute extremly the Statut*is cum omni rigore et sine misericordia* uppon hys godeson: and to enserten hym of hys godsone lowly be hauyour, not only in obeyng the Statut*is* of the Vniuersyte but also for the satysfaccion made to the partes. In all this mater I haue fownd my ʒung lord full lowly, and so wyll I sertyfy my lord off Wynchestyr by the next messanger: trustyng he wyll sende me hys wepun and to haue xˢ ¹ for conuyccion to the Vniuersyte. Thys done, my wrytyng shall be so made that my lord of Wynchestyr shall be well plesyd with my ʒung lorde, and also ʒe to be thankyd of hym for ʒur good dylygence and honorabyll delyng. ʒe know, and my lord hade not wryte to me, my ʒung lorde and ʒu be bownde that he shuld obey such correccion and reformacion as I thowte most metly: the wych bonnde wold be lokyd upon that satysfaccion ys made; for perellys that myth fall. Ferthermore the ʒung man that of hys good wyll p*ur*veyd loggyng and browt hys beddyng in,² wold be sen to: and as for my senddyng up to London, the wych cost xxᵈ the horse her and xxᵈ my seruant, the satysfaccion theroff ys made by the jentyll wrytyng my lord of Wynchestyr sende me. I prey ʒu of an answer by wrytyng, or ellys to speke with me ʒur sylff; and thus fare ʒe well.

by ʒur feythfull louer the commyssary.
On to mastyr Cleymude of Brodʒatt*is*.

¹ The statutory fine for wounding: the weapon also to be confiscated.
² This suggests some form of confinement.

** 35. FROM WOLSEY

BM. Cotton MS. Titus B. i. 104 vᵒ.   Windsor.
Brewer i. 880 (3443).   30 September ⟨1511⟩.

[Wolsey's writing is sometimes misleading, his *a* being open like *u*, his *e* dotted like *i*. R. Fiddes printed this and no. 37 in his *Life of Cardinal Wolsey*, 1724, collections pp. 8–11. The year-dates are conclusively indicated by the contents.]

Aftyr moste humbyl comendacions with lycke desyre of yowr helth and perfygth recouery, pleasyt yowr good lord-shyp to vndyrstand that on Sonday laste paste the Kyng reseyuyd letter*is* from Sir Robert Wyngfeld datyd the iiijth of thys moneth: by the contynue wherof he aduertysyd the Kyng that the Emperror[1] had nat onely worde from the cowrte of Rome but from dyuers other placys that owr holy father the Pope[2] shuld be in suche danger of lyfe that ther ys no hope of hys recouery; for all the lower partys of hys body from the mydel downward wer ded mortyfyd and as colde as any stone.

Wherfore the Emperror myndyng and intendyng to hys beste the auancement of the Cardynall Adryan[3] *ad papatum*, hath sent the Bushope of Gurce[4] to Rome, effectually to solycyte the same; and to the yntent that thys hys p*ur*pose shuld the better be browgth abowth, he hath ioynyd with hym Sir Robert Wyngfeld, wych also at the ynstant desyre of the Emperror intendyth to go to Rome.

Yesterday at masse I brake with the Kyng in thys matter, and shewyd on to hys grace how mych honor and also furtherans of all hys afferys in tyme to kome shuld insue to hym, yf that by hys comendacion sume Cardynall mygth atteyne to be Pope; and seyng that the Emperror was

---

[1] Maximilian.

[2] Julius II was unconscious on 21 Aug. 1511, but recovered: †20 Feb. 1513.

[3] de Castello, an Italian; bp. of Hereford 1502, of Bath and Wells 1504–1518.

[4] Matt. Lang, bp. of Gurk in Carinthia 1505, cardinal 1511, abp. of Salzburg 1519.

effectually intendyng the preferment of the Cardynall
Adryan, wych in maner ys as the Kyng*is* bownden subiect,
with hys gracyous help the matter shuld ⟨be⟩ mych the
sonner browgth to passe. I fownde hys grace very con-
formabyll and aggreabyll to my sayyng. Howbeyt I durste
nat further wade with hys grace as towchyng yowr letter*is*
of recomendacion, as well for the renouelyng of yowr other
letter*is* and the datys of the same, as also that we haue no
suer knowleg of the Popys deth other wyse than ys before
seyd. Yowr lordeshyp, I trust, ys no thyng myscontent with
that I presumyd to breke yowr instruccions; for assurydly
except Mr Tresorer,[5] no herthly man ys nor shalbe made
preuy to yowr letter*is*. I am half afrayd that ye be dysspleasyd,
for as myche as I haue resseyuyd no wryttyng from yow
thys longe season. I truste ye woll take my doyng (wych
procedyd of good wyll, thynckyng that yt was for the beste)
in good parte.

My lorde, in comynycacion at the large, I haue felt how
that my lorde Chambyrleyn[6] and of Duresme[7] be myche
inclynyd to the Cardinall of Seynt George,[8] and in all ther
talke they kan nat speke to myche honor of hym, dyss-
preysyng the Cardinall Adrian affor. Yf yowr lordshyp
war here, thys matter wold be sone browgth to yowr
purposse. And my lorde, for dyuers vrgeynt causys yt ys
thowgth very exspedyent that ye shuld repare to the Kyng;
for all hys gret matters be defferryd on to yowr commyng:
wych ys dayly lokyd for and desyryd of all thos that wolde
the Kyng*is* causys shuld procede in a good trayne. The
Maister of the Roll*is*[9] ys commyn to Douer: we loke for
hym dayly. He hath wryttyn hyther that neuyr man had
wers chere than he in France. No thyng ha⟨th / he done
further than I wrot on to yow in my laste letter*is* as
towchyn⟨g / hys charge.

The Ambasador of Arragon hath lyberally delte with my

5 the Earl of Surrey; see no. 29.
6 Charles Somerset (†1526), lord Herbert; lord chamberlain since 1505.
7 Ruthall.   8 Riario.
9 John Yonge; master of the Rolls 1508–†1516.

lorde Darcy.[10] He hath gouyn to hym allowance for one
hole moneth aftyr vj^d the day, and for xv days aftyr viij^d
the day, for euery solger, more than of very dute he cowde
demavnde. And the Kyng owr master hath for hys par⟨te /
gouyn to hym the thowsand pow⟨n⟩d*is* wych at hys departyng hys gra⟨ce / lent on to hym. Thus the Kyng*is* money
gothe awey in euery korne⟨r./ And as towchyng the Kyng*is*
abode here he intendyth nat to departe hens tyll within
fower or[11] fyve days affore Alhallowtyd. One Monday next
commyng hys grace purposyth to ryd to London to se hys
shyp /, ther to tary two days, and so retorne hyther ageyn.
My lord Stuar⟨d[12] /ys nat yet commyn to the Cowrt. Withyn
iij or iiij days he intendyth to be here.

My lorde Tresorer at hys laste commyng to the Kyng,
wych wa⟨s / thys day sennygt, had suche maner and cown-
tynance shewyd on to hym that on the morowe he departyd
home ayeyn, and as yet ys nat retornyd to the Cowrte. With
lytyll help nowe he mygth be vtterly, as towchyng loggyng
in the same, excludyd: wherof in my poore iuggement no
lytyll goode shuld insue.

The Kyng ys myndyd as yet to send Mr Deane of Wynd-
sore[13] to the Kyng of Scott*is*, as well to declare the cause
why he hath takyn hys shyppys and thus intretyd hys
subiect*is*, as also to bere the Quenys bequest; for the wych
she hath instantly wryttyn. Mr Howard meruelusly
incendyth the Kyng ayenst the Scott*is*: by whos wantone
meanys hys grace spend⟨yth / mych money, and ys more
dyssposyd to ware than paxe. Yowr pre⟨sence / shalbe very
necessary to represse thys appetyte.

Other nuys we h⟨aue / none here, but that yt ys thowgth
that the Quene ys with chyld. Whe⟨n / other shall occure,

---

[10] Sent in March 1511 to aid Ferdinand in a holy war against the Moors.
When he reported his arrival at Cadiz in June, Ferdinand replied that 'now
no arrangements are made for the said war' and that he had better go home.
    [11] of *MS*.
    [12] George Talbot (1468–1538), earl of Shrewsbury. He was returning
from an embassy to the Pope.
    [13] West: see no. 49.

I shall aduertyse yow of the same, as knowy⟨th / God: who preserue yowr good lordshyp in good helth.

At Wyndsor ⟨in / haste the laste day of Septembre with the rude hand of yowr l⟨ouyng / and humbyll prest.

As towchyng the preferment of Mr Yng,[14] I nede nat wryt on to yow; for I s⟨uppose / he hath aduertysyd yowr lordshyp at the leyngth in that behalf, a⟨nd / also desyryd yowr cownsell, now that the Kyng hath shewyd hym hy⟨s / pleasure how for the exspedicion of hys matter he shalbe fe⟨r⟩ther orderyd and demeanyd. And owr Lorde send yow helth and str⟨eyngth. /

Thomas Wulcy.

To my synguler goode lorde, my lorde of Wynchester.

‖36. FROM THE UNIVERSITY OF OXFORD

Bodleian MS. 282, f. 10 v⁰.   Oxford.

21 December ⟨1511⟩.

[From the University Letter-book: Register FF, which follows Register F (see nos. 4, 17, 18). The year-date can be supplied from the chronological arrangement of the book. Barnacke was a Fellow of New College who had been appointed University Scribe in 1508. It appears that Fox was already contemplating some educational foundation in Oxford.]

REVERENDO IN CHRISTO PATRI AC DOMINO, DOMINO RICHARDO DIVINA PROVIDENTIA WINTONIENSI EPISCOPO, CANCEL-LARIVS VNIVERSITATIS OXON. VNIVERSVSQVE MAGI-STRORVM REGENTIVM SENATVS IN EADEM S.P.

Oxoniensium tuorum negligentie vel potius ingratitudini merito inputare ascribereue potes, dignissime Presul, quod nec litteris nec alio quouis officiorum genere tuam paterni-tatem v⟨n⟩quam vel raro visitauerint. Animus enim tuus omnino nobis fuit beniuolentissimus; nec adolescentulorum more quodam vel amoris flexibili ardore, sed stabilitate potius atque constantia tuam nobis semper contulisti beniuolentiam. Imitatur enim tua paternitas ipsos fertilissimos agros, qui multo plus afferunt quam acceperunt. Cuius rei argumentum euidentissimum pre se ferunt opera factaque tua benignissima. Quod enim libentissime non perfecisti, a te petiuimus nichil.

---

[14] Canon of Wells 1501; Bp. of Meath 1512; Abp. of Dublin 1521; †1528.

Nunc etiam (vt aiunt, et nos aliqualiter experimur) non solum inanimatos nobiscum splendidissime coniungi facies verum etiam viuos edificabis lapides; opus certe preclarum, pium munificentissimumque. Nobis tuis Oxoniensibus commodum et profectum, tue autem paternitati honorem, gloriam et nominis immortalitate⟨m⟩ et, quod maius est, anime salutem conferes. Ad rei igitur incepte consummationem vel commouere vel incitare opus esse non duximus; prudentissimi enim atque excellentissimi animi tui constantiam satis satisque cognouimus. Quare in benignitatis liberalitatisque tue perseuerantia firmiter confidimus. Et cum ipsi tue beniuolentie corespondere non valeamus, quotidi⟨a⟩nas nostras pollicebimur preces, vt sic in longum vsque euum perseueret tua dignissima paternitas.

Oxon. e domo Senatus nostri xxi Decembris.

Barnacke.

** 37. FROM WOLSEY

BM. Cotton MS. Titus B. i. 105.   Farnham.
Brewer i. 1356 (3388).   26 August ⟨1512⟩.

[The lamentable action between the Regent and 'the gret Caryke of Brest' took place on 10 Aug. 1512, under Sir Edward Howard, admiral.]

Aftyr moste humble comendacions, my lorde, I beseche yow to arrect[1] no blame to me that sythyns my departyng from yow I haue nat wryttyn to the same all suche nuys as hath occurryd for the tyme. For in fayth on to thys day I cowde atteyne no tyme so to do onles I shuld haue wryttyn but half a tale. Suyr I am here of ye wol meruel; but at owr next metyng yowr lordeshyp shal knowe the cause. And as for the materys of Spayne, howe the same do goo, I am suyer ye haue beyn aduertysyd by suc⟨h / wryttyng*is* as hath beyn sent to yow from thens. Howbeyt ye shall by Mr Knygtt*is* lettre, wych I nowe send on to yow, knowe in substance all that ys wryttyn by my lorde Marques, John Style or any other. By the wych lettres I nowe perceyue yowr olde sayng to be trewe, towchyng the ordyr and payne wych

---

[1] impute: cf. Brewer i. 1357 (3387).

Inglyshe men wole abyde ⟨and / indure. I trowe ther desyre
to returne hom shalbe to the hynderance of the ynterprise of
Gyen, equyualent to the Kyng of Arragons slacnes.

From whom the gentylman wych was sent hyther in tyme
of the Parlyament to vyeu the Kyngis artyllery, a man full
of wordis, ys lately comyn to the Kyng. The substance of
whos chargye restyth onely in excusyng the Kyng hys
mastere that hys army hath nat joynyd with the Kyngis
army hytherto, allegyng that the danger of Nauar with the
colorable delyng of the Kyng of the same, hath beyn the
cause of thys longe delay. Howbeyt nowe he dare geoport[2]
hys lyff that bothe armys be joynyd. The Kyng hys mastere
affermyth by the othe of a prynce that he shal neuyr desyste
from the warre nor leue the Kyng, on to suche tyme as hys
grace hath recoueryd and atteynyd to the crowne of France;
with many other plesant wordis. I pray God the dedys
may followe and insue accordyngly. And as towchyng the
state of Itally and howe also owr ambasadors do in ther
maters, yowr lordeshyp shal perceyue by suche lettres as
I send to the same in thys pacquet. Wych whan ye haue
rede, I beseche yow to send ageyne.

And to asserteyne yow of the lamentabyll and sorowfull
tydyngis and chance wych hath fortunyd by the see, owr
folkis, on Tuysday was fortnygth,[3] met with xx gret
shyppys of Frawnce, the best with sayle and furnyshyd with
artyllery and men that euyr was seyn. And aftyr innumer-
abyll shotyng of gunnys and long chasyng one a nother, at
the last the Regent moste valyently bordyd the gret Caryke
of Brest. Wherin wer fower lordis, ccc gentylmen, vɪɪjᶜ
solgers and marynes, ɪɪɪjᶜ crosbowe men, c guners, cc tonne
of wyne, c pypys of befe, ʟx barellis of gonepowder and
xv gret brasyn cortawdis,[4] with to meruelose a nombyr of
schot and other gunys of euery sorte. Owr men so valyently
acquyt them sylf that within one ower fygth they had
vtterly venquyshyd with schot of gonnys and arows the

---

[2] For this word Wolsey first wrote *jeop*.
[3] 26 Aug. was a Thursday.   [4] Short cannon.

I

sayd Caryke and slayne moste parte of the men within the same. And sodenly as they war yeldyng them sylf, the Caryke was one a flamyng fyer, and lycke wyse the Regent within the turnyng of one hand. She was so ankyrryd and fastyd to the Caryk that by no meanys possybyll she mygth for hyr salfgarde depart from the same. And so bothe in sygth within thre owerys war burnt, and moste parte of the men in them. Sir Thomas Knyuet, wych moste valyent⟨ly / acquyt hym sylf that day, was slayne with one gonne; Sir John Carewe with dyuers others, whos namys be nat yet knowne, be lycke wyse slayne. I pray God to haue mercy on ther sowlys.

And, my lorde, at the reuerens of God, kepe thes tydyng*is* secret to yowr sylf; for ther ys no lyuyng man knowyth the same here but onely the Kyng and I. Yowr lordeshyp knowyth rygth wel that yt ys exspedyent for a whyl to kepe the same secret. To se howe the Kyng takyth the matere and behauyth hym sylf, ye wold meruell, and myche allowe hys wyse and constant maner. I haue nat on my fayth seyn the lycke.

And thus with heuy harte and sorowfull penne I make a ende, besechekyng God to preserue yowr good lordshyp.

From Farneham thys mornyng in wonderuse hast the xxvj day of August with the rude hande of[5] yowr assuryd chapleyn,

Thomas Wulcy.

The resydue of the Frenche flete aftyr longe chassyng was by owr folk*is* put to flygt and drevyn in to Brest hauyn. Ther war vj as gret shyppys of the sayd flete as the Regent or Souerayn. Howbeyt as cowar*dis* they flede. Sir Edward[6] hath made hys voue to God that he wyl neuyr se the Kyng in the face tyl he hath reuengyd the dethe of the nobyll and valyant knygth Sir Thomas Knyuet.

The lettres of thanck*is* to my lorde Cardynall Adryan I send to yowr lordshyp in thys pacquet.

---

[5] of of *MS.*

[6] Howard, second son of the Earl of Surrey (no. 29). He fulfilled his vow by losing his life in an action against the French, 25 April 1513.

**38. FROM JOHN DAWTREY

RO. S. P. 1: 3, f. 197.   ⟨Southampton.⟩
Brewer i. 1845 (4007).   5 May ⟨1513⟩.

[Dawtrey, collector of customs at Southampton and overseer of the port, was now helping Fox to provide transports for France and victual the army: see nos. 39-46.]

Please it your good lordeshippe to haue knowlege,

I send you herewith your letter and the copy of the Kyng*is* letter. My lord, we haue here all redy iij ship*pis* of the Westcountrey, whiche wyll bere abowt ccc tonnys of vytayle all redy, and also one hoye; and I loke euery day for our vytalers of the Westcountrey to comme agayne— I meane them that went to the trade¹ fro hens. Also here be comen yn evyn now vj crayers² and certeyn Spaynysshe ship*pis* lade with vytayle fro London. Also the xxvj saylys of vytayle that lay at the Cowe,³ be by this tyme with the army. For Echyngham⁴ came yesterday yn here: whiche met with Gunson and the said vytalers past Portland thedyrward.

To morowe⁵ I wyll wayte on your lordeshippe: as knowythe allmygty God, who ever preserue your good lordeshippe.

Wret*en* this Assencyon daye by your seru*au*nt

John Dawtrey.

To my syngeler good lord, my lord of Wyncheste⟨r, / be this delyueryd yn hast.

¹ The sea off Brest and the Breton coast; cf. no. 39 and see Brewer i, index.
² small trading vessels.   ³ Cowes.
⁴ A ship-captain, knighted after Flodden.
⁵ Fox came to Southampton on 6 May: see no. 46.

**39. TO WOLSEY

RO. S. P. 1: 4, f. 4.   Portsmouth.
Brewer i. 1858 (4056).   11 May ⟨1513⟩.

[The group, nos. 39–46, is mainly concerned with preparations for the attack on France in 1513; Fox being required, with the assistance of Dawtrey (no. 38) to provide transports to carry the army across the Channel. Later on he himself went over to Calais with the King.]

Broder maistre Aulmosner,

Yistredaye abouts iiij of the clok in the afternone I receyved your lettres dated at Baynard Castell the ix day of May; and haue by the same vndrestond that the Kyng*is* grace by thadvise of his counsell hathe ordeygned Sir Charles Brandon[1] with iiij m¹. men vnder hym to goo to thadmirall, and for that propose to take shippyng at Hampton the xviij daye of this present moneth. For the vitayleng wherof and of thadmirall and his compaignye ye haue writen bothe to John Dawtrey and to me to doo all diligence possible; acertayneng vs that ye trust to send as much beer, flesshe, bisquyt and fisshe from thens as shall suffise the said iiij m¹. men for oon moneth.

As towcheng preparacions of vitails heer for the said propose, ye shall vndrestand what may be done at Hampton by John Dawtrey is lettres; in whom ye may be sure neyther lacketh nor shall lacke noo diligence. And I trust he woll faile of noo vitayls, soo ther may be had ships for the fettyng therof and foysts[2] for beer: wherof fewe comme hidder, as ye haue be enformed in tyme past. And albe it that bothe ye, as ye write, and we also haue writen for them, both to thadmirall that was[3] and to thadmirall that nowe is,[4] yit haue we noo remedye. Albe it that for the tyme of my lord Admirall that nowe is, ther hathe be noo wynd, nor yit is, to bryng them; but ye must fro tyme to tyme call

---

[1] A member of Henry viii's household, who commanded against France also in 1523 and 1544; Duke of Suffolk 1514; married Mary Tudor 1515; ✝1545.
[2] casks; also, barges.   [3] Sir Edward Howard; see no. 37.
[4] Lord Thomas Howard (1473–1554), elder brother of 'thadmirall that was'.

vppon my said lord Admirall for the sendyng of them hidder, and specially the empty pipes,[5] and we woll doo the same. Ther can noo great vitaile be shipped in the fewe ships that nowe be, or herafter shall comme to Hampton, byfor the commyng of Sir Charles and his compaignye, for such causes as John Dawtre sheweth by his lettres; and I fear that the said holl noumbre woll not be ⟨at⟩[6] Hampton, neyther the said xviijth daye nor iiij or v dayes after, and thought it is by men of experience that they can not be shipped with theyr vitails and bagages by the space of viijth dayes after. And thus I feer that it shalbe the first daye of Jung byfor they shall mowe depart fro Hampton. Ye knowe well ther must be oon wynd to bryng the ships out of the Themmys into the Downys, and a nother to bryng them out of the Downys into Hampton Watre, and the third wynd to bryng the ships out of West contre into Hampton Watre. I praye God that the lacke of thies wynds tract not the tyme farther then shalbe expedient.

Thus ye may see ther may be many chaunces to retarde the departyng hens of this newe armye. Neuerthelesse I shall from hens addresse me streight to Hampton, and accordyng to your writeng and the Kyng*is* commaundement remaigne theer till the said army be past; and in the moyne tyme doo my possible as well for the spede of the said vitails as also for my attendance gevyng vppon Sir Charles and his compaignye, and for the fortheryng of theyr shippyng; and afterward drawe me with my compaignye tawards the Kyng*is* grace as spedely as shalbe to me possible. Yt wer well doo that ther wer soom intelligence bytwyxt them that prepayre vitails in the West parties and John Dawtrey and his compaignye, to thentent that euery of them myght knowe what other doo. It myght, I thynk, be to the Kyng*is* profite that it soo wer.

I see also in my mynde oon great aduenture towcheng the said vitaileng of this army when they shalbe in the

---

5 Casks for beer; in nos. 37, 46 for meat.
6 This insertion, in the middle of a line in the original, seems necessary.

trade,[7] and that is this. Ther is noo vitaile fette hens but fro tyme to tyme, and that is not for any long tyme, as not past for ıɪj wekes at the most; and if the wynd after the commyng of the vitailers to thadmirall, serue them not to retorne hidder till the said vitaill be spent, ther shall therof followe a great inconuenient. Yt shall therfor be well done that my lord Admirall be writen to, to acertayne John Dawtrey howe he is furneshed of vitaill, and for how long. And amongs other maters faill not continually to write to hym to cause euery ship to kepe theyr emptye pipes; for vndoubtedly they haue brent and lost many of them. Except this be done, I assure you ther wolbe lacke of them heer. And thus fare ye hertely well at Portesmowthe the xj daye of May with the shakyng hand of your lovyng broder

Ri. Wynton.

/ To⟩ my broder the / K⟩yng*is* Aulmosner.

** 40. TO WOLSEY

RO. S. P. 1: 4, f. 19.   Southampton.
Brewer i. 1881 (4073).   15 May ⟨1513⟩.

Broder maistre Aulmosner,

I am pr*e*uye to the lettre that John Dawtrey writethe to you; and except I wold write the same, I can shewe noon other newes hens. And I praye God that the compaignye that shall comme hidder, put theyr folks in such ordre as they comme not nyghe this toune by ıj dayes journaye at the leest; and if they doo otherwise, ther shall many inconuenients ensue. And also God knoweth when we shall haue shippeng heer sufficient for tharmye. It is to vs great m*e*rvaile that ther comme noon hidder out of the West parties. If we hade had them heer byfor the commyng of tharmye, they myght haue take in such vitails as they shalbe chargied with byfor the commyng of tharmye: which myght

7 Cf. no. 38.

haue be thadvaunsyng of tharmy peraduenture by iiij or
v dayes or mor.

Heer lyethe the Lyon without takelyng, and is like to be
lost, without warant made to John Dawtrey for takelyng
to be deliuered for hir. Albeit I advise that she shuld be
sold, rather then to bestowe newe takelyng vppon hyr.
I thynk ther may xl^li or ther abouts be had for hir. Ye may
write the Kingis plaisure in this behalue to John Dawtrey;
and thus fare ye hertely well at Hampton the xv daye of
Maye with the hand of your lovyng broder

Ri. Wynton.

After viij of the clok in the evenyng.

To my broder the Kyngis Aulmosner.

**41. TO WOLSEY

RO. S. P. 1: 4, f. 22.   Southampton.
Brewer i. 1885 (4075).   16 May ⟨1513⟩.

Broder maistre Aulmosner,

This afternone comme hidder Fitz William[1] commyng
streight to the courte; and as he saithe, thadmirall wolbe
heer with the next wynd with all his flete. And thus what
with hym and what with Sir Charles and his compaignye,
heer woll faile noo businesse. Asfor newes, ye shall haue
them by Fitz William, and therfor I write none; savyng that
I knowe for certaynte that the treuxe[2] of oon yere is taken
and proclamed bothe in Spaigne and France bytwyxt the
Frenche and Aragonesse Kyngis with theyr adherents,
as ye knowe better then I. And I feer that themperor woll
daunce the same daunce. I require you, though I knowe
well ye haue noo laisure to write me your newes yourselve,
make Bryan Tuke[3] by your enformacion write me soom.

---

[1] Later Lord High Admiral and Earl of Southampton, †1542. He was
wounded in the action when Sir E. Howard (no. 37) was killed; and was
doubtless now returning to report.

[2] 1 April 1513: see Rymer xiii. 350–352.

[3] A secretary; first 'master of the King's posts' 1517; †1545.

Thadmirall writethe to me that he lacketh c maryners, and heer be noon to get. Also he wold haue bowes, spekyng of noo noumbre certayn; item m¹. m¹. sheves of arowes; v m¹. shot for hakbusshes; iij m¹. shot for serpentyns and fawcons; item goonpowder, not nameng how much: and what is heer, ye knowe by the post of yister evyn. If this journay be entended as great as is spoken, it woll not be feneshed shortely. I pray God send good and honorable effect therof, for it is right weyghtty; and thus fare ye well at Hampton this Witsommonday abouts v of the clok in the ouernone with the hand of your lovyng broder,

Ri. Wynton.

And yit agayn I thynk the noumbre of iiij m¹. to fewe, and if ther be any lesse noumbre appoynted to land then x m¹., it shalbe to littell.

To my broder the Kyng*is* Aulmosner.

** 42. TO HENRY VIII

RO. S. P. 1: 4, f. 30.   Southampton.
Brewer i. 1898 (4095).   19 May ⟨1513⟩.

Please it your grace, Sir,

This selve heure I receyved a lettre fro my broder your Aulmosner, by the which he sheweth me that your grace for diuerse consideracions hathe latly writen to my lord your Admirall to comme with your holl armye beyng vnder hym to Portesmuthe, ther to make his abode to the commyng of Sir Charles Brandon. Wherfor he writeth to me that it is your commaundement that if the said Admirall with your said armye be comme theder byfor this Thursdaye or vppon the same daye, I shuld then aduertise your grace therof by post to Wyndesore; to thentent ye myght secretely comme to the said Portismuthe, not only to see thestate of your armye, but also to see the same spedely sette forthward.

Please it your grace, Sir, neyther my said lord Admirall nor noo ship of that armye be yit comme hydder. And as I am credebely enformed, he with the holl armye and theyr vitaylers lighe soo far within the haven of Plymmouthe, that they can not comme out of it without a northe west wynde: and the wynde hathe be suthwest continually iij dayes past, and yit is. And if he myght haue comme with that wynd, he wold by liklihod haue be heer ij dayes past. And soo myght he haue bee, seyng that the wynd wold haue served hym soo to haue be, if he had be out of the said haven; and thus, Sir, we loke not for hym till the said north-west wynd doo serve hym. And whensoeuer he commeth, your grace shalbe therof aduertised with all spede. And if your grace shall comme into thies parties, it shalbe mor conuenient that ye comme to this toune then to Portes-muthe; for ther can be noo prouision for you, specially for haye, nor in the contre nygh therabouts.

Sir, heer is noo ship yit mete for the shippyng of Sir Charles Brandon and his compaignye, savyng oon Spaynyard[1] of ccc and a nother of vj^{xx}: which John Dawtrye and I haue appoynted to serve the said Sir Charles; who has not yit comme, but we heer by his seruaunts that he wolbe heer this daye. And seyng the said lak of ships heer, he shall comme yit all in good season. And after tharmye be holly comme hidder, the depechyng therof, what for layeng in of vitails for soo many ships and what for payment of wagies and what for shippyng of Sir Charles compaignye, woll require a right good tract of tyme. Albe it I doubt not ther shall such diligence be done that ther shall noo tyme be lost, specially if[2] wynd will serve.

Diuerse souldiers be comme and logied in the contre abouts ij dayes journayes on fote hens and therabouts; and soo we entend to ordre the remenaunt till such tyme as ship-pyng be redye for them, for spareng of vitails in this toune and nyghe herabouts. And asfor the vitayleng of my lord Admirall and his compaignye, your seruaunt John Dawtrye I trust be sufficiently prouided. If ther shal be any lacke, it shalbe of empty pypes: which comme with my lord Admirall, as we trust, and ellis we shalbe greatly disap-

---

[1] See no. 43.　　　　　　　　[2] of MS.

poynted. Asfor the vitaileng of Sir Charles and his compaignye we vndrestond that theyr vitailes shall comme fro
London; for the which and also for the commeng of my
lord Admirall I praye God send vs sone convenient wynds.
And thus the holy Trinite send your grace thaccomplisshe-
ment of your most noble desires.

At Hampton this Thursdaye the xix daye of Maye
abouts ix of the clok byfor none with thand of your most
humble subgiet

Ri. Wynton.

To the Kyng*is* grace at Wyndesore.
Hast, post, vppon thy lyfe!

** 43. TO WOLSEY

RO. S. P. 1: 4, f. 29.   Southampton.
Brewer i. 1899 (4094).   19 May ⟨1513⟩.

Broder maistre Aulmosner,

This daye abouts viij of the clok in the mornyng I
receyved your lettre dated at London the xvij daye of this
moneth: and thus ye may see what spede our posts make.
And forthwith the same heure accordyng to your said lettre
I wrot to the Kyng*is* grace, acertayneng the same that
neyther my lord Admirall nor noon of that armye vitailers
nor other be yit comme, neyther to Portesmuthe nor hidder;
and we vndrestond heer that they be soo far within the
haven of Plymmouth that they can not comme out of it
with this wynd. Which of liklihod is true; for yf they
myght haue comme thens with a south west wynd, they
myght haue be heer ij dayes past. And also ther is not oon
ship vitailer nor other comme out of the Themmys nor fro
Sandwiche; and when we shall haue wynds to bryng them
hidder out of all thre places, God knoweth. All other
thyngs towcheng ships, vitaileng or payement of wag*is* ye
shall vndrestond by John Dawtreys lettres.

And asfor sendeng of ships for the scowreng of the narowe
see and waftyng of the hoyes that goo to Calis, I pray God

send you them in tyme; for it is to great a shame to leese
the ships that be lost. And I trust ye woll noo mor aduenture, neyther thordnaunce, artillerye, vitailes nor men, till
ye haue wafters.[1] Me semeth that ye myght man soom of
the Spaynyards[2] that be at Sandwyche, and make them
wafters till other may comme to you. And when my lord
Admirall commeth, I woll call vppon hym to send such
shippes into the narowe see as be named in your said lettre;
but I feer that ye shall not haue them yit.

    Neyther Sir Charles nor noon other capitaigne is yit
comme hidder saving Brug*is*. Soom of theyr seru*auntis* be
comme; and John Dawtrey and I caused them stop theyr
compaignyes, and laye them ij dayes journayes hens, and
soom of them farther. And yistre even camme hidderwarde
therbergier;[3] and by our advises he hathe appoynted
logeyng*is* in the contre about ij dayes journays hens for
the said compaignyes. And when the ships be comme, ye
may be sure ther woll lak noo diligence in John Dawtrey.
I praye God that lak of conuenient wyndes stop them not.

    I thank you for your newes of Spaigne, which I knowe
assuredly be true; and if the fault be not in the Frenche
Kyng, the Kyng of Aragone I doubt not woll kepe his
bargyn, notwithstandyng his ambassador is worke to the
contrarye. And asfor themperor I thynk his will be good,
but powayre woll faile hym. And by that I heer, he shall
haue ⟨e / noughe to doo with the Venycians, which I trowe
be confedered ⟨with / the Frenche Kyng, and then haue at
Mylayn agayn. Which peraduenture shall doo vs good;
for soo shall the Frenche poway⟨re / be devided, and the
lesse shall it be vppon vs. But then gette we noo helpe,
neyther of the Pape, themperor nor the Kyng of Aragon;
for euery of them shall haue much e nough to doo for hym
selve in the parties of Italie, except themperor and the Kyng
of Aragon wold with theyr werre makeng, eyther of them

---

[1] Ships to act as escorts, like destroyers.
[2] Perhaps some of the transports which Ferdinand had supplied for the
English army in 1512, on the expedition to Guienne. Cf. no. 42.
[3] The billeting-officer.

on his quarter, vppon soom groun⟨de / of France prevent
the sendeng of the Frenche armye into Italie. But euer I feer
that themperor for lacke of substance shalbe enforced to
fall to a treuxe.

A substanciall wise man hathe told me that he see the
Kyng*is* lettre writ⟨ten / to my lord of Buk*ingham*,⁴ to haue
the middell warde, and to be redy to ship hym selve and
his compaignye the xv day of Jung; which was bif⟨or /
appoynted for the Kyng*is* grace and his compaignye. Wherof
I am oon, and I appoynt my selve to kepe that daye. I pray
you, lat me knowe by the next wherunto I shall dispose me.

And thus fare ye well at Hampton the xix daye of May
abouts none with the hand of y⟨our / lovyng broder

Ri. Wynton.

To my broder the Kyng*is* Aulmosner.

** 44. TO WOLSEY

RO. S. P. 1: 4, f. 67.   Southampton.
Brewer i. 1912 (4103).   21 May ⟨1513⟩.

Broder maistre Aulmosner,

Hidder be comme yit noo ships, neyther fro tharmy⟨e /
that is vnder thadmirall nor fro Sandwyche nor London. I
praye God send them sone hidder. And ellys I feer that
it shalbe nyghe the xv daye of Jung, which is my daye
assigned to be with my compaignye at Dovorre and Sandwyche, byfor I can depart hens. This mater trowbleth me
not a littell, and therfor I praye you lat me vndrestond your
mynde therin.

I rekyn that thoughe the first of the Kyng*is* warde begyn
to ship the said xv daye of Jung, it shalbe xv dayes after
or mor byfor the last of the said warde be shipped. And
I thynk that my soo long tarieng heer considered, the Kyng*is*
grace not displaised, I shall mowe comme to Dovor or
Sandwyche to take shippeng all in good season, with them

⁴ See no. 29.

of the King*is* warde that shall take theyr last shippyng, that is to saye xv dayes or therabouts after the said xv daye of Jung. Wherof I require you lat me knowe your mynde by the next post, for I haue great nede soo to doo, to thentent I maye ordre me therafter. And if ye may not haue the lais*ure* to write to me yourself, as I knowe well ye haue full littell, I praye you make Bryan Tuke to write to me by your instruccion, as I haue desired and prayed you to doo in tyme past. For without knowlege hade fro you of the premisses, I can not ordre my selve to serve heer and theer.

Also my lord of Devonshire[1] by the King*is* licence went to my ladye his moder[2] byfor Mydlent, wher he hathe be euer sens, saveng that he in the moyne tyme comme hidder oonys and loked vppon me. My said ladye wold gladly vndrestond whedder it shalbe the King*is* plais*ure* that he remaigne still with hir for the tyme that the King*is* grace shalbe be yond the see, or ellys that she shall send hym to the King*is* grace to passe to Calis with the same, and then to goo by the King*is* ordinance and sendyng to the Prince of Castell. I praye you vndrestand the King*is* plais*ure* in this mater and aduertise me of the same, to thentent my saide ladye may dispose for hir said soon therafter.

The Capitaigne of thisle of Wight hathe desired me to praye you be good maistre to hym in a mater that is in your hands towcheng hym not a littell, as he saithe. What it is I can not tell, and therfor I dar not write depely in it, but yit *rogatus rogo*.

Soom of the capitayns vnder my lord Lisle[3] shewe me that of theyr noumbres they had appoynted soom to goo to Calis with theyr cariagies, horses and bagages: the which not withstondyng, they be commaunded to bryng theyr holl noumbre hidder, and soo they saye they woll doo. And I thynk it be expedient that they soo doo, and then and in that case they praye to haue wagies for theyr folk*is* that shall

---

[1] Henry Courtenay (c. 1496–1538), cousin of Henry VIII; executed later on a charge of aspiring to the Crown.

[2] Katherine, sixth daughter of Edward IV.

[3] Brandon (no. 39), who was created Visct. Lisle in 1513.

attend vppon theyr cariagies to Calis, which shalbe a bove theyr noumbres assigned to them. And they thynk it shall not be the Kyng*is* plais*ure* that they shalbe chargied of theyr owne purses with the wagies of theyr said folk*is* that goo with theyr cariagies: which they pray you and my lords of the Counsell fauorabely to considre, and they woll send theyr said folks to you for theyr said wages.

All other thyngs worthe the writeng John Dawtrey writethe to you: wherto I am pr*e*uy. And except ther comme moo emptye pypes fro tharmye vnder my lord Admirall then is like to doo, I assure you it shall not be possible to furnesshe that army with sufficient beer. I feer that the pursers woll deserve hangyng for this mater: if any of them comme to you, speke with them accordyngly. Heer can lak noo beer, if ther comme foystes and empty pipes to receyve it; and if they comme not in season, the lak of them shall m*e*rveyleuxly hyndre the breweng of beer: which con-sequently must retarde tharmye. This is a daungereux mater, and much remembrance haue we made therof to thadmirall that was, and often prayed we you to doo the same. If ther fortune any lak in this behalf, it shall not be imputed of raison to vs; for I assure you heer wolbe beer mor then e nough for this armye, soo we may haue pipes: the which I praye God send vs with spede, and soon deliuer you of your outragieux charge and labour. And ellis ye shall haue a cold stomocke, littell slepe, pale visage and a thyn belly *cum rara egestione*: all which and as deffe as a stok, I hade when I was in your case etc.

At Hampton the xxj daye of Maye with the hand of your lovyng broder

Ri. Wynton.

To my broder the Kyng*is* Aulmosner.

**45. TO WOLSEY

RO. S. P. 1: 4, f. 78.   Southampton.
Brewer i. 1960 (5757).   4 June ⟨1513⟩.

Broder maistre Aulmosner,

Yistre nyght in my bed and in slepe after x of the clok I receyved your lettres with the lettre to the Kyng of Scots, a minute for a warant for the deliuerance of Steward out of the Toure, and thenstructions for Thomas Spynell: the which, with a lettre directed to Mr Compton to gette them signed of the Kyng*is* grace, I deliuered to the post forthwith, sittyng up in my bed. Soo that by this heure, which is vj in the mornyng, he myght be with the Kyng*is* grace at Gilford. They wer lost bytuyxt Alton and Waltham and afterward recouered; and that was the cause of theyr long taryeng by the waye. In like wise the lettres for themperor, the Venicians and the Bisshop of Worcestre[1] had such a chaunce by the waye that it was Thursdaye after none byfor they comme to my hands; and the same heure I retorned them to you. Ther hathe be, what by slewghe of the post*is* and what by other chaunces, evill fortune for conveyance of lettres sens the Kyng*is* commyng hidder; but by me, I assure you, ther was noo taryeng.

I also receyved this nyght past the copie of the lettre that the Kyng of Scots writeth by Isley: wherof the words sound well, but what his mynde is, it is vncertayne.[2] But it appereth well that the Frenche Kyng meneth, that in case the Kyng our maistre accept not the treux of Aragon, that then the Kyng of Scots shuld be at large; trustyng that he woll take his part. But the mynde of the Kyng of Scots can not be knowen by this lettre. Yt shuld rather be knowen by Mr West,[3] my lord Dacre and Sir Robert Drury and theyr workes; and by his workes, and also by the Kyng*is* dealyng tawards hym. Which I knowe not, but me semeth that the lettre that is nowe writen to hym, shall littell plaise hym;

---

[1] Sylvester, nephew and successor of John de Giglis (no. 1).
[2] Before long he entered upon the invasion of England which ended in his death at Flodden, 9 Sept.   [3] See no. 49.

albe it the lettre that Rosse brought, as it shuld seme by the rehersall therof in the Kyng*is* lettres, deserved noo better. But such mutuall accusacions and relacions of vnkyndenesse be not the moynes of entreteygnement of good love and amite. And yit I thynk it shalbe knowen at leyngh that he woll make noo actuall werre, but rob and spoyle the Kyng*is* subgiets, specially by water. And I thynk he woll not take well with the appoyntement of the next daye of dyet in Octobre, he woll rekyn craft therin. And in my opinion it myght haue be assigned better in the myd of August, and with much lesse suspicion.

Thinstructions for Thomas Spynell I am sure shall not content my ladye of Savoye:[4] but as for that mater, *habuit a principio malum fundamentum, et postea deteriorem super-edificacionem, et male arguitur a malis exemplis.*

Asfor the repaireng of the ships to the cost of Britaigne, I doubt not ye knowe thyssue of my Lord Lysle is mater. It was sent to you vppon Thursdaye in the mornyng. And asfor my lord Admirall, I warant you he woll not slepe his maters. But he lacketh many thyngs, as ye may see by his lettres of yistredaye; and he hathe had a great lette by my lord Lisle is maters, and nowe for thorderyng of many other maters far out of goode frame, I warant you: the which he woll reforme, I doubt not, to the Kyng*is* honour, profite, good seruice and better obeissance. And he woll noo longar byde then verye necessite shall require, and soom what he is embusied abouts reddyng of my lord Lisle is compaignye by land, and takeng into his ships and devideng the vitails that camme fro you, and dischargeyng a great noumbre of ships to the Kyng*is* great adu*au*ntage.

And thus fare ye hertely well at Hampton the iiij[th] daye of Juny abouts vj in the mornyng.

Your lovyng broder
Ri. Wynton.

I feer that it wolbe Mondaye byfor I may depart hens.

To my broder the Kyng*is* Aulmosner.

4 Margaret of Austria.

** 46. TO WOLSEY

BM. Egerton MS. 2603. 5.   Southampton.
Brewer i. 1976.   8 June ⟨1513⟩.

Broder maistre Aulmosner,

I haue great mervale that I haue noon answer fro you of the last lettres that I wrote to you, seyng that soom part of them wer mater of charge. And wher ye wrote to me to helpe sette forthe Delabere with certayne of the Kyng*is* garde and other seru*au*nts and folk*is* of my lord Haward*is*, soo it is that Delabere was with me at Sayncte Crosse[1] vppon Ascension daye[2] at dyner, and incontinent after dyner departed tawards Hampton; and the morrowe after I went thidder. And the same daye[3] comme thidder Rote with soom of the garde, and as yistredaye[4] comme the remen*au*nt, and this daye comme also with yong Braye certayne of my lord Haward*is* folk*is*; but the full noumbre be not yit comme. Delabere and Ichyngham,[5] Rote with all his compaignye, and soom of my lord Haward*is* folk*is* be departed hens this day. The wynd is good for them, and I trust they woll make good spede. Rote made great diligence in commyng hidder, and well and wisely hathe he ordred and shipped his compaignye. John Dawtrie hathe bothe shipped, vitayled and depeched them in the spedyest maner, and the same woll he doo for the remen*au*nt of my lord Haward*is* folk*is* when they comme. And in like wise he woll prouide as many ships as may be had in thies parties ayenst the xv daye of this moneth, accordyng to your last writeng: as ye shall mor playnly vndrestond by his writeng.

Yistredaye comme hidder a very good and goodly ship of Spaigne of ccc and above out of Flaundre, to lade wols heer. I haue advised that she shalbe reteigned for the Kyng*is* seruice, and soo John Dawtrey woll doo; and except

---

[1] See no. 58.   [2] 5 May.   [3] 6 May.
[4] 7 June.   [5] See no. 38.

the Kyng commaunde the contrarie, she shalbe oon of them that shalbe appoynted for such seruice as ye write of to be done, at and after the said xv daye of this monethe. And if she shall not be entreteigned therfor, ye must with all spede possible so certefie John Dawtrey, to thentent he may the rather discharge hir, soo that she put the Kyng to noo great cost.

This nyght I propose to goo to Sayncte Crosse, and to morrowe to Portesmowthe to see howe the brewehowses theer goo forthwarde: wherof I shall aduertise you by the next.

And forasmuch as ther gothe much vitaile out of the Thammys, much from hens and much out of the West-contre, and all to[6] to tharmye, and noon knoweth what another dothe, nor what yche of them sendeth thidder, it shalbe wisdomme that thadmirall be writen to, for to cause it to be soo distributed that euery ship haue that he ought to haue, and that the remenaunt may serve for a newe vitaileng; and that the Kyng be not dowble charged nor ouerchargied with the vitaileng of any of them. Also thadmirall must be writen to that as sone as the vitailers comme to hym, that he depeche them and send them forth-with hidder agayn, and that they bryng empty vessels with them. And ellis I assure you they can not be served of beer heer: like as ye shalbe mor playnly acertayned by John Dawtrey. And also they must haue wafters bothe commyng and goyng, and ellis ther is good liklihod that they shalbe take vp by the waye. Ye had nede also write to them of the West contrey that they send hidder part of the empty foystes that be left theer with them. For if they shall reteigne all theer, and that noon shall comme hydder, it can doo noo seruice to brewe beer heer. Also I vndrestond that heer is much old piped[7] befe in right great substance, left heer by Edward Ratclif:[8] which is like to be lost. Wher-for it shalbe good that ye commaunde Edward Ratclif to

---

[6] Perhaps=altogether: or cf. no. 37, n. 5.   [7] Cf. no. 39 n.
[8] or Hatclif, a clerk comptroller, and second clerk of the kitchen.

comme hidder and loke vppon it, and doo the best profite
that can be doo therof.

And thus fare ye hertely well at Hampton the vⅡⱼth daye
of Jung⁹ with the hand of your lovyng broder
Ri. Wynton.

** 47. TO WOLSEY

BM. Cotton MS. Galba B. III, f. 165.　　　　　Esher.
Brewer i. 2811 (4796).　　　　　　17 April ⟨1514⟩.

[The MS. has suffered in the Cotton fire, at the top and on both edges. To
help conjecture, the lines of the original are followed in printing. We have
had the benefit of Mr R. H. Brodie's ingenious reconstruction, based on
Rymer, in the new edition of Brewer i. The year-date can be assigned with
certainty from the age of Prince Charles, who was born on 24 Feb. 1500.
The King's sister, Mary, whom by treaty he was to marry, was born on
18 March 1495. As Fox expected, the Prince's governors repudiated the
marriage: see Brewer i. 3139 (5319).

As Wolsey was now bishop of Lincoln, the style of Fox's address changes;
but there is no lack of cordiality, nor in the later years, when Wolsey's
powers as legate were being used to the full.]

My singular good lord,⟩
　　　　　　　After⟩ my departyng ⟨from you . . .
I haue somew⟩hat mused for thinstru⟨ccions wher
of ye⟩ haue the charge, if it soo comme to ⟨pass that
ye hi⟩t vppon the mater that the same instr⟨uccions be
vp)pon. I praye you loke vppon them and a⟨duise me
as ye shall see cause. But shewe them yit ⟨to noo man,
for it is yit noo season; and soom folks peradu⟨enture that wold
see them, wold saye that we wer much busyar ⟨than is nede.
And if noon effect comme therof, they myght g⟨eue cause
of mokery. Neuerthelesse if the Kyng*is* grace ⟨woll take
the labour to see them at a goode leasure, I thy⟨nke it woll
doo good: for littell make we but by his ⟨fauour, wherin
is soom amends. And to make the mater the ⟨suerer,
it shuld not be a mysse if ther wer a commis⟨sion with
glasse wyndowes¹ *ad² tractandum et concludendum*, and ⟨in like
wise a salueconduyt with glasse wyndowes hade forthwith this s⟨ame moneth,
bycause the tyme is very short. And much I m⟨eruale
that ther comme noo newes fro Mr Ponyngs of ⟨the lettres

---

⁹ A correction from *Juyn*.
¹ Mr C. T. Onions suggests that this must mean 'transparently to be
trusted': and compares Vitruvius 3 pref., 'oportuit hominum pectora
fenestrata et aperta esse'.　　　　　　　² at MS.

that wer sent to hym by Thomas Pawlet. Me seme⟨th ther
myght soom thyng haue be doo vppon them by th⟨e way.

Also it ys not to be liked that my lady of Savoy⟨e 3
maketh noon answer for the mariage appoynt⟨ed to
be at Calis. And in case she make noon answer, ⟨or
that she woll put it ouer to soom other tyme and place, ⟨this
is a playne mater wherwith to prove theyr entent⟨ions in
the said mariage, and whedder they woll performe it ⟨as is
conclud⟩ed vppon that treatie 4
wherin is⟩ oon article conteyneng pro⟨uision: *quod
Princeps per proc⟩uratorem vel procuratores suos, ad h⟨oc post
quart⟩umdecimum etat*is *sue annum sufficienter auct⟨orisatos,
infra* XL *d⟩ies postquam dictam etatem* XIIIJ *annorum imp⟨leuerit
proximo s⟩equen*tes, *ad dominam Mariam in regnum Angl⟨ie missos,
cor⟩am duobus apostolica et imperiali auctoritate notariis et ⟨testibus
ad⟩ hoc specialiter vocat*is *et rogat*is, *cum eadem domina Mar⟨ia
m⟩atrimonium per verba de presenti ad hoc apta real⟨iter
contr⟩ahet et cum effectu.*

This article is not derogat by ⟨the
tre⟩atie made at Lysle,5 as may appere in the end of ⟨the
sa⟩me. Also the said XL dayes be past, as may apper⟨e
b⟩y accompt makyng fro saynct Mathies daye 6 last past hiddert⟨o.
And for as much as they haue not obserued this art⟨icle,
it shall in my mynde be right expedient if they
woll not performe the mater of Calis, or make n⟨oon
answer, but dryve the tyme, then forthwith require ⟨the
ladye to performe the said article. And if she refuse soo ⟨to
doo, it is playne mater that they entend noo mar⟨iage,
or ellys that they woll protract yt vncertaynly &c. Much ⟨do I
muse of the worde that the Gouernor of Bresse said, *scilicet* that within
IJ moneths it shuld be seen &c. shuld do harme.

And thus,
my nowne good lord, I pray God send you aswell to fare
as I wold wisshe my selve to doo.

At Essher this mond⟨ay
in Ester weke with the hand of your lovyng broder

Ri. Wynton.

---

3 Margaret of Austria.　　　　　　　4 of 1507–8: Rymer xiii. 173.
5 15 Oct. 1513; Rymer xiii. 379–381.　　6 24 Feb.

‡ 48. FROM DARCY

RO. S. P. 1: 230, f. 177.   Templehurst.
Brewer i. 2914.   18 May ⟨1514?⟩.

[Darcy's difficulties for money appear frequently in the pages of Brewer.
In March 1517 he buys the wardship of two heiresses (ii. 3034). In Jan. 1519
he borrows from a London draper. In June 1521 he writes to his agent,
'Remember Northern purses be thin' (Suppl.).
Templehurst is in Yorkshire, s. of Selby. The year-date is conjectural.]

My verrey good lord,

After most herty recomendacion and like thank*is* for
yowr costly good cheir*is* and humanite shewd too me and
my frend*is* att dyver*is* tymes, and specially att my retourne
from ⟨Sp⟩ayn;[1] my good lord, of my faith vnfenyd, eveyn
of verrey syngler faffour and trust that I hav in yow, I doo
nowe send my trusty seru*aun*tt*is* Lawrence Baynes and John
Halile vnto yow, thatt for a sesson I may bee yowr storer
by waye of lone of a certayn sowm of money: wich, if itt
so be yowr pleas*ure*, they shall deliuer vnto yowr good
lordship my bond for in duble the sowm.

My lord, I hav nott ben vssed to thes ways, ne trust nott
much to be. Yowr often kynd offir*is* and word*is* to me
and the many good actt*is* and succowr*is* that I hav knawen
by yow don to dyver*is* yowr neybour*is* in ther nessessites,
boldyns me that never deserued such a pleas*ure*, thus to
writ and desir it of yow.

My lord, with warres and hasty p*ur*chaiss*is* of ward*is*
& cet. I hav ouershott my selff, with paymentt*is* to be mayd
in ouershortt tym; and loth I wer to breke my credence as
any poir man. I beseich yow, gif as faste credence to this
berer and his felloo as ye wold too my selff, if I wer present
with yow: as I can fynd in my hertt often to wissh me.
And what they, ar ather of them, doth or deliuers for my
ded, I shall withowt dowtt perfowrm, and, God woillyng,
not breke onne day.

My lord, ye had my hert inwardly (?) to yow befor; and if

                    [1] Cf. no. 35.

yowr lordship doo this for me, mor ye can not hav, butt
bynd me eftsones; and all that may ly in me, shalbe redy
for yow when I may do yow ples*ures*. And thus yowr
goodly desir*is* God send yow.

Written at my caben of Tempilhirst the xviij^the day of
May.

* 49. FROM NICHOLAS WEST

RO. S. P. 1: 10, f. 128.   Paris.
Brewer ii. 306.   6 April ⟨1515⟩.

[Nicholas West (1461–1533), Fellow of King's College, Cambridge 1483–
1498, was now employed in diplomacy.   He had long found a refuge and
strength in Fox; having received from him the rectory of Egglescliffe in
Durham in 1499, in 1502 the rich living of Witney (see no. 51): both of which
he held till his 'promotion' in 1515 to the see of Ely.]

My singlier good lord,

Humble recommendations premised, I hertely beseche
you to contynue my good lord. *Et perfice opus manuum
tuarum*; for without your helpe at this tyme I see not how it
is possible for me to obtayn the promotion that the Kyng*is*
grace hath now named me to. For your lordship knoweth
my pouertie; and also now in myn absence I can make no
shyfte. Wherfore I haue non other refugie but to your good
lordship; and therfore I haue sent my seru*au*nt John Archer,
and desired maister Clyfton to wayte vpon your lordship
and my lord Archbusshop of Yorke,[1] not only to desire
your helpe but also to be ordred by your commaundement*is*,
aduise and counsell in all myn affaires.

My lord, I beseche you to pardon me that I am thus bold
vpon your lordship; and sithens I can not otherwise recom-
pence your goodenes toward me, I wol daily pray to almighty
God, as I am bounden, for the preseruation of your good
lordship.

Writen at Parys the vj^th day of April

your dayly bedman

Ni. West.

To my singlier good lord, my lord of Winchester.

[1] Wolsey.

** 50. TO WOLSEY

RO. S. P. 1: 11, f. 21.   Esher.
Brewer ii. 730.   20 July ⟨1515⟩.

[The Benedictine Abbey of St. Augustine's at Bristol was founded by a
Fitzharding, and under the patronage of that powerful family had acquired
a patrician character. Abbot John Newland died on 12 June 1515; his
successor, Robert Eliot, received the temporalities on 4 August. Out of the
Abbey the see of Bristol was founded at the Reformation.
  Wolsey had been given the archbishopric of York in Sept. 1514. From
Fox's reference of this matter to him, it might seem that his cardinalate was
already impending. He was actually created in Sept. 1515.]

My singular good lord,

  After my best recommendacion I send you herin enclosed
a lettre that I receyved this day by this berar fro Mr Haniball;[1] by the which ye may vndrestond the inordinat, hedye
and vnreligiose dealyng of the chanons of saynct Augustyne
besidis Bristoll. Yf I wer within the diocese of Worcestre,
I cowde by calleng the evill disposed persons byfor me sone
remedye the mater. Mr Haniball myght doo the same if
he durst, but I perceyve well that he is a ferd. I vndrestond
also that Lloyd of the Kyngis chapell is the auctor of much
of this busynesse. I see well he wold make thabbot to gette
hym a fee.

  I see noo remedye in this mater but that Mr Haniball reteigne in his handis the Kyngis lettres patentis de libera eleccione:
which shall cause soom of the chanons to resort to the courte
to sue for it, and then shall ye mowe ordre them after your
wisdomme. Or ellis that it may plaise the Kyngis grace to
send a doctor of his counsell with a gentilman of his house
to the President and covent with his lettres, chargeyng them
by the same to procede peaxibely and quietely to theyr
eleccion, and in the same to be directed and ordred by theyr
ordinaries Vicar generall; and the Kyngis said seruauntis to
see all folkis avoyded out of the monasterye dureng the
tyme of the eleccion, and that the iiJ yong folys which sue
for licence to haue voyces in eleccione, not withstandyng that

  [1] Thos. Hannibal, a lawyer; afterwards Master of the Rolls; †1531.

they be not *in sacris*, be vttrely excluded in the tyme of the eleccion. And I woll vndretake that the covent shall paye theyr costs. This is a perliese mater, for the evill example that may comme therof; and therfor accordeng to your good begynnyng I beseche you hold your good hand to it.

Ther is also a nother waye and that is this: *scilicet* that Mr Haniball suffre them to procede to theyr eleccion and lat them cheese at theyr perill; and if they doo amysse, to reforme it at the tyme of the confirmacion. I beseche your good lordship to ordre this mater after your wisdomme, and lat me haue knowlege therof, and I and Mr Haniball shall conforme vs to the same; and thus I commit your good lordship to the Holy Trinite.

At Essher the xx daye of July

assuredly yours
Ri. Wynton.

If it may like you to examyn this berar, he can shewe you much of the mysdemeanour, bothe of the chanons and of Lloyd, which shuld be put to silence.

To my lord of York*is* good lordship.

** 51. FROM RICHARD RAWLYNS

Corpus MS. ⟨Oxford.⟩
⟨1515–16?⟩

[Part of the site of Corpus, namely Corner Hall at the NW., Nevyll's Inn in the centre and w., and the Bachelors' Garden on the s., was bought from Merton College for an annual payment of £4 6s. 8d. (perhaps in addition to a capital sum: see T. Fowler, *History of Corpus*, OHS, 1893, p. 66), charged by Fox upon the living of Witney, which was in his gift. This agreement was expressed in an indenture dated 20 Oct. 1515; see *Merton Muniments*, OHS, 1928, no. 20.

This letter from the Warden of Merton asks for security that the annual payment shall be made with as little trouble to the College as it had previously had in receiving rents. In the indenture Fox covenants that Merton shall 'have and perceive' the annual payment. The scroll mentioned at the end here (now in the Corpus Archives) has as its first article that Corpus shall pay the sum or cause it to be paid 'in Oxford': a stipulation which accords with this letter, and suggests that it is later than the indenture. Subsequent articles require that there shall be no windows, no sinks coming from the kitchen, stable or draught, to the 'displesure' or 'noianse' of Merton, no door in the wall; and that the bounds shall be clearly expressed before Easter. Thus this letter may be dated conjecturally between 20 Oct. 1515 and Easter 1516.]

Ryght reverent fadur in God and my especial good lord,

Aftur dew and moost hvmble recommendacions had, pleasith yow to wnderstond that I have, acordyng to yowr honorabul letturs sent to me by yowr chapelayn, reshevyd sich wrytyngis which your discret counsel and myn hath concludyd for the perfoormans off your gracius and blessid mynd concernyng yowr College callid Corpus Christi; and aftur and acordyng to youre mynd, my Felows al hath endeverd them sylff to seale al sich wrytyng*is* which ye have send, wyth moost diligence. And hartyly in the moost humble maner that they may or can, they recommendith them to your good lordship; besekyng yow that forasmych as the sum off iiij^{li} vj^s viij^d, which hath ben a fore payd to Merton College wyth out eny trobul, expensis and further labor, bi cause the land which your lordship hath off vs, is in the Wniuersite, they therfore most mekely desiryth your goodnes that notwythstandyng that the church[1] is bound for the payment off the same, that ther may be a articul made be tuixt yow and vs expressid bi a indentur, that the forsayd sum may be payd in the Vniuersite wyth out eny further labor or expensis.

And forasmych as I can not expresse in wrytyng my Felovs myndis, I have shewyd it moor largly to yowre chaplen, to whom I pray yow geve credens: which hath bound hym silff bi obligacion to me and the Felows off my House, that the forsaid sum off iiij^{li} vj^s viij^d shal be yerly payd in Oxford to oon off the Felovs or Offisars off my House, as oure counsel wol diuise sufficient wrytyng for the same. For as yet my cumpany can not persheue the seurte off the recovere and off sych othur wrytyng*is*, tyl that othur men bi side oure counsel geue them further instruccion. There mynd is so blyndyd wyth scrupulus consciens, as your sayd

[1] of Witney.

M

chaplen can shew youre good lordshyp: by whom ye shal
haue also a scrow off sich articuls which they require for
the klene kepyng and seurte off our College, as God knowyth.
Who preserue your good lordship long to continew to se
the increse off werteus clerkis in your College off Corpus X^i
Your bedman and continual orator
Richard Rawlyns
Reverendissimo in Christo patri et domino singulariter-
que de se benemerito domino Wyntoniensi episcopo
tradantur.

** 52. TO WOLSEY

RO. S. P. 1: 13, f. 121.   Winchester.
Brewer ii. 1814.   23 April ⟨1516⟩.

[After 29 years' service to the Crown, Fox was permitted to resign the Privy
Seal. The actual date when he gave it up is not known: probably 18 May
1516, when it was handed to Ruthall, bishop of Durham. He was now an
old man; and he wished whole-heartedly to devote his remaining years to
the duties of his spiritual office, especially within his diocese. A first fruit
of his new intention may be seen in no. 55: within a year, too, his College
in Oxford had come into being. But his work in the State had been too important for him easily to be let go. His memory and experience are often
called for (cf. nos. 57, 81); and he is frequently required to come to Court
and attend the Council (cf. nos. 67, 71, 75).

The year-date to this letter can be assigned from the mention of the joint
attack by Maximilian and the Swiss on Milan in March 1516; which was
supported by English gold. Fox's estimate of 28 years' negligence must
therefore be regarded as inaccurate.]

My very singular good lord,

In my most humble wise I recommaunde me to your good
lordship. And wher I vndrestand by my fellow William
Purde that of late your said lordship diuerse tymes asked
of hym when I entended to be theer, and that finally ye
commaunded hym to send to me for my commyng thidder:
my lord, yf my impediments and the causes of my absence
fro you wer not bothe resonable and necessare, and that
I hade not the King*is* licence to be occupied in my cure,
wherby I maye doo soom satisfaccion for xxvɪɪJ yeres
negligence, I wer greatly to be blamed; and to your good
lordship I shuld be vnkynde, consideryng and remembryng

your great goodnesse of tyme past. And as I haue said to
your selve and to soom other also, I hade neuer better
wyll to serve the Kyng that was my maker (whos saule God
pardone), then I haue to serve the Kyng his soon, my
soueraigne lord that nowe is. And specially sens your good
lordship hathe hade the great charge that ye haue in your
hand: perceyveng better, straghttar and spedyar wayes of
justice, and mor diligence and labour for the Kyng*is* right*is*,
duties and profitz to be in you then euer I see in tyme past
in any other; and that I my selve hade mor ease in attendance vppon you in the saide maters then euer I hade bifore,
albe it I trust I gave you such attendance as ye woll not
complayne of me.

But, my lord, to serue wordly with the damnacion of my
saule and many other sawles wherof I haue the cure, I am
sure ye woll not desire. And as it shall please God to geve
me grace, I shall endevor me to doo bothe God and the Kyng
some seruice, and soo I tendrely beseche you, my nowne
good lord, to be contented. I assure you, my lord, my
absence fro you is neyther to hunt nor hawke nor to take
noon other wordely plais*ure*, nor for ease of my bodye,
nor yit for quietenesse of mynde: which is trowled nyght
and daye with other mens enormites and vices mor then
I dar write. Wherof I remembre ye shewed me ye hade
soom knowlege, when ye wer bisshop of Lincoln:[1] and
of them I assure you ther is playntye heer with moch mor.
But I haue prouided the medicine which I trust shall doo
good seruice. Nor verely, my lord, I seke noo lucre of
money. I pray God I may *lucrari animas*.

Also, my lord, I considre well that ye haue as much
labour of bodye and busynesse of mynde as euer hade any
in your roumes, and moor; and neuer noon hade lesse helpe.
But of great weighty cause heer I noon. And soo themperor
and the Swyshes spede well (wherof I haue as great desire
to heer as of any mater), I trust ye shall haue noo great
trowbeleux maters. But your paynes be neuer the lesse.

[1] in 1514.

And I require you and hertely praye you, laye a part all such busynesses fro vj of the clok in the evenyng forthward: which, if ye woll vse it, shall after your intollerable labours greatly refresshe you. And, good my lord, when the terme is done, kepe the Counsell with the Kyng*is* grace whersoo euer he be. Thus, my lord, I presume *docere Mineruam*: but I write it of goode mynde and to goode entent, our Lord be my juge. Thus, my lord, I humbely and hertely beseche you to spare me of my commyng vp yit, and pluk me not fro the necessite that I am in, till I haue fyneshed it. And I shall make all diligence possible.

And for farther declaracion of my mynde in this behalue and to thentent I doo you noo mor encomberance with this my long tediose lettre (wherof I beseche you, my lord, of pardon), it may plaise you to geve credence to William Purde and benignely to considre all that he shall shewe you on my behalue. And I shall as hertely daily pray for you as any preste lyvyng.

At Wynchestre the xxiij daye of Aprill with the hand of your assured prest and bedeman

Ri. Wynton.

To my lorde Cardinall of Yorke.

** 53. FROM THOMAS BARKER

Corpus MS.   ?

22 December ⟨1516⟩.

[The College Archives show that Fox bought the land of Dorsett and Newlond in the first days of January 1517: so that Barker was justified of his haste and his consequent miswritings.

Arborfield is in Berkshire, 5 ms. SE. of Reading.]

Ryght reuerend and my syngular gode lord,

In the moste humble wyse that I can, I recommend me on to youre gode lordshyp as yowre own bedman, thankyng youre gode lordshyp of your grete benyuolens and kyndnes schewyd onto me at all tymys, and specyallye that ye be so goode lord on to my powyr ladde:[1] of whom I truste in

[1] No doubt Ant. Barker, from Berkshire: disc. 21 Oct. 1517, sch. 1519.

God ye schall haue a trewe bedman duryng hys lyfe, and my seruys and prayour.

And where as hyt hath pleasyd youre gode lorshyp to wryte on to me to a vewe a howse with certen lond lyyng in the parisshe of Erberfeld, of Thomas Dorsett, I haue seyn hyt, and hyt ys worth xiij^s iiij^d by the yere. The howse ys sumwhat at reparacion, and ix acre of gode land lyyng there to and inclosyd. And he schwyth me that he hath spokyn on to Thomas Bullokk for an acre of mede and *di.*,[2] the wyche he schuld haue in hys me;[3] and he made answer, yf he kowde schewe a de[4] ther of, that he schuld haue hyt.

Aiso I haue spokyn on to a nothyr man callyd Richard Newlond; the wyche hath iij croft*is* of arrabull lond lyyng in the same parisshe, nye on to the howse of the seid Thomas Dorsett. The wyche he wull selle after xvj yere purches, and that he schall haue hyt to ferme for vj^s viij^d by the yere; and he to bere all maner charg*is*, and to serue the Kyng and lord.

Also I haue comynyd with the same Thomas Dorsette, to vnderstond what he wuld haue for hys howse and lond. And he seyth that he wulnat selle hyt vnder xx^{ti} marke, for he seyth he maye haue so of dyuers of hys neybors. And his neybor Richard Newlond wulnot selle hys vnder viij marke; the wyche ys after xvj yere purchys.

Also where as Thomas Fest and Thomas Creswell where infeffyd in the seid howse and lond to the vse of hym and hys wyfe, the same feffeys hath delyueryd the same dede to the same Thomas Dorsette. And yf I can haue knowlege of anye othyr land that wull be shold in our cuntre, your lordshyp schall haue knowlege ther of schortlye: with the grace of Jhesu, who preserue ⟨you⟩ to hys plesure.

Wretyn in haste the xxij^{ti} daye of Decembre.

By yowre own to hys powyr

Thomas Barker.

To the reuerend fathyr in Godd and moste syngler gode lord, my lord of Wynchester, thys bylle be delyueryd in haste.

---

[2] *dimidium.*   [3] *sic.* ? mede.   [4] *sic.* ? dede.

‡54. FROM CLAYMOND TO ISABELLA BRAYNTON

Corpus MS. Oxford.

17 January ⟨1517⟩.

[Evidently Claymond was assisting Fox in acquiring sites for his College. Nun Hall occupied a position, 18 × 40 feet, on which part of the west side of the front quadrangle now stands: to the south of Corner Hall, which was at the NW. angle of the College. As it was the town-house or refuge of the abbey of Godstow, there can be no doubt as to the person addressed.

As the College is sufficiently near completion for its seal to be contemplated, a year-date may be conjectured with some security.

Isabella Braynton was abbess (1494–†10 March 151⁶⁄₇, Brewer ii. 3052) of the Benedictine nunnery at Godstow on the Thames, a few miles above Oxford. She is mentioned as dining with the President of Magdalen in 1497 and 1502–3: see W. D. Macray's *Register of Magdalen*, N. s. i, 1894, pp. 29, 32.]

Madame,

After deue recommendation, I shall move my lord of Winton that ye shall have his whriteng with his seele; bi the which he shall bynd hym and his College to discharge you and your monastere of all rent*is* and seruice that canne be rightfulle hasked and demandit of Nonhale, os of IIIJ^s claymed by the Prior of Frideswidis.[1] And after, when he hath made his College a body and gyven them a seele, thei shall make to you and your monastere a lyek whrytenge by ther seele: and thus God send you prosperus helth.

Fro Oxferth the xvij day of Januarij

Joannes Claimondus.

55. TO THE READER

Rule of seynt Benet, f⁰. A². ⟨Winchester.⟩

22 January 151⁶⁄₇.

[The preface to a translation of the Benedictine Rule made by Fox at the request of four houses of holy women in his diocese. After presenting manuscript copies to them, he had it printed for wider circulation, with the title *The Rule of seynt Benet*, London, Pynson, *s.a.* The dates at the end should strictly refer to the printing; so that the translation may have been made at any time before. But it seems likely that it was a fruit of his leisure on retirement; cf. no. 52.

For Fox's vigilant care of nunneries see also no. 87.]

For asmoche as euery p*er*sone ought to knowe the thyng that he is bounde to kepe or accomplisshe, and ignorance

[1] See no. 56.

The Rule of Seynt Benet, 22 Jan. 1517, title-page, recto

The Rule of Seynt Benet, 22 Jan. 1517, title-page, verso

of the thynge that he is bounde to do, cannot nor may not
excuse him; and for so moche also as the reding of the
thynge that a persone is bounde to do and execute, except
he vnderstande it, is to the executinge therof no thyng
vailliable but only thyng inutile, trauell in vayne and tyme
loste:

We therfore Richarde, by the permission and suffrance of
our lorde God bisshope of Winchester, reuoluinge in our
mynde that certayne deuoute and religiouse women, beinge
within our diocese and vnder our pastorall charge and cure,
haue not only professed them to thobseruance of the Rule
of the holy confessoure Seinte Benet, but also be bounde
to rede, lerne and vnderstond the same, when they be
nouices and before they be professed, and also after their
profession they shulde nat onely in them selfe kepe,
obserue, execute and practise the sayd Rule but also teche
other their sisters the same; in so moche that for the
same intente they daily rede and cause to be red somme
parte of the sayd Rule by one of the sayd sisters amonges
them selfe, aswell in their Chapiterhowse after the redinge
of the Martyrologe as somme tyme in their Fraitur in
tyme of refeccions and collacions: al the which reding*is* is
alwayes don in the Latin tonge, wherof they haue no
knowlege nor vnderstondinge but be vtterly ignorant of
the same; whereby they do nat only lese their tyme but also
renne into the euident daunger and perill of the perdicion
of their soules:

We the sayd Bisshope, knowing and consideringe the
premisses, and rememberyng that we may not without like
peryll of our sowle suffer the sayd religious wemen, of
whose sowles we haue the cure, to contynue in their
sayde blindenesse and ignorance of the sayd Rule, to
the knowlege and obseruance wherof they be professed;
and specially to thentent that the yonge nouices may first
knowe and vnderstande the sayde Rule before they pro-
fesse them to it, so that none of them shall mowe afterward probably say that she wyste nat what she professed,

as we knowe by experience that somme of them haue sayd in tyme passed:

For these causes, and specially at thinstant requeste of our ryght dere and welbeloued doughters in oure lorde Jhesu, thabbasses of the monasteris of Rumsay,[1] Wharwel,[2] Seynt Maries within the citie of Winchester,[3] and the Prioresse of Wintnay,[4] oure right religious diocesans, we haue translated the sayde Rule into oure moders tonge, commune, playne, rounde Englisshe, easy and redy to be vnderstande by the sayde deuoute religiouse women.

And by cause we wolde not that there shulde be any lacke amongis them of the bokis of this sayd translation, we haue therfore a boue and besyde certayne bokes therof, which we haue yeuen to the sayde monasteris, caused it to be em-printed by our welbeloued Richarde Pynson of London, printer, the .xxii. day of the monethe of January, the yere of oure Lorde .m.ccccc.xvi., and the .viii. yere of the reigne of our souerayne lorde kynge Henry the .viii., and of our translacion the xvi.

*56. TO CLAYMOND

Corpus MS.   Esher.
                                  25 February ⟨1517⟩.

[As in no. 54, it appears that the site was only just acquired; but as Claymond's successor was already appointed at Magdalen, and the institution of the President and Fellows in the new College was imminent, only 1517 is possible.

It appears that the first list of Fellows was drawn up by Claymond and approved by Fox. The second list, sent with the letter which this answers, differed; but to oblige Claymond, Fox agrees to get round his own Statutes.

The 'Fundacion' which Fox sent down by Coke does not exist. But the College Archives possess the copy 'new writen', with the 'addicions of Maisters and Bachelers'; dated 1 March 151⁶⁄₇ from Wolvesey and with his

---

[1] A Benedictine house, founded in x°. The abbess at this time was Anne Westbrooke.   [2] See no. 65.

[3] A Benedictine house, founded c. 900, in the E. part of the city. A ms. Order for the profession of Nuns, in English, presented to St. Mary's by Fox, is in the University Library at Cambridge, Mm. iii. 13.

[4] A Cistercian house, founded in xi°: N. of Winchfield.

seal intact. Under it the following six Fellows were instituted with Claymond
on 5 March:

    Thomas Fox, dioc. London., 'my pore kyndesman'.
    John Garthe, M.A. ⟨1512, Univ. Coll.⟩, dioc. Dunolm.
    Richard Clerkson, M.A. ⟨1516, Durham Coll.⟩, com. Ebor.
    Robert Treguilion, B.A. ⟨1512⟩, dioc. Exon.
    Thomas Welshe, dioc. Winton.
    Robert Hoole, com. Linc.]

Brother maister President,

    I haue receyued your lettre by your seruaunt this berer,
for the which I hertely thank you; for it was to my great
comfort, and in maner revived me out of many dumpes and
perplexities that I was in, by reason that I had no sonner
writing frome you. I was in great doubt that the Prior[1] by
some invyous counsaill had chaunged his mynd; but now
I thank God and your diligent and wise ways, I am brought
in to good suerte of the pouer grounde and syte of our
Colleige. And by Humfray Coke,[2] which shalbe here with
me vppon Sonday,[3] and departe towardis you vppon Monday, ye shall receyue the Fundacion vnder my seall. And
therwith and in thesame a graunt of the said syte, with a
lettre of attornay to the Warden of the New Colleige[4] and
the President of Mawdelayn Colleige[5] to bring you and your
company in to the possession therof.

    And whereas ye sent me at this tyme the names and order
of suche as shalbe Felowes and Scolers of our Colleige,
wherof two be Maisters of Arte and oon Bacheler, this order
dooth far vary frome the names that ye left with me, and
that ye wrote your self in the mynite of the Fundacion. And
of theym there is noon named neither Maister of Arte nor
Bacheler; and as ye left theym with me, and in thesame
order, they be written in the Fundacion, without namyng

    [1] John Burton, prior since 1513 of St. Frideswide's; from whom Fox
bought Urban Hall and garden and Beke's Inn. The indenture for this,
9 Feb. 1517, is in the College Archives.
    [2] Carpenter and master of the works since 1513, when Fox began to
build on the site: see T. Fowler, *Hist. of Corpus*, OHS, 1893, pp. 61, 65.
He was present at the Institution on 5 March 1517.
    [3] 1 March.   [4] Wm. Porter, warden 1494-1520.
    [5] Jo. Hygdon, president 1516-1525.

of any of theym [6]Maistre or Bachelar[6]: and this ye must take in worth at this tyme. And to save our honestie in that behalue, ye must cause suche a discrete person to rede the Fundacion at the tyme of the possession taking, as by your good instruction may and can subuerte the order, and rede theym as ye haue ordered theym, with their addicions of Maisters and Bachelers; saving that it shalbe noo great inconuenience[7] to rede my pore kyndesman in thesame order that he is now in in the Fundacion. And as soone as ye may, cause ye[6] the Fundacion to be new writen with a good large substanciall hand. And therin ye may order the names of thesaid Felowes with their addicions of Maisters and Bachelers, diocises and shires, in thesame forme that ye sent theym to me at this tyme; saving that I will that mysaid kyndesman be the first.

And in this new writing adde the childe that my lorde of Wynchecomme[8] writeth to you for, called Kenelme Aden[9] of Glocestershire, if ye fynde hym hable therfor; and ell*is* not. And if he be to yong or otherwise vnhable to be a Felowe, leve hym oute and reserue hym for a disciple, and soo take hym in to you when ye list, [6]so he be hable[6]: and by hym ye may excuse you to Sir Robert Poynes for his childe, saying that ye can haue b⟨ut oon / for Glocestershire. And when ye haue new writen thesa⟨id / Fundacion, send it to me with the other, and I shall seall it ⟨and / sende it to you agayne. And to excuse you to my lorde of Wynchecomme for the Maister of Arte that he writeth to you for, ye may say that by the Fundacion there be noo Maisters of Arte eligible; which is true. And as for those Maistres[6] that ye haue now taken in, ye may say ye haue soo doon of necessite to make theym Officers;[10] and to make your saying true, I pray you make theym either Deanes or Bursers, and take noo moe Maisters of Arte to you herafter. For frome hensforth I wol that in that poynt ye obserue the Statut*is*: which

---

[6] added by Fox.   [7] inco͞uence MS.

[8] the famous Richard of Kidderminster.

[9] left out of the new Fundacion, but admitted disc. 4 July 1517, sch. 1519

[10] Garthe was made bursar, Clerkson dean.

be not yet redy, and I think it wilbe yet xv days or I can send theym to you.

And let your company begynne commyns vij or viij days bifore your departing in to the North Countrey.[11] And I shall send you more monay by Humfray Coke, for they must yet for a season lyve vppon my purse; and in your absence I doubt not your Vicepresident[12] will order theym accordingly, and bydde hym as he shall nede any thing, ⁶that he⁶ write and[13] send to me, and soo will I doo to hym.

The barge departed frome West*minster* vppon Fryday last with your kechyn stuff and other thing*is*; and with it commeth to you Robert, baillief of Savoy, which shall deliuer you oon parte of thindenture conteygnyng the particulars of thesaid stuf. And at my commyng to Wynchester which shalbe about the later ende of the next weke, I shall send yow more stuff. And I pray you depart noo sonner Northward then ye shalbe enforced to doo of pure necessite; for I wolde gladly that bifore your departing ye see your company somme what metely establisshed. And certifie me of suche of your matiers as there shalbe frome tyme to tyme occurraunt. And thus fare ye well.

At Essher the xxv day of February.

Your lovyng broder
Ri. Wynton.

To Maister John Claymond, president of Corpus Christy Colleige in Oxford.

---

[11] to his living of Norton, by Stockton-on-Tees, to which Fox had appointed him in 1498. Seemingly some residence was required of the rector, for Claymond resigned it in 1518.

[12] Morwent; see no. 60.

[13] and *Fox*: or *sec*ᵛ.

* 57. TO WOLSEY

BM. Cotton MS. Faustina E. vii, f. 121.   Winchester.
Ellis, Ser. 2, no. 96: Brewer iii. 2207.   30 April ⟨1517⟩.

[Nos. 57–59, are evidently connected; for the first two are concerned with Calais, and all three ask for the wages of the gunners and the keepers of the brewhouses.

No. 57 is placed by Brewer in 1522; the other two, which have only recently been found, are dated in 1517 in the supplementary volume of Letters and Papers which is being prepared.

In favour of 1517 are:
1. the identification of 'the matere of London' (no. 58) with 'Evil May Day'.
2. the dispatch of a commission to Calais in May 1517 with Mr. Sandis as one of its members (Brewer ii, p. 1475); which may be regarded as an outcome of the present enquiry.
3. Fox's estimate of almost 30 years for his neglect of his cure—a date which agrees with his appointment to Exeter in 1487. His figure, 28 years, in no. 52, has been shown to be inaccurate; but nos. 52, 57 cannot be far apart, unless he is to be regarded as quite vague in his calculations of time.

If 1517 be accepted, Fox's statement of his own age, '70 years and above', is about one year in advance of that which he gave in his examination at Wolvesey, 5–6 April 1527, '79 years old'; see no. 89 introd.]

My verye singular good lord,

After my humblest recommendacion, I haue receyved your lettre sent to me by Mr Sands. In the whych it hathe pleased your good lordship to shewe me that, after dyuers communicacions had by the King*is* grace with hys Counsell vppon thestate and condicion of the toune and marches of Calis and other fortryses within the same, and of theyr ruynes, decayes, mutacyons and alteracions fro the auncyent estatutz and ordinances, his grace for remedye in that behalue, by thaduyse of hys said Counsell, hathe determyned to send thidder with conuenyent diligence certayne hys Commissioners: not only to vieu the said ruynes and decayes, and theruppon to aduertyse hys grace what reformacions, reparacions and fortificacions be necessar*e* to be made in that partye; but also substancyally to examyn thabuses of the sayde auncient ordinancies, and the insufficienties of the souldiours, wyth all other thyngs that may sounde to the daungier of the sayd toune, marches and fortryses. And

therof to make relacion and reaport to hys grace and hys
Counsell for spedye remedye to be prouyded for the same.
And ouer thys your good lordship sheweth to me by your
sayde lettre, that forasmuch as I haue at sundry tymes taken
travayle in the saide maters, and haue knowlege of theme,
and that the Kyng*is* grace is also enformed that I haue
certayne bok*is* concernyng the sayde maters, hys grace therfor willeth that, all other thyngs set apartt, I doo repaire
incontynent to hys grace, bryngeng with me all such bok*is*
as I haue concerneng the premisses.

My very singular good lord, in my humblest wyse I beseche you that withowt your displeasor I may frely shewe
you the trowble that your saide lettres hathe put my
mynde in.

Truely, my singular good lord, syns the Kyng*is* grace
lycenced me to remaigne in my chyrche and therabowts
vppon my cure—wherin I haue be almost by the space of
xxx yeres so negligent, that of iiij seuerall chathedrall
chyrches that I haue successiuely had, ther be two, *scilicet*
Excestre and Wellys, that I neuer see, and innumerable
sawles wherof I neuer see the bodyes—; and specially sens
by hys licence I left the kepyng of hys pr*e*uy seale; and most
specially sens my last departyng fro your good lordship and
the Counsell: I haue determyned and, bytwixt God and
me, vtterly renouncyed the medlyng with wordly maters,
specially concernyng the werre or any thyng to it apper-
teigneng. Wherof for the many intollerable enormytes that
I haue seen ensue by the said werre in tyme past, I haue
noo littell remorse in my conscience; thynkeng that if I dyd
contynuall penance for it all the dayes of my lyfe, though
I shuld lyfe xx yeres longar then I may doo, I cowde not
yit make sufficient recompense therfor.

And nowe, my good lord, to be called to fortificacions
of townes and plac*is* of werre or to any mater concerneng
the werre, beyng of the age of LXX yeres and above, and
lokyng daily to dye—the whych if I dyd, beyng in any such
medlyng of the werre, I thynk I shuld dye in dispeyr—; no

marvayll, my lord, the premiss*is* considered, if thys my present vocacion to such maters trowble not a littell my spirits. I fere that I shall not by raison therof be in such quyetnes that I shall dar say masse thies next v or vj dayes.

And yit, my nowne good lord, I am not vnremembred of my deutye tawardis the Kyng, my most drad kynde soueraigne lord, the soon and successor of the Kyng that was my maker and promotor to the dignytie that I vnworthely doo occupye, and to all that I haue in erthe. And therfor if hys grace call or commaunde me to doo that thyng that may becomme soo old a preest to doo, verely, my lord, to spend my lyve and all my pouer substance, I shall neuer refuse it. But by licence of your good lordship, the maters for the whych hys grace wolleth me to comme to the same, be all of a nother sort, qualitie and nature. It becommeth me noo thyng nowe to medle, neyther by way of counsell nor faict, wyth municions or fortificacions of townes and places of werre. Also, my lord, I had neuer commission, charge, nor commaundement, by wryteng or worde, to medle wyth the saide fortificacions, neyther of Calys, Hams, nor Guynes; nor neuer dyd I medle wyth theme in deed.

Trowthe it is, that byfore the siege of Boleigne[1] I and other, to ryght a good noumbre, as ambassadors met and hade many treaties and communicacions with thambassadors of France, some tyme at Boleyng, some tyme at Calys and somtyme at Sandyngfeld. And after all my compaygnye except Sir John Doon and Sir John Troblevyld were retorned into England, they two and I mette at Boleigne dyuerse tymes wyth the lord Quardis: all whych season indured frome abowts Mychaelmas to it was abowts Candelmas then next ensueng. And in the moyne tyme, besyds the tymes of the said metyngs, I contynued allwayes at Calais; and dureng that tyme, by the Kyngis ordynance that ded is, whos saule God pardon, I medled wyth the haven of Calice, and in my mynd brought it to that condicion, that if the scluse that I caused to be made, hade not be destroyed

---

[1] in 1492.

by Sir John Turbrevyle, then thresorier of Calice, it had be
nowe a good havyn. And also in the meayne tyme I rode
to Hams and Guysnes, to make good chere with the capy-
tayns; but farther dyd I neuer medle in noon of the saide
places. And asfor the bok*is* that it is supposed I shuld
haue, verely, my lord, noon I haue, nor neuer had nor neuer
see noon, savyng suche as be wont to remaigne in the
Counsell house of Calice, and in the hand*is* of thofficers and
the Counsell ther, concernyng the ordre of the retenue, and
the rule of the toune: wherof I neuer had copye, nor noon
desired to haue.

My singular good lord, in my most humble wyse I beseche
your good lordship fauorabely and beningly to interpretate
and take the premisses; and in consideracion of the same,
to be soo good lord to me as by your good meanys thys my
excuse, grounded vppon resonable causes, may be acceptable
to the Kyng*is* grace, to you my lord, and all other of the
Kyng*is* most honorable Counsell.

Also, my lord, I haue not soo sklenderly buyldyd my
selue, nor soo weykly estableshed my house in thies parties,
that I can honestely or conuenyently so sodenly depart hens,
nor incontynent come theder. I haue also many causes in
my hand*is*, bothe of correccions and justice, that if I shuld
sodenly relinquyshe theme, I shuld vnresonabely and in-
honestly disapoynt many maters and persons to my great
rebuke and sclaundre. And oonys in xv dayes I visit my
cathedrall chyrche, and the monasterye of Hyde;[2] whych
may not soo sodenly be discontenued.

Finally, my lord, I also beseche your good lordship, that
in case thies advised fortificacions and municions of Calice
and the other places be ordeyned to be doo for suspicion of
werre or siege, that then the reparation and ryggyng of ships
be in lyke wyse auaunced; for if owr enemyes be lord*is* of
the see, Calice may not long hold. In lyke wyse the Isle
of Wyght, whych hathe no Capitaigne bydyng within it,
and is full sklendrely inhabit, and wors fortifyed and pro-

2 See no. 90.

uyded of artillarye, and also Portesmowthe,[3] shalbe oon of
the fyrst thyngs that owr enemyes woll loke vppon; for as
your good lordship well knoweth, if the werre fortune, it
shall do great seruice. And in thys partie I beseche you, my
lord, to remembre the warant that I left with you for the
wag*is* of ij goonners for the towre and the blokehowse,
and the keper of the brewe howses theer, whych must be
regarded, be it werre or peaxe. Thus doo I presumptuosely
encombre your good lordship with thies rude maters; but
they be necessar*e*, and I do make me sure ye knowe and
considre the same better then I can wryte. And thus I shall
daily pray the Holy Trinite to send you, my lord, as good
lyfe and long as I wold wyshe to my self.

At Wynchestre the last day of Apryle.

Your humble bedeman and preste
Ri. Wynton.

*58. TO WOLSEY

RO. S. P. 1: 232, f. 23.   St. Cross.
                                        10 May ⟨1517⟩.

[The disturbances at Southampton reported here and in no. 59 do not seem
to be mentioned in any other source.]

My singular good lorde,

After my moste humble wise I recommaund me to your
good lordship. Please it the same to vnderstond that I haue
of late receyued from you thre lettres.

The first by my poure chapeleyn Mr Mils: by the which
I vnderstond to my grettest comforte that ye haue beningly
accepted thexcuses that I made to your good lordship for my
noncommynge to you at that tyme, and that it woll please
your good lordship so to declare and shew my said excuses
to the King*is* grace as his highnes shalbe contented.

My lorde, your good lordship hath don more for me in
this behalf then I can write or think, and for the same in my
moste humble wise I thank your good lordship; assuringe
the same that I rekyne me singularly bounden to you that

3 Cf. no. 65.

it hath pleased you, no lesse to my grete comforte and quietnes of mynde then also for the surety of my helth, to be so
good lorde to me as ye haue ben in thacceptynge of my
said excuse. Albe yt, as I wrote to you by Mr Sand*is*, I
shalbe alwais redy at your commaundement*is*; and so moste
hertely I beseche you to think and truste.

And wher ye desire that I write to you my poure opynion
and aduyse in the maters of Calice, verely, my lorde, I haue
shewed theym to Mr Sand*is* in the largiest wise that I can:
as he can, and I doubte not woll, shewe you, when ye shall
demaunde him. And as in other maters concerninge the
Kinge and his realme, though my wit be but poure and
small, yet my hert and good will is as large as any creaturs
liveing; and your good lordship so contented, I entend sum
tyme to encombre you with writynge my poure mynde to
you in the said maters. For vndoubtedly, my lorde, I think
no lesse nor no seldomer devise of theym in my mynde and
with my self, then I wolde doo if I were daily attendynge
vpon you in the King*is* Counseill.

The other two lettres I received by Mr Sand*is*. Wher of
the oon was wrytten with your own hand: for the which
I moste humbly thanke your good lordship. And much I
merveill when ye cowde fynd the laisure to write it your
self. I knowe perfectly, it com of your speciall good herte
and affection toward*is* me; and ell*is* for your contynuall
busynes yt cowde not well haue ben don. And therfor I woll
kepe it and sum tyme loke vpon it for my comforte.

And as towchynge the matere in your lettres comprised
concernynge the riot of Suthampton, your lordship hath
taken a better way for the redresse therof then the govern-
ours of Hampton and I cowde haue deuysed or wisshed;
and a more propice or mete persoon then is Mr Sand*is* for
thorderynge of that matere, cowde ye not haue found. For
beynge amongs theym he is ther Mayre, balif and all the
holl ruyller of the town; and with thaucthorite that he hath
vnder the Kyng*is* grace, the love and credite that he hath
among*is* the peple, when he is present, he may more doo

o

with theym then may doo the Mayre and all officeres that
bilongith both to the town and to the porte. And what he
hath don there for thexecution of the Kyng*is* commaundement, I nede not to encombre you with the wrytynge therof,
seynge that he woll playnly and truly reporte yt to you.
And that he hath don, hath be with out any trowble or
stirrenge makynge among theym; with right wise demonstration of the matere of London with the circumstances of
the same, to the great comfort of all wellordered persons
and the great feer of all thoes that be evill entendynge or
maliciously disposed. And with his indifference bytwixt
bothe parties he hath left the holl town in a sure quietnes,
rest and peaxe.

I doubt not also he woll shewe you that the matere was
not so grevouxe nor so haynouxe of it selff, as was wrytten
in the two lettres that I sent to your good lordship enclosed
in my lettre. The which I besech your good lordship to
considre in the punishment of thoffenders brought vp at
this tyme; albe it they must haue soom what the grevouser
punyshement, for the yevynge of feerfull example for tyme
to com. And though they make not the holl noumbre of
the bill delyuered to Mr Sand*is*, ther be as many as nedethe,
and sum for feer be voided.

And if it shall please you, my lorde, that the Kynge by
his estraicte lettres commaunde the Mayre and his brethren
to fynde this riot by due enquisicion, and after it be found,
to punyshe a certeyn of the chiefe riotters not sent vp at
this tyme by enprisonment and fyne, and to bynde theym
by recognoysance for ther good aberynge; this shall make
a suer peax and restfulnes, not oonly in that town but in
all the holl shier and ferther.

And, my lorde, I thynk that if it fortune hereafter any
commotion to be made in this shier, Wiltshier, Barkshier or
Somersetshier, yt shalbe by the meanes of weavers, fullers,
sheremen and other jorneymen artificers and serua*untis* for
cloth makers. Wherfore if ther be proclamations sent and
made in the said shiers, that clothyers shall haue their

libertie in byenge of woll, and that the said artificers and
jorneymen be paid for ther labores and workes by the said
clothyers in redy money and not in wares, acordynge to the
statutes in both cases prouyded, I doubt not it shall put
theym in great quietnesse and confort and avoide thocca-
sions of all such commotions. Wherof within iij dayes last
past I had soom experience emongs my neighbours of the
citie of Winchestre and my tenauntis of the soke of the
same: emongs whome I found som variance for the said
two maters, but I doubt not it is now appeased.

Also, my lorde, though I assuredly knowe Mr Sands
fastenesse, kyndenesse, and love to the Kyngis grace, and
also his redynesse allwais to spende his liff and lond in his
seruice as any gentilman within this realme, yet it is to my
great comforte that your lordship by your said lettres written
with your own hand doith afferme the same. And albeit
I knowe certaynly, as well by his reporte as your dedys, that
ye be his good lord, yet must I, my lord, for my partie
beseche you allways so to contynewe; assurenge you ye shall
fynd hym as fast, true and deligent, bothe to the Kynge and
your self, as shalbe any gentilman of the Counseill. And
eftsones I be seche you, my lorde, to remembre the bill
concernynge the kepers of the Kyngis brewhowses, and
gunners of the towre and blokhowse of Portismowthe;
which had no wages by a longe season. And nedis they
must be had. And I shall perseuerently pray the good Lord
to send you, my lord, as good liff and longe as I wold wyshe
to my self.

Wrytten at my poure howse of Seincte Crosse[1] besidis
Winchestre the xth day of Maij.

Your faithfull continuall bedeman

Ri. Wynton.

To my singlere good lorde, my lorde Cardinall of Yorke,
chaunceller of Englande.

---

[1] An ancient almshouse founded by Bp. Henry of Blois c. 1136: a mile
s. of Winchester. Fox as bp. had the appointment of the master, and used
it as a place of residence.

* 59. TO WOLSEY

RO. S. P. 1: 232, f. 27.   St. Cross.

12 June ⟨1517⟩.

My veray singler good lorde,

In my mooste humble wyse I commaunde me to youre
good lordeship. Please it thesame to vnderstande that nowe
lately by thand*is* of oon of the King*is* messagers I receyued
aswell the King*is* lettres missiues directed to me, the lorde
Awdelay and certain other gentilmen of this shire of
Southampton, as alsoo his commission vnder his halue seall,
with certain instructions annexed to thesame; and where it
hath pleased his grace to commaunde vs by his said lettres
to assemble our self and take suche ways, orders and direc-
tions among*is* vs, as herafter there ensue noo commocions,
dissentions or vnlaufull assembles among*is* his people of
this his said shyre. My lorde, as touching this matier, I trust
there shalbe doo suche diligence as the King*is* said commaundement shall spedely and diligentely be executed, and
the said inconuenienc*is*, as far as shall ligh in oure powers,
be exchewed. And as I shall fynde disposicion in the people,
soo shall I frome tyme to tyme after thexigence of the case
aduertise youre goode lordeship. And as touching thesaid
commission, it extendeth to iiij shires, viz. Suth*ampton*,
Wiltshire, Somerset and Dorset; and there be noo moe commissioners named therin, but oonly my self, with a voyde
space scant hable to receyue iij names, or not soo many
with honest additions. And the namyng of the said iij
persones and the entering of their names in to thesaid commission is, by writing made vppon the bakke syde of thesame commission, commytted to my discretion.

Please it you, my lorde, me semeth vnder correction that
for thesaid iiij shires which, specially Wiltshire and Dorset,
be veray large, and for thexecution of thesaid commission
within thesame, I with iij other commissioners be not sufficient in nowmbre; and after my pouer estimacion iiij commissioners were scant sufficient for the leest of thesaid iiij

shires. And if my self were adioyned with other, though it were in a right great nowmbre, to execute thesaid commission through out thesaid iiij shires, and that I shulde all ways be oon of theym by vertue of thesaid commission, I think it coude not ligh in my power to travell thesaid shires for the due execution of thesaid commission withoute intollerable labour bitwixt this and All Halowtyde: and noo day in the meane season to be in myn awen howse, and alsoo to take soo moche travell this hotte season[1] of the yere, withoute it were in a case of greater necessite. I trust neither the King*is* grace nor youre good lordeship intende not to put me to the jeopardy of my pouer body that might therby ensue; which may better suffer and endure the travell of oon moneth in colde wedder then of oon weke in the hotte season of the yere. And alsoo for thexecution of thesaid commission within this shire it shalbe right expedient that I goo my self in to the Isle of Wight: which wol aske noo lytell leas*ure*. And ouer this, my lorde, I think I shulde do the King*is* grace better seruice by my byding still in this shire for the keping of it in good peax and quietnes then to be soo long absent for thexecution of thesaid commission in the iij other shires.

In consideracion wherof I beseche your good lordeship to commaunde iiij seuerall distincte commissions of like effecte and tenour to thesaid commission, or at the leest iij suche commissions, that is to say, oon for this shire of Suth*ampton*, the secounde for Wiltshire, and the iij^de for Somerset and Dorset, which be both vnder oon shreif; and to adioyne to me for this shire the lorde Awdelay, Sir John Lysle, knight, Sir William Gifford, knight, Sir John Dawtry, knight, John Newport, serieaunt at lawe, William Pawlet, squier, and William Frost. And in the other two commissions, the oon for Wiltshire and the other for Somerset and Dorset, to put suche other as shall please youre good lordeship: wherof there is moche good chose in thesame shires. And if it shall please your good lordeship to sende me

---

[1] Nine years later Fox begs to be excused from travelling in winter also.

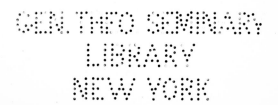

thesaid commissions with thinstructions to theym apperteynyng, I shall conuey theym accordingly; beseching your good lordeship not to think that I deuise this for myn awen ease or for exchewing of cost, which I shall neuer ponder in the King*is* seruice. But ver26ily, my lorde, I think the King*is* intent about*is* the execution of thesaid commissions can not be otherwise duly, surely and sufficiently accomplisshed and performed.

It may alsoo please youre good lordeship to here the reporte of Sir John Dawtrye, this berer, concernyng the good demeanour and towardnes of the commons of the towne of Southampton: which be now repentaunt for that they haue doon, and haue conformed theym self to all suche order as the rewlers of thesaid towne haue ordeyned for thestablisshing of the King*is* peax and the keping of good rewle among*is* theym self. Wherfor I vnderstande thesaid rewlers of thesaid towne by their lettres haue besought your good lordeship, and soo doo I in like wise, to be good and gracious lorde to the pr*i*soners of thesaid towne, now being in the Marshalsye, for thenlargement of theym out of thesame pr*i*son. And if it may please your good lordeship that bifore their departing they be bounde euery of theym for other for their good abering; the good order and rewle of thesaid towne shall therby be moche the better establissed, and good example therof ensue herafter.

My lorde, there is soo grete difficultie and variaunce among*is* the people, not oonly of this shire but alsoo of diuerse other, about*is* the taking and refusing of pennys, that if it may please your good lordeship to commaunde proclamacions to be made in euery shire like to the proclamacions that were last made for that matier, I doubt not it shall moche content vniuersally all the King*is* subgiett*is*. It may alsoo like your good lordeship to yeue your thank*is* to this said berer for the diligent regarde that he taketh for the good rewle not oonly of thesaid towne but alsoo of the countrey. He can, may and will doo as good seruice in suche matiers as any in his quarter about*is* hym. And as he

can shew you, if there be noo waraunt for the payment of
the gunners and keper of the brewhowse at Portesmouth,
they will departe and the howses stande vnloked to: which
is not to be suffered. Wherfor I beseche your good lordeship soo to remember thesaid waraunt that thesaid maist⟨re
Da⟩wtry may bring it with hym. And I pray you, my
lorde, alweys to commaunde me your good plea*sure*.

At my pouer howse of Saynt Crosse bisid*is* Wynchester
the xijth day of Juyne.

Your assured continuall bedeman
Ri. Wynton.

To my moste singler good lorde, my lorde Cardinall of
Yorke, chaunceller of England.

|| 60. TO THE PRESIDENT AND
FELLOWS OF CORPUS

Corpus MS.   Winchester.
                                          22 June 1517.

[Copied in the earliest College Lease-book, f. 3.

  At the time of the Institution (no. 56) the Statutes were not ready; but on
20 June, sitting in the church at St. Cross, Fox formally delivered the first
draft of them to a notable company. Two days later he named as Vice-
President Robert Morwent, whom he regarded as a trained man of affairs,
likely to be useful for the business of the College in its beginnings. Morwent
held a life-fellowship at Magdalen; and as it was proposed that he should
retain this, he could not be a Fellow of Corpus, only 'Sociis compar'.

  At the conclusion of the formal document, Fox passes to encourage the
Scholars to whom he felt so affectionately.]

RICARDVS PERMISSIONE DIVINA WINTONIENSIS EPISCOPVS
    FVNDATORQVE ET PATRONVS COLLEGII NOSTRI CORPORIS
    CHRISTI IN VNIVERSITATE OXONII FILIIS NOSTRIS CHARIS-
    SIMIS PRESIDENTI ET SOCIIS EIVSDEM VNIVERSIS SALVTEM
    ET BENEDICTIONEM.

Quum nos magistrum Robertum Morwennum, Collegii
Magdalenensis socium perpetuum, ab illo Collegio, in quo
plurimis commodis sine magno negocio aut labore frue-
batur, abstraximus, nostrique Collegii fecimus et constitui-

mus Vicepresidentem; in quo ad multos annos, tum quod
ipsum Collegium nouum sit et recens, tum quod reliqui
eiusdem Socii et Officiarii haud multum in rebus eiuscemodi
sint experti, plurimos sit labores subiturus, quibus emolu-
menta que in eius commissione ei concessimus, imparia sunt
et indigna:

idcirco volumus atque precipimus vt ad omnia emolu-
menta que nos ei, vt prefertur, concessimus, vos etiam eidem
M. Roberto pensionem annuam quattuor librarum a Collegio nostro per manus Dispensatorum eiusdem, quousque
ad summam decem mercarum[1] sumptibus ordinariis deductis
promotus fuerit, soluendarum vestro scripto authentico,
vestro communi sigillo confirmato, concedatis; Statutis nostris, que premissis vel eorum cuipiam aduersari videntur,
etiam iuramento confirmatis, non obstantibus: cum quibus
ac etiam vestris iuramentis quo ad ea, sed hac du*n*taxat vice,
authoritate nostra quam nobis vt Fundatori reseruauimus,
dispensamus per presentes.

Dat*um* Winton. decimo Calendas Quintiles. anno partus
virginei millesimo quingentesimo septimodecimo et nostre
translationis sextodecimo.

Reddet autem vobis hic noster nuncius Statutorum nostrorum volumen:[2] exquibus cognoscetis quemadmodum et
quibus legibus vos in nostro Collegio conuiuere obporteat.
Quas suscipere, venerari et vt sacrosanctas et non sine pia-
culo violandas seruare, vos omnes hortamur, obsecramus
et, que nostra est authoritas, iubemus; quo non solum in
bonis literis ac moribus admodum haud dubium proficietis,
verum etiam efficietis vt amplioribus vos beneficiis indies
afficiamus. Ad quod nos omnem nostram operam et studium
i*m*pendemus, si vos omni vigilantia et industria ad has
nostras leges seruandas propensissime incumbatis. Valete.

Studete virtuti, et bonis literis omnibus viribus certatim
operam i*m*pendite, filii non minus quam si vos genuissem
nobis charissimi.

Winton. quo et superiora.

[1] £6. 13s. 4d.   [2] Bodleian MS., Laud. misc. 621.

*61. TO CLAYMOND

Corpus MS.   Winchester.
                                                        17 July ⟨1517⟩.

[A visitation of the sweating-sickness had carried off Thomas Fox; but
Claymond, though taken ill, had recovered. A letter from London, 6 Aug.
1517, states that 400 students died at Oxford in a week (*Calendar of State
Papers, Venice*, ii. 945). Cf. nos. 62, 63.]

Broder maister President,

    I commaund me hartely to you; and to exhorte you to
take patiently the great tempest that hathe lately ben emong*is*
your company, I can no better say then to desyre you to
take it as I haue euer vsed to take such thyng*is* my self:
*videlicet speraui semper me felicem habiturum exitum, vbi durum
et graue erat principium.* And also I wold ye shuld thynk that
in this case God provyth you, *et tunc beatus vir qui suffert
temptacionem.* And as towchyng my self, seth it hath pleased
God to leve me your persoon, I woll yeve hyme dowble
thank*is*; the oon is that he hathe left me your self, and the
secund is that he hathe so provyd you, and in the same
prove taken to hys mercy my pouer kynsman,[1] your disciple,
whyle he was, as I trust, in the state of grace.

    As touchyng the procuratys that ye haue sent me, they
be not sufficient for so great a mater. And therfore Mr
Myls shalbe with you shortly to accept more large constitu-
tions. And then he shall shew you the specialties of the
maters, and when the sade Mr Myls commeth to you, I shall
send you more money for your beeldyng. And thus fare ye
hartely well. At Wynchestre the xvijth day of July

                    your lovyng broder
                           Ri. Wynton.

    To my broder the President of Corpus Christi College
in Oxford.

              [1] Thos. Fox: see no. 56.

*62. TO CLAYMOND

Corpus MS.   St. Cross.
                                      18 August ⟨1517⟩.

[Ammonius, a native of Lucca, Latin secretary to Henry VIII, friend and confidant of Erasmus (cf. no. 21 introd.), died on 17 Aug. 1517 at 9 p.m. The news reached Winchester next day; and with the promptitude customary in those days, Fox at once presented Claymond to the vacant living of Bishop's Cleeve, near Cheltenham. In the College Archives are three deeds of presentation, all dated 18 August. With equal promptitude Claymond on 19 August resigned the living of Westmonkton, near Taunton, to which Abbot Bere (no. 69) had presented him in 1506. Fox's reason for enjoining secrecy was probably that he wished to put forward a candidate of his own, and secure the Abbot's consent before any other candidate could appear (cf. no. 63).]

Brother maister President,

After hertie recommendacion, soo it is that by the visitacion of God, maister Andreas Ammonius in this sweting sekenes is departed oute of this worlde, and by his deth is comme to my collacion the benifice of Bisshops Cliff in the diocise of Worcester, the which I gave to hym within xv days last passed by the deth of Maister doctor Porte, which died at London in the said sekenes. And now with as free hert and good mynde as euer I gave benifice to any person, I yeue it to you, and send you in a box by this berer the collacion therof with the *mandatum ad inducendum*. After the recepte wherof I aduise and require you to goe theder in your awen person with all diligence possible and take possession therof, and set suche order therin as shalbe thought good to you, aswell for the cure as for your awen prouffite.

I feare that ye shall not haue thys hervest, bicause thesaid Maister Porte died syns Our Lady Day: but ye shall neuer thelesse fynde the benifice to your plea*s*ure.

And bifore ye take possession, resigne the benifice that ye haue of my lorde of Glastonbury is yeft, and send me the resignacion pr*e*uely when ye retourne fro Bisshops Clif, and make the notary that shall make thinstrument to kepe it secrete.

I send you alsoo in thesaid box the collacion and *manda-*

tum ad inducendum of the parsonaige of Tarring,[1] which is now yours as clerely as euer ye had any, and without pension with a vicar indewed. I trust it shalbe worth to you clerely yerely xx[li]. I send you alsoo in the said box a collacion with the *mandatum ad inducendum* for John Fox[2] for tharchediaconry of Surray,[3] praying you to kepe theym for hym. And when ye be retournede out of Worcestershire, ye shall doo well if ye make a start hither; for it is necessary for many causes that ye soo doo.

This berer goeth to Guytting,[4] and therfor let hym not tary with you. And thus fare ye well, at Saynt Crosse the XVIIJ day of August.

your broder
Ri. Wynton.

To my brother the President of Corpus Christi Colleige in Oxford.

*63. TO CLAYMOND

Corpus MS.　　　　　　　　　　　　St. Cross.
25 August ⟨1517⟩

[In sequence with no. 62.]

Brother Mr Presidente,

I commaunde me to you, and haue received your lettre by your seruaunt this berer: to the beginnynge wherof *pleno bili* I woll make non answer at this tyme, but differ it till our next metynge, *quia satis sudamus sine invectiuis*. And I pray you let this be a matier for your scolares to make mo verses vpon; for ther last verses wer so pleasaunt that I am very desirouse to haue mo of theim.

I marveyle why ye sent me your collacion, *mandatum ad inducendum*, and proxye of your benifice of Cliffe. Yf ye hade not taken possession ther of, I wold haue thought ye hade be

---

[1] in Sussex.
[2] No doubt a kinsman. He presented books to the Corpus library in 1519, as 'archideaconus de Surray'. In 1521 he was Archdeacon of Winchester.
[3] in Winchester diocese.
[4] in Worcestershire. Fox gave the College the manor and great lands, which it still holds: 'not an estate but a principality,' J. M. Wilson.

mynded to haue refused yt. I send you them ayeyn, and also a lyke collacion and *mandatum* vnder the seale of my lord of Worcestre: and when ye haue both, I cannot tell wheither ys the better. Never thelesse kepe theim both.

Henry Saunders hath appoynted the law day at Guyttynge to be holden the Tewysday[1] next be fore sayncte Mathew day: wher he desireth to haue your selff the same day; and so yt ys good ye be, the rather to thentent ye may take personall possession of your said benifice, and ordre and dispose yt to your profeite. He shall passe by you, and therfore make you redy ayeyn the same day; and at your retorne com streight heder to me and brynge hym in your companye, and then we shall haue comodite and leas*ure* for the dissposynge of my pourchest lond*is* to that my Colleige.

And as for the manor that Mr Almosner[2] enformed you of to be sold in Cambrigeshire, I pray you acordynge to your wryttyng cause good serche to be made ther of by men goyng to Strubrigefayer;[3] for I haue no knoleige ther of.

Also as towchynge the lond lieinge bysid*is* Guyttynge, the which ye say oon Mr Morton of Haifford offerith to sell, Henr*e* Saunders never spake word to me therof. And ther-for I pray you cause good serch to be made for yt, and in me ther shall lake nether good will nor money.

I haue wrytten to thabbote of Glastonbury for the pre-sentacion of Westmonkton, but neuerthelesse kepe the resignacion secrete; for thabbot of Glastonbury hath no knoleige ther of by my lettres, and iff he or any other cause the question to be asked of you, let hym haue no knoleige ther of. And thus fare you well with all your scollars.

Wrytten at Sayncte Crosse the xxv day of Aust.

your broder

Ri. Wynton.

To my brother the Presidente of Corpus Christi Colleige in Oxford.

---

[1] 15 Sept. 1517.   [2] the Warden of Merton, Rawlyns: see no. 51.
[3] Held at Sturbridge, 1½ ms. NNE. of Cambridge, in September.

** 64. FROM LINACRE

Galen, 1517, tit. vᵒ.   ⟨London.⟩
Johnson p. 316.   ⟨c. September 1517.⟩

[Linacre's Latin translation of Galen's *De sanitate tuenda*, printed in Paris, G. Rubeus, 22 Aug. 1517, under the supervision of Thomas Lupset, was dedicated to Henry VIII with a long preface dated 16 June 1517; but the verso of the title-page being blank gave convenient space for ms. letters of presentation to other patrons. One such copy of the book, inscribed to Wolsey, is in the British Museum, C. 19. e. 15; another, offered to Fox, belongs to the Royal College of Physicians (see J. N. Johnson, *Life of Linacre*, 1835). It has the following inscription, which is possibly autograph.]

REVERENDO IN CHRISTO PATRI ET DOMINO, DO. RICARDO,
DIVINA PROVIDENTIA WYNTONIENSI EPISCOPO, THOMAS
LINACRVS MEDICVS SAL. PLV. DICIT.

Cum tu, Praesul amplissime, ita studiis consulis vt corporis quidem alimenta non exiguo studiosorum numero deesse non possint, animi vero etiam toti gymnasio abundent; quorum sicuti priore nulli vsquam nostratium quos simile studium habuit, cedis, ita secundo plane omnes qui hactenus fuere, superas: neminem arbitror, Anglici praesertim nominis, studiosorum esse qui se frugiferum aliquid ex studiis prompturum speret, qui tibi eius aliquid non quasi iustum debeat, quo tibi, dum se non ingratum probet, sanctissimum pientissimumque hoc tuum institutum magis magisque tibi commendet. Ego certe quae proxime lucubraui, tum hoc communi nomine debere tibi me censeo, tum illo priuato, quod sanitati tuae, cui litterati omnes bene precari debent, nonnihil his consuluero.

Mitto igitur ad te hoc codice sex Galeni de tuenda Sanitate libros, quos proxime, vt potui, Latinos feci; optaremque lectione tua dignos, nisi id omnino vota superaret. Nunc agi mecum praeclare putabo, si a doctorum quos in contubernio tecum habes lectione non abhorrebunt: ii enim, nisi fallor, multa in his deprehendent, quibus si vsus fueris, non sanitate modo magis integra, verum etiam longiore vita ad ea perficienda quae magnifice simul et summa cum pietate

coepisti, fruere. Quod vt tibi foeliciter contingat, ipse certe
a Deo Optimo Max. omnibus votis fere contendere non
desino.

Vale, Antistes humaniss. et grauissime.

*65. TO WOLSEY

RO. S. P. 1: 16, f. 145.   St. Cross.
Brewer ii. 3952.   15 February ⟨1518⟩.

[Wharwell was a Benedictine nunnery, 3 miles s. of Andover. The new
abbess, Avelena Cowdrey, was installed in March 1518.]

My mooste singular good lorde,

In my moste humble wyse I recommende me to your good
lordeship; right soo thanking thesame for your gracieux
expedicion of the King*is* lettres vnder his great seall, being
in youre keping, for the fre election of a newe abbasse
within the monastery of Wharwell. And forasmoche as the
conuent haue now chosen suche oon of their awen sisters
by the way of the Holy Gooste as I doubt not shalbe
pleasaunt to God, true to the King*is* grace, and prouffitable
to the monastery, thesaid conuent sendeth at this tyme this
berer to pursue and obteigne the King*is* royall assent necessary in that behalue; and for the gracieux expedicion of
thesame I beseche you, my moste singuler good lorde, to
be good and gracieux lorde to the said monastery, and they
and I shall assuredly be youre contynuall bedefolk*is* and
orators.

My lorde, the long brute and rumour of the preparacion
of an armye and a navy in Normandy hath caused me to
serche by the meanes of marchaunt*is*, aswell Englisshe as
Frenche, what the said preparacion shulde purtende. And
as far as I can lerne, it is to set over the Duke of Albeny[1]
in to Scotland: which, as it is said, intendeth to punisshe
the murderers of his lieuten*au*nt;[2] and bicause he trusteth

---

[1] John Stewart (1481–1536), grandson of James II; Regent after Flodden.
[2] a Frenchman, Ant. de la Bastie, Scottish warden of the east Marches.

not moche to the countrey men, he purposeth to goo theder in the better strength.

My lorde, it is my dutie to aduertise you of this matier as I can be enformed, praying you to take it as shewed to you of good zele; and as marchaunt*is* goo and comme, I shall make further serche and frome tyme to tyme aduertise you of the informacion that it shall fortune me to haue in that behalue. And my lorde, if the said warre be intended against the King*is* grace and his royme, as I trust it be not, the Isle of Wight and Portesmouth[3] be full feble for defense or resistaunce; and the rather bicause our maner is neuer to prepaire for the warre, to our enmyes be light at our dores. And vndoubtedly, my lorde, neither the Isle nor the countrey be well furnisshed of hable men for the warre, nor yet greatly of harnes. And therfore if there be veray likely-hod of warre, it shalbe right necessary that they haue warnyng to prepaire theym for warre; and yet shall they be founde bothe to slakke and to slowe; as knoweth our Lorde, who haue you all weys, my moste singulare good lorde, in his blissed keping.

At my pouer howse of Saynt Crosse the xv day of February.

your assured dayly orator and preste
Ri. Wynton.

To my most singler good lorde, my lorde Cardinall of Yorke, chaunceller of Englande.

* 66. TO WOLSEY

RO. S. P. 1: 17, f. 146.   Marwell.
Brewer ii. 4540.   30 October ⟨1518⟩.

[Fox, as usual, stands up for his servants; but the Bishop of Winchester makes no claim to have the law stretched, if they have acted 'contrary to the statute in that case prouided'.]

In my moste humble wise I recommende me to youre grace; right soo thanking thesame for my licence of biding at home for attendaunce yeuyng vppon the King*is* highnes this somer

3 Cf. no. 57.

season. Wherin your grace did noo lesse for me then if ye
had deliuered me of an inevitable daunger of my lief. For
the which, among*is* other your great goodnes and com*fortis*
shewed to me in tyme passed, I reken me bounden not oonly
to pray for youre grace but alsoo during my lief to owe you
my seruice to the best of my power; and soo I beseche your
grace to trust and vse me.

And noon Englisshe man gladder then I of this honour-
able and prouffitable amytie and alyaunce [1] with the royme
of Fraunce. I doubt not there be some *inuidi et maliuoli
obtrectatores*; but vndoubtedly, my lorde, God contynuyng
it, it shall be the best dede that euer was doon for the royme
of England; and after the King*is* highnes the lawde and
prayse therof shalbe to you a perpetuall memory.

Please it youre grace, I am enformed by my lerned counsaill that where they haue made answer bifore your grace in
the King*is* chauncery, that thinquisicions founde against me
for inclausures of arrable land contrary to the statute in that
case prouided, be all and euery of theym vntrue; youre grace
demaunding my said counsaill how they knew that it soo
was, they answered that they had credible informacion by
the Stieward and other my hed officers of my land*is*, and
by presentment*is* of the homaig*is* in my court*is*, and that
I might prove thesame by sufficient witnes, as youre grace
wolde awarde. Wheruppon it pleased youre grace of your
olde accustumed fauour toward*is* me to take this direction,
that is to say that I vppon my pouer honour by my lettres
shulde aduertise youre grace of the veray trouth in this
matier on this syde *crastino Animarum*; [2] and ell*is* to runne
in suche daunger as other men doo.

My lorde, in my moste humble wise I thanke your grace
for this your fauourable direction, and specially for the trust
that ye can yeue in suche a matier to my writing. Veraily,
my lorde, bifore Michaelmas last passed I caused serche to
be made twise vppon the grounde, whether thesaid inquisicions were true or not; and when my Stieward and Surveyor

---

[1] 2 Oct. 1518.   [2] 3 Nov.

of my land*is* and other myn officers after Michaelmas departed frome me to kepe the court*is* and law days, I charged theym as effectually as I coude, to enquire effectually whether thes said inquisicions were true or not. And soo they did, aswell by examinacion by mouth as by the homage; and they haue certified aswell me as alsoo my said lerned counsaill attending vppon your grace in the Chauncery, that thesaid inquisicions and euery of theym be vntrue.

Nathelesse, my lorde, for asmoche as I haue not be personally present vppon the grounde and land*is* surmised to be inclosed, to take the vew of theym with myn awen yen, I dar not take vppon me to certifie your grace by my writing*is* that thesaid inquisicions be vntrue. But vppon my faith and trouth that I owe to God and the King*is* grace and vppon my pouer honestie I veraily suppose and faithfully beleve that thesaid inquisicions be vntrue; and thus dar I take vppon me to make certificat to your grace in the premisses. And if it shall please you, my lorde, to accepte this my certificat, I know well ye shall in that behalue shew me a speciall grace, and I trust veraily doo the King*is* grace noo wrong.

The Stieward of my land*is*, called William Frost, is a sadde, substanciall, feithfull man, and well lerned in the lawe; and the Surveyor of my land*is* called William Pownde, being a man of an hundreth pownd land and a boue, is in like wise a right substanciall true man, and somewhat lerned. Thes twoo persones with other of myn officers haue certified me as a boue. They be men of as good credyt within this shire as any other within it, and to theym haue I yeuen credence in greater matiers of tyme passed, and soo I doo in this. Nathelesse, my lorde, as it shall please youre grace torder me in this matier, I shalbe right well contented therwith, and gladly obey thesame.

The land*is* be copy holde. And what it is worth by the yere to the copye holders and ten*au*nt*is* therof I know not; but to me, as my said officers shew me, they be noo better in value by the yere then an hundreth sheling*is*. And if it shall please your grace to deliuer me of all this busynes, and to assesse the fyne according to thesaid value and the statute, I shalbe right well contented to pay it; and in soo doing repute you my veray singuler good lorde, as ye haue allways contynually been in all other my matiers. As knoweth our Lorde: whom I shall daily beseche to sende youre grace as good lief and long as your noble hert can desire.

At my pouer howse of Marwell3 the xxxth day of Octobre.

your humble bedeman and daily preste

Ri. Wynton.

To my moste singler good lorde, my lorde Cardinall of York, legate of England and chaunceller of the same.

* 67. TO WOLSEY

BM. Cotton MS. Faustina C. vii, f. 216.   Marwell.
Brewer iii. 1122.   2 January ⟨1519⟩.

[Brewer places this often-quoted letter in 1521; but that conflicts with no. 74, the year-date of which is confirmed by the date of Fox's translation. This letter is no doubt Fox's reply to Wolsey's general letter to the Bishops, dispatched at the end of Dec. 1518, and summoning them to a conference on reform of the Church, to be held at Westminster on the first Monday in Lent 1519 (Brewer iii. 77. 3 and 1). This is corroborated by Fox's calculation, 'hoc fere perpetuum triennium', since his retirement from the Privy Seal in April 1516 to the care of his diocese: see no. 52, and cf. no. 71.

This letter was printed by J. Strype, *Ecclesiastical Memorials*, 1721, i. app. p. 18; and by D. Wilkins, *Concilia*, 1737, iii. 708.]

Reuerendissime Pater et domine mihi vnice semper obseruande, salutem plurimam et optatum votorum omnium successum !

Ingentem atque mirificam, Pater amplissime, ex proximis vestris ad me literis cepi consolationem atque voluptatem; quod ex illis intellexi D.V. reuerendissimam vniuersi cleri reformationem secum instituisse, et ad eam inchoandam atque aggrediendam diem breui futurum praefinisse et praescripsisse. Eum namque profecto diem iamdiu non

---

3 At Marwell, 6 ms. SE. of Winchester, Henry of Blois (see no. 58) founded a small college of secular priests: part of which still survives in a modern house and the barns of a farm. Fox used it much for his residence in his later years.

minus quam Symeon ille Euangelicus expectatum Messiam,
votis omnibus videre expetiui; et ex quo illas D.V. reuerendissimae literas legi, reformationem ampliorem et multo
exactiorem vniuersae Anglorum ecclesiasticae hierarchiae
mihi videor tantum non sentire et palpare, quam ego hac
hominum aetate vel faciundam vel ineundam diuinare
potui, nedum sperare. Conatus sum enim facere, quod
mearum erat partium, in ditione hac mea peculiari et
exigua, quod vestra praestantissima dominatio instituit in
vtraque amplissima huius regni prouincia; et hoc fere perpetuum triennium illi vni negocio diligenter incubui,
omniaque mea studia, labores, vigilias, sudores, in ea fere
vna collocaui: vbi, quod prius non putassem, depr⟨e⟩hendi
et animaduerti omnia quae ad antiquam cleri et praecipue
monachiae integritatem spectant, adeo vel licentiis et
corruptelis deprauata vel temporum malignitate et diuturni-
tate abolita et corrupta, vt aetate mihi confecto voluntatem
et studium auxerint, spem vero omnem sustulerint, per-
fectam et absolutam vnquam videndi reformationem in hac
vel mea diocesi priuatam.

Nunc autem ex optatissimis illis v. reuerendissimae
dominationis literis veni in certissimam spem summamque
expectationem breui videndi vniuersalem et publicam.
Exploratissimum nempe habeo multisque experimentis
luculentissime perspectum, quidquid D.V. reuerendissima
moliatur, instituerit et susceperit, id eam omne prudentis-
sime et constantissime, citra negocium aut contationem,
confecturam et felicissime absoluturam. Tam incompara-
bilis extat in ea diuinarum humanarumque rerum peritia,
tamque singularis apud serenissimum N. Regem sanctissi-
mumque dominum Pap⟨am / gratia et authoritas. Quibus
quum v. circumspectissima dominatio hactenus ita perfuncta
s⟨it / vt summam inde laudem amplissimamque per vniuersum orbem famam sit assequta, ex hac profecto sua clarris-
sima Legatione,[1] quam compositis et sua vna opera inter
Christianissimos principes confirmatis federibus, ad statum

---

[1] Wolsey had been appointed *Legatus a latere* 17 May 1518.

et ordinem ecclesiasticum reformandum et componendum decreuit conuertere, solidam et immortalem apud Deum et omnem posteritatem gloriam reportabit: tanto caeteris omnibus qui nostra memoria quouis gentium a summi Pontificis latere missi sunt, prestantiorem et celebriorem quanto vel pax bello expetibilior vel clerus populo sanctior et veneratior. Nam si quamplurimis pontificibus maxim⟨is/ vel obliuione vel silentio preteritis, bini illi olim huc Legati² omnium ore vbique terrarum hodie celebrantur, idque tantum ob nonnullas sanctiones, quas praematuro Romam reditu infirmiores reliquere, quae aetas aut quae malignitas v. reuerendissimi nominis laudem et celebritatem vel delere possit vnquam vel offuscare? quum vniuersum Angliae clerum et monachiam suae integritati et dignitati restituerit, et leges ad eam tuendam et inconcusse seruandam condiderit, conditasque moribus et consuetudine comprobari et confirmari fecerit.

Quod D.V. reuerendissimae, non dubito, eo multo facilius feliciusque succedet, quod Rex noster Christianissimus, cuius hortatu et auspiciis, arbitror, hanc prouinciam recepit, omnem suam authoritatem et opem ei ad votum impertiet; omnesque prelati, presertim episcopi, suos assensus et studia alacres, ni admodum fallor, adhibebunt.

Et vt de meipso saltim pollicear quod animus meus ferre prestareque gestit, sic mihi videtur haec reformatio cleri et sacrorum omnium oblatrantem diu populum placatura, clerum illustratura, Regem ipsum serenissimum et optimates omnes clero conciliatura, ac Deo in primis Optimo Maximo plus omnibus sacrificiis vsque adeo placitura vt quidquid reliquum sit mihi huius vitae curriculi, id in eam lubentissime impenderem atque consumerem: vti D.V. reuerendissime apertius coram declarabo ad diem in illius literis prefinitum, si mihi viuo et sano illum videre detur.

Interim vero, imo dum vixero, Deum benignissimum cotidie assidueque inter sacrificia ⟨mea/ precabor vt D.V.

---

² Otho le Blanc and Ottoboni Fieschi; who in 1237 and 1268 revised the Canon Law for England.

reuerendissimam diutissime seruet, omniaque illius instituta
secundet et feliciter et fauste.

Ex Marwellis postridie Calendas Ianuarias.

E. v. reuerendissime dominationis deuinctissimus orator
Ri. Wynton.

* 68. FROM JOHN FITZJAMES

Corpus MS.   Redlynch.

12 January ⟨1519⟩

[This and no. 69 deal with the purchase of land by Fox at East and South
Brent in Somerset; both Fitzjames and Abbot Bere of Glastonbury (no. 69)
being concerned. The College Archives contain a number of original documents about the sale, dated in January 10 Henry VIII ⟨1519⟩; among which
are a demise by 'John Fitzjames senior' dated 8 Jan., a confirmation sealed
with the Abbey seal 12 Jan., and an indenture of 13 Jan. signed by Bere.

John Fitzjames the elder, father of the Lord Chief Justice, held property
at Redlynch, SE. of Bruton; and with his brother Richard, successively
Warden of Merton and Bishop of London, was joint-founder of Bruton
School.

The College still owns land at Brent.]

Right reuerent Fader yn God, my syngeler good lord,

After moste humble recommendacion had to your good
lordship, pleasse it the same to knowe that ther was neuer
ony wretyng made bitwene my lord of Glaston*bury* and me
for this land*is* that I p*ur*chesid yn Est Brent and Southe
Brent; but at request of my saide lord I was content he
shulde haue theym at his pleasure. And how be it that I
receiued of hym suche money as I payed for the saide lande,
yet forasmoche as he intendid to haue put the said lond to
oon almeshouse[1] of late new made by hymselfe, he willed
me alwey to contynue my possession therof, and so I haue
don yet hetherto, and he hathe taken the profitt*is* apon oure
saide agrement. And now at this tyme at his commaundement, for asmoche as I was seasid of the lande, and no other
bargeyn made bitwene my saide lord and me, but as is
aforewreten, I haue made a dede of feoffement to suche

[1] On the E. side of Taunton; showing Bere's arms and monogram.

persons as your seru*au*nt² this berer named to me: whiche
dede of feoffement is executed, and for your ferther suertie
I haue made indentures of sale and bargeyn of the said lande
betwen your good lordship and me.

And for discharge of the dower of my wyfe, whan so euer
ony Justice shall next come yn to this qwarter, if it shall so
pleasse your lordship, she and I shall knowelege the note
of a fyne of the premisses before the said Justice at youre
cost*is* and chargg*is*: whiche fyne shall discharge hir dower.

Item, as towchyng ferther suertie ageyn*st* Sir William
Bouthe, it shall appiere by the indenture made bitwene hym
and me that he is bounde at all tymes to make suche suertie
as shall be aduysed by me and my councell; and whan I shall
wayte apon ony of your lernyd councell at London, I shall
requyre suche ferther suertie of the saide Sir William Bouthe
as shall be aduysed by your said councell. And if he will
not performe it, I shall than seu hym as I haue bounde my
selfe by myn indenture.

Item for discharge of suche vsse as my lord of Glaston-
bury had yn the saide lande, he will seale a confirmacion to
your feoffees, whiche Master Portman and I thynke sufficyent
for this mater: whiche confirmacion and other wretyng*is*
suche as my saide lord of Glaston*bury* and I had, or now be
made, concernyng the said lande, youre seru*au*nt this berer
shall delyuer your good lordship.

Item, as towchyng my saide lord*is* licence to amortise
the saide land*is*, how be it that he is some whatt scrypulus
yn that mater, yet at your commaundement, as fer as I
perceyue, he will be content to doo it. But forasmoche as
your seru*au*nt was yn dowte whether thes feoffees be seasid
of suche other land*is* as ye haue p*ur*chesid ther, whiche be
holden of my said lord as this is, I aduysed your said ser-
u*au*nt to spare the said licence to tyme I had the certentie
therof. And than I dowte not my said lord will doo theryn
as ye shall requyre hym. And I shall helpe therto the best
I can with my hartie seruyce yn that and all other att your

² William Fletcher.

commaundement as knoweth God: who longe preserue
your good lordship.

At Redliche the xijth daye of Januarie.

your moste humble and assuride seruaunt

John Fitzjames.

To the reuerent fader in God and my syngeler good lord,
my lord of Wynton is good lordship, be this delyuerd.

* 69. FROM RICHARD BERE

Corpus MS.   Glastonbury.

13 January ⟨1519⟩

Bere (†20 Jan. 152⅘) had been abbot of Glastonbury since 1493, and had
been installed by Fox's Vicar-general. He was a great builder, at various
places in Somerset (cf. no. 68); and after a visit to Italy in 1504 introduced
into England the new fashionable cult of Loretto, for which he built a chapel
in his abbey church.]

My very singler goode lord,

Bothe I and all my powre brothers in our moost humble
maner with our dayly prayers recommend vs vnto your
goode lordshipe. And right so thanke you for your honorable gyfte and moost loving remembraunce send vnto us by
your seruaunt this bringer: whiche is farre better then we
haue or can deserue of your goode lordshipe. But we take
your said honorable gyffte to be a contynuall memoriall
amongest vs in our powre churche, and we all therfore to
be youre perpetuall orators.

My goode lord, as touching your principall mater[1] ye send
vnto me for, I trust I haue endevoured my self to my litle
power taccomplissh your godly mynde in that behalf, els
shall I be sory. And also I hartely thank you for youre
newes ye send me. Albeit I thinke thei be trew, yet thei be
not moost plesaunt; if they com to passe as Criste seith in
his gospell, *Venient ante tempus torquere nos.* In the reuerence
of Jhesu, be ye mery and, as the tyme woll geve, vse your
great wisedom and let not your substaunciall stomache
faill you.

[1] See No. 68.

My lord, as tyme requireth, so shall I write vnto you.
Within half an howre bifore I began to write this letter,
ther was a gentilman with me which hath maryed Turgeus'
wiff, and he shewed me that he had paied to Dan Edmund
Coker, late my monke, iiij^{xx}. pownd*is* this yere, whiche
Turgeus owed vnto hym.

My lord, ye may now see bothe for the discharge of your
conscience and myne also whate maner a man he is. It hath
be told me diuers tymes of credeable persons he had fowre
hundred mark of my predecessor's goodes. It is not like
that Turgeus had all his substaunce, he is to crafftye therfore. Blessid be God, many goode ded*is* and goode reformacions haue be doon in oure howsse, whiche I fere me wold
not with ease haue be doon if he had taryed amongest vs.
I fere me leste your honorable chaplayn Master Stokesleigh[2]
be displeased with me for hym, albeit ther is no cause, our
Lord knoweth: who euer preserue youre goode lordshippe
to your hartys desyre.

At Glastonbury the xiijth day of January.

Ric. abbat of Glastonbury.

To the reuerend fader in God, my lord of Wynchester.

70. FROM ERASMUS

Farrago Epistolarum, 1519, p. 156.   Antwerp.
Erasmus, Ep. 973.   25 May 1519.

[An appeal for protection against vexatious criticism of Erasmus' New
Testament (see no. 21 introd.), uttered at Louvain by a young man who had
been at one time in Fox's household.]

ERASMVS R.P.D. RICARDO EPISCOPO WINTONIENSI S.P.

Reuerendissime Praesul, si vnquam placuit tibi animi mei
studium in te, hoc tantum praemii reposco, ne quid temere
credas sycophantiis de me, quibus nunc fatali quadam peste
feruent omnia. Eduardus Leus si demonstrat argumentis se
melius sentire quam ego sentiam, nunquam offendet animum

---

[2] Vice-President of Magdalen 1505–1507; bp. of London 1530–†1539.

meum. Caeterum quod hic et apud suos scriptis, dictis, per
se, per suos, omnia implet inimicis rumoribus, nec suae
famae recte consulit. Iampridem palam prae se fert plus-
quam hostilem animum, nullo vnquam dicto aut facto
lacessitus a me. Iuuenis est, ardet cupiditate famae: sed
praestabat hanc melioribus auguriis auspicari. Noui prudentiam tuam, quae non facile pronunciet, praesertim in
malam partem. Tempus omnia proferet in lucem. Veritas
laborare potest, vinci non potest. Si tua autoritas consulet
Leo vt aut in totum desistat ab istis sycophantiis, quibus
seipsum magis traducit quam me, aut argumentis duntaxat
mecum certet, illius famae consuluerit. Nunc enim odio,
ceu morbo animi lymphatus, fertur.

Erasmus olim ambiit tuum fauorem, non successit: nunc
non orat vt sibi faueas, sed vt Leo tuo. Bene valeat T. R. P.;
cui me totum consecro dedicoque.

Antuuerpiae. Octauo Calen. Iunias. M.D.XIX.

**71. TO WOLSEY

RO. S. P. 1: 18, f. 278.   Southwick.
Brewer iii. 414.   14 August ⟨1519⟩.

[Wolsey's meeting of the Bishops in Lent 1519 (see no. 67) was adjourned
to the autumn. But about this time he resolved to summon the heads of
monastic houses to state their case before him at Martinmas (cf. Brewer iii.
475). The Bishops' meeting was therefore postponed to Lent 1520.

Fox was perhaps visiting the Priory of Austin canons at Southwick,
N. of Porchester.

So far as we know, this is the last letter surviving which he wrote entirely
with his own hand.]

My most singular good lord,

After my right humble recommendacion, I haue receyved
your lettres by this berar; wherby I perceyve that for diuerse
causes mencioned in your said lettres, your grace thynketh
expedient to prorogue the daye appoynted for like attendance to haue be yeven vppon your grace, as was in Lent
last: wherin it hathe plaised the same to will me by your said
lettres to shewe you my mynde.

R

Plaise it you, my lord, me semeth the said causes be grounded vppon great wisdomme, and next Lent to be mor propice tyme for such treaties then any other. And in the moyne season your grace by your wisdomme shall the mor assuredly knowe the resolucion of the religiose persons in such thyngs as towcheth theyr reformacion. I thynk also that to attend vppon your grace at any tyme bifor the said resolucion be had, shall litell profite, and peraduenture shall not be honorable. And therfor after my pouer witte the said prorogacion shalbe not only expedient but also necessare.

My lord, wold God that the pouer logeyng of Essher[1] did content your grace as much as it reioyseth me that it can plaise you to vse yt; and in good faythe, my lord, the mor and the longar that ye doo vse it, the mor comfort shall it be to me. And therfor I beseche your grace as hartely I can, vse it all wayes as often and as long as it shall plaise you, right as your owen, and make yt a selle to Hampton Courte: as the Kyng that deed is, whoes saule Good pardone, made Hampton Courte and it selles to Richemont.[2] And I shall pray God send you as much good helthe, plaisure and comfort in yt as I wold wisshe my selve to haue.

From Suthwyk the xiiij day of August with the hand of your assured daily preste and bedeman

Ri. Wynton.

To my most singular good lord, my lord Cardinall of York, legat of England and chauncelar of the same.

[1] Wolsey left London, apparently for a short outing, about the beginning of August 1519: Brewer iii. 407.
[2] Cf. no. 22.

‖ 72. FROM THE UNIVERSITY OF OXFORD

Bodleian MS. 282, f. 41 vº.   ⟨Oxford.⟩
                                              ⟨Spring 1520.⟩

[From the same source as no. 36; following letters to the Bishops of Lincoln
and Durham (Atwater and Ruthall), asking them similarly to plead for
Wolsey's intervention. Once more (cf. no. 19) the complaint is of flooded
meadows; to which Fox's scholars at Corpus are nearer than any one else.]

EPISCOPO WYNTON.

Quod homines bonarum litterarum auidos maximi ingenue
nonnunquam feceris, Pater venerandissime, spe nimirum
vegetiore ducimur, in omni negocio quod ad studentes
pertinet, tue amplitudinis beneuolentiam accersire, tuam fisi
pietatem in nos longe calentiorem esse quam vt nostra velit
⟨refrigerari⟩[1] temeritate. Ad hoc etiam magis incitamur
quod tua munificentia Oxoniensis Academie non paruam
partem erexerit: quam vt tuteris ac incolumem conserues,
non minus firmiter, speramus, studebis quam ad eam primitus
construendam nonnullis o⟨m⟩nino parcebas impensis. Nec
quicquam certe a tua celsitudine implorari nostra intentio est,
cuius ipsi tui scholares participes non erunt. Verumenim-
uero, si id quod res est fateamur, in rem suam potius quam
alienam, quod aquis viciniores sunt, futurum erit.

Te igitur vnum nobis aduocatum ante alios duximus
elegendum, cuius authoritas, vt creditur, apud colendissi-
mum dominum Cardinalem, penes quem non ⟨minus⟩[2] vis
secularis quam ecclesiastici iuris est, quammaximi fit.
Verumtamen quanticunque apud eum haberis, hoc vnum
constat, illustrissimo Principi nostro neminem te acceptio-
rem, aut vllum etiam in fauore parem vix, verum certo,
ducimus. Nemo igitur te melius nostram causam aget:
quam vt luculentius agnoscas, non pauca nobis incom-
moda afferentem, paucis enarrabimus.

Sunt in finibus nostris aquarum quidam obices, non
quidem antiquitus solum sed et recentius constructi: quorum

---

[1] Some such word is needed.   [2] coni. Garrod.

abusione et dominorum licentia alii qui suam rem communi preponunt, ducti similes fieri fecerunt. Hi fluctibus adeo obstant quod spatiosa prata que gramina fenaque passim et abunde parere solebant, aquis vndique cooperta suam luxuriem in sterelitatem mutarunt. Homines iumentaque nefandum scelus clamant, quia paucorum questu numerosa plebs oppressa gemit, paruique pisciculi non tam humili et fetoso pecori quam robustis et pinguibus beluis sua loca surripuerunt.

Quantam rerum omnium penuriam hec mala nobis afferent, tua prudentia discutiet. Addunt preterea his magis nociua. Stagnare quidem lacunas faciunt, spurcicias procreant, obscenos fetores generant, qui nares simul et precordia infestant, et horribili pesti, tabifico[3] sudori ceterisque id genus aliis fomenta prebent. Eos denique qui nos precesserant egre molestabant, cum tunc temporis tamen longe mitius fuerant ferendi; illi namque armata manu obices ipsos diremerunt. At nos contra non vi sed pace et pia prece, tuo freti auxilio eos subuertemus et, vt spes est, funditus demoliemur.

Cui rei tua bonitas primo enitatur rogamus; dehinc excellentissimum patrem Cardinalem ad id officii munus horteris petimus. Postremo ceteros omnes qui in hac re quicquam possunt, ad id ipsum alliceas obsecramus; et nos tui obseruantissimi, quod alia rependere nequimus, pro tua salute sedulo fundemus preces.

[3] tobifico *MS*.

73. FROM ERASMUS

Epistolae ad diuersos, 1521, p. 492.   Louvain.
Erasmus, Ep. 1099.   5 May 1520.

[Continuing the matter opened in no. 70.]

ERASMVS ROTERODAMVS R. P. RICARDO EPISCOPO
WINTONIENSI S.D.

Reuerende Praesul. Quod Eduardus Leus tam manifestis
conuiciis debacchatus sit in famam meam, dici non potest
quam displiceat probis omnibus. Nec enim tam mihi nocuit
quam omnibus bonarum studiosis literarum, quorum vtilitati desudat hactenus nostrum ingenium. Tot amicorum
literis, tot monitis meis non potuit deterreri quo minus suae
non minus quam meae famae maculam inureret. Exiit liber
malis auibus; nonnullo detrimento nominis mei, sed multo
maiore ipsius. Ad conuicia respondimus moderatius quam
vellent quidam. Ad argumenta sic respondimus vt ille nunquam sit responsurus, sat scio, et tamen vbique tempero
a conuiciis.

Nec his contentus Leus adornauit, vt aiunt, alterum
libellum multo etiam virulentiorem, quem misit Lutetiam
excudendum. Non audit amicorum sana consilia, nec
vnquam finem facturus est nisi tua autoritate coherceatur.
Atque vtinam id esset factum antequam hoc incendium
erupisset! Subornauit Londini Cartusiensem quendam,
opinor nomine Ioannem Batmanson, iuuenem, vt e scriptis
apparet, prorsus indoctum, sed ad insaniam vsque gloriosum.
Quod si Leum ab his furiosis tumultibus compescuerit
autoritas tua, non meis tantum studiis consulet, sed etiam
Eduardi; qui nunc et suum perdit ocium et meum. Bene
vale.

Louanii .III. Nonas Maias. An. M.D.XX.

‖ 74. TO EDWARD WOTTON

Corpus MS., Liber Admissorum i, f. 6.   Esher.

2 January 152$\frac{0}{1}$.

[Edward Wotton (1492–1555), having begun as a Magdalen schoolboy, passed through the College to his B.A. in 1514, and was Fellow in 1516; so that he had ties with Claymond before coming to Corpus. He used the dispensation here granted to study at Padua, and proceeded there M.D.: a degree on which he was incorporated at Oxford, 3 March 152$\frac{5}{6}$ (cf. no. 84). With the revival of classical studies Greek medicine was displacing the Arab medicine hitherto in vogue; and Galen in particular was receiving much attention (cf. no. 64). Possibly therefore Wotton is to be identified with the Englishman Odoardus, who in company with Clement and Lupset, both of Corpus, helped to correct the proofs of the Aldine Galen in Greek, 1525. He became President of the College of Physicians in 1541, and in 1552 published his celebrated work *De differentiis animalium*, Paris, M. Vascosanus.]

RICARDVS DIVINA PROVIDENCIA WINTONIENSIS EPISCOPVS AC
     CORPORIS CHRISTI COLLEGII IN VNIVERSITATE OXONIENSI
     FVNDATOR EDWARDO WOTTON SALVTEM

Cum ante omnia bonarum literarum in vtraque lingua[1] exoptamus perpetuum incrementum et felicem perseueranciam, teque adolescentulum preclare indolis ac magne expectacionis ex nostri[2] Collegii Presidente, cui fidem habemus non modicam, accepimus; ex mea vnius authoritate te in nostrum Collegium, non vt socium, quod non permittunt Magdalenensia statuta,[3] sed socio comparem admittimus et assumimus; tibique concedimus facultatem discedendi in Italiam ad ediscendas bonas literas et precipue Grecas, illicque triennio post Calendas Maii proximo consecuturas moraturo:

ita vt triennio exacto ad nostrum redeas Collegium, nisi tibi amplius prorogandum tempus ego, aut me defuncto, Presidens et maior pars seniorum permiserint et concesserint;

illicque lectionem Grecam aut Latinam aut vtramque, si videatur predictis commodum et oportunum, per quin-

---

[1] Greek and Latin.   [2] nr̃e *MS.*
[3] So too with Morwent: cf. no. 60.

quennium, nisi prefati aliquid temporis relaxarint, prosequaris, protrahas et continues nostri Collegii sumptibus et
impensis.

Ac durante hoc triennio quo a Collegio abfueris, singulis
annis a me quinque libras et totidem a nostro Collegio
accipies; in reditu accepturus que nostra iubeant Statuta.
Bene vale, bonis literis indies profecture.

Ex nostris edibus Essheri postridie Calendas Ianuarii anno
Domini millesimo quingentesimo vicesimo et nostre translationis anno xx^{mo}.

* 75. TO CLAYMOND

Corpus MS.　　　　　　　　　　　　　　Winchester.
　　　　　　　　　　　　　　　　17 February ⟨1521⟩.

[This accords so well in date with no. 77 that they may probably be placed
together. They show happy relations between Fox and his College.]

Brother Mr President,

Soo it is that I am commaunded to goo to the cowrte
and to attende vppon the Counsell. Wherfor I intende by
God*is* grace to departe hens thetherward to morow; and
full glad shall I be to haue you with me at Esshere in the
weeke byfore Palme Sonday:[1] prayng you to dispose you
to the same and to abyde with me all the Estur season.
And thus fare ye well.

At Wynchestre the xvij^{th} day of February.

　　　　　　　　　　　　　　　　Your brother
　　　　　　　　　　　　　　　　　　Ri. Wynton.

To my brother the President of Corpus Christi College in
Oxford.

[1] 24 March 1521.

* 76. FROM WILLIAM STAFFORD

Corpus MS.   ⟨Bradfield?⟩
                                          25 February ⟨1521⟩.

[Sir William Stafford of Bradfield in Berkshire had acquired through his
wife Ann, daughter of Sir John Langford, the estate of Langford in Devon,
between Cullompton and Plymtree. In the College Archives are preserved
various documents about the transfer of the estate to Fox, dated 12 Nov.
1518–13 March 1520, in which Sir Thomas Fetiplace appears; and finally
a receipt from William Stafford for the £10 asked for, dated 25 April 1521
(13 Henry VIII), from which a year-date can be assigned to this letter.
  Langford is still in the possession of the College.]

My dute humbly remembred, pleaseth it your gode lordeship to vnderstonde that at the tyme of bargayn makyng
bitwene the Maister of Savoy and me for the manoire of
Langeford to your vse, Y shewed hym that there was certeyne woddes there which Y was in mynde to haue solde;
and at the tyme of commvnycacion bitwene Sire Thomas
Fetyplace and me, in lyke wise. Wherfore it was agreed
bitwene hym and me as one of the articles of couvenauntis,
that Y shulde haue for the seid wodes x^{li}.: which was gevyn
to my wif. And so the Maister of Savoy feithefully promysed
me to speke vnto your lordeship for the same. And bifore
Cristemas, when Y was laste with your lordeship at Seynt
Mary Overeice[1] at London, at the tyme of arbitrement
bitwene Sire Thomas Fetiplace and me, at my departyng
from you Y moved your lordeship for it; and then you seid,
when all the mater was fynysshed bitwene hym and me, Y
shulde haue it.

   So it is, my lorde, accordyng to the awarde made bytwene
vs, Y haue paide hym his hole monney which was cccccxij^{li}.,
which was xxx^{li}. more then euer Y receyved of hym; beside
all other charges of costis of myn attendance: which Y
assure your lordeship Y am the worse fore by c^{li}. In consideracion wherof Y besche your gode lordeship to
remember me with the seid x^{li}., with ferther rewarde as best
shall like you. And duryng my liffe Y shalbe yours with my

                    [1] See no. 23 n.

seruyce and preyer: as knoweth oure Lorde, who preserue
you longe to his plesure.

Wretyn the morne after Seynt Mathias day by your
humble seru*au*nt and bedeman

Wylliam Stafford.

To the right reuerend fader in God, my lorde of Wynchester.

‡ 77. FROM CLAYMOND

Corpus MS.   Oxford.

⟨April 1521.⟩

IESVS . AMPLISSIMO IN CHRISTO PATRI AC DOMINO RICARDO
    WINTONIENSI EPISCOPO IOANNES CLAIMONDVS SA. PLV.:
IN QVO EST OMNIS SALVS.

Profectus abs te omnia domi inueni ex sententia: videbatur
mihi nihil mutatum. Tanta est diligentia Vicepresidis [1]
tantaque aliorum obseruantia. Nihil igitur est hic quod
cures. Cura itaque teipsum, neque temere te comittas
incerto aeri. Expecta magnam partem Maii, vt membra
respondeant omnia. Solent volucres deplumes non ante
euolare e nido, donec et plumas et temperatum nacte sunt
aerem.

Sed hec satis prudenti. Teipsum in tua valitudine consule
solum: quanquam sit tibi mediculus noster Lepton, qualis
aliis nullus. Est enim medicus perpaucorum medicorum,
incognitus vulgo: quod est eis salutiferum, ne multos
interimat. Vrinas perspicit sed non discernit. Tui famuli
cubicularii non miscerent, vt faciunt (obtenebrescunt enim
eis oculi), sed cribro in faciem diffunderent, vt inuitus
collachrimans et purgans oculos diiudicet. Et hec ioco: cui
in tempore annitere, postpositis seriis.

Obiit Noui Collegii custos.[2] Quis ei sufficiatur Deus scit,
non Claimondus: qui non est augur nec Oedipus. Vale et
cura vt olim valeas: tibique magis quam medico prospicias.
Oxonii.

[1] Morwent; see no. 60.
[2] John Rede, †1 April 1521. His successor, John Young, was elected
c. 13 April.

*78. TO SIR ARTHUR PLANTAGENET

RO. S. P. 3: 3, f. 11.   Winchester.
                                            5 November ⟨1522?⟩

[Plantagenet (c. 1480–1542) was a natural son of Edward IV. He was attached to Henry VIII's bodyguard; and on 25 April 1523 was created Viscount Lisle.

As he has not yet this title, the letter cannot be later than 1522; but Fox's signature is so weak, that the date must be put as late as possible.]

After my right herty recommendacion, I haue this day receyved your letters of diuerse content*is*.

Wher of the first is that ye desire me to be good lorde to your cosyne John Wayte. And as to that matier, I trust he be my warde; for, as far as I can vnderstonde, it shalbe Candelmas[1] before he be xxj yere of age. I haue seased hym and offered hym mariage; and what shall comme ther of, I cannot tell tyll Candelmas be past. I haue don hym no wronge, nor non indendith to doo, and glade I shalbe to doo hym good; and the rather at your desire.

Secundly ye wryte in your said letter that I haue an indenture and obligacion of old Mr. Kingismyll*is*. Which is trew; and iff ye had wrytten to me to haue sent it you, I wold so haue don, and am redy so to doo when ye will wryte for yt.

Therdly ye desire by your said wrytyng to haue the obligacione that I haue of you for the delyuerance of the store[2] of the manor of Segyngworth,[3] accordynge to the will of John Wayte dissesed. As for that matier, for ase-muche as I haue yet no certeyntee wheder ye haue fully delyuered the said store, or whether ye haue delyuered ⟨yt/ accordyng to the condicions of the said obligacion or not, I pray you take pacience for a season; makyng your selff well assured that nether for that matier nor any other I seke note nor desire to put you to any besynes.

And fourtely and fynally, wher ye wryte by your said

---

[1] 2 Feb.   [2] furniture.
[3] Segenworth, N. of Titchfield. In 1528–9 John Wayte leased the manor to Arthur Plantagenet: V.C.H., Hampshire iii. 229.

letter that it was the will of the said John Wayte that if his sone Thomas now dissessed died byfore he cam to the age of xxij yeres, that then the said store shuld remayne to hys next heyer: I thynk that such was the will of the said John Wayte. And therfore yf his sone and heyer Thomas now discessed died before he wer fully the age of xxij yers, his brother John Wayt owght to haue the said store. And for the recouerye ther of he hath his accion only ageynst the late wyfe of his said brother; for she hade ⟨it⟩, as far as I can vnderstond, after his discesse. And I doubt not he hath non accion a yenst you as excecutor, seyng that ye deliuered it to the vicar of Tychfeld⁴ to the vse of Thomas Wayte: which receyved yt of hym, and after his discesse left it with his said late wyfe; which of reason must awnswer for yt. And thus I haue aunswered your said letter: wherwith I trust acordynge to reason ye wilbe contented.

And thus fare ye hertely well at Whynchester the vth day of Nouember.

Ri. Wynton.

To the right worshipfull Sir Arthure Plantagenet, knyght.

*79. TO WOLSEY

RO. S. P. 1: 29, f. 7.   Winchester.
Brewer iii. 3491.   October 1523.

[This and no. 80 are identical in form; concerning two different counties. In spite of their official character, they are included here as illustrating the work which the Bishop of Winchester was required to do.]

My most syngular good lord,

In my right humble wyse I recommende me to your grace. Pleas it the same tonderstand that the iiij^{th} day of this moneth I receyvede the Kyng*is* commyssion dated at Hampton Court vndre his great seall the iiij^{th} day of Septembre last past. By the whiche his grace commaunded me that, forasmuche as Sir Arthure Plantagenet, nowe Vicecount Lisle, John lord Awdeley, Sir William

---

⁴ Titchfield, in Hampshire, near Portsmouth.

S⟨and*is*, now⟩e Lord Sand*is*, Sir John Wallop knyght, Richard Lyster, William Paulett, James Worsley, Richard Sa⟨nd*is*, Richar⟩d Norton, William Vuedall, John Wyntershull, William Hawles, and Thomas Well*is*, late commyssio⟨ners within the counte / of Hampshire for the practysyng of a certayn loone and prest, haue not yet for th⟨ere owne parties aduaun / ced to his grace any summe or summes of money by way of prest or loone, I sh⟨ulde therfor aswell call the / sayd late commyssioners and euery of them byfore me and assesse them for ⟨a like loone; as also soo to endeuer / me for the levyeng of the same, as it myght be payd to the Treasorer of the Kyng⟨*is* Chambre in the xv^{cim} / of Saynt Michaell then next folowyng.   And over this that I shulde by my wry⟨tyng certyfy your grace / and other of the Kyng*is* Counsell at Westm*inster crastino Animarum* then next cummyng of my ⟨demeanour in thexecution / of the sayd commyssion: as more largely is conteyned in the same.

Accordyng whervnto ⟨by my seuerall lettres / directed and delyuerd to the sayd late commyssioners, I by vertu of the sayd commyssion desyre⟨d and requyred / them for the causes aboue rehersed, to come to me assoone as they goodly myght vppon the ⟨recept of my / sayd lettres. Whervnto euery of them, except my lord Awdeley, whiche is not nowe resedent withi⟨n the counte / of South*ampton* but dwellyth in London or nygh thereabowt*is*;

my lord Sand*is*, whiche is byy⟨onde the see / in the Kyng*is* werres;

Sir John Wallop knyght, whiche is in likewyse byyonde the see in the ⟨Kyng*is* / werres;

Richard Sand*is*, whiche is in likewyse byyond the see in the Kyng*is* werres;

and William H⟨awles /, whiche is abydyng at London in Lincolns Inne,

haue answerde as p*ar*tycularly foloweth:

Fyrst my lord Lisle hath affirmyd that the yerely valo*ur* of his land*is* excede not the summe of ⟨   , /

and therafter he is assessed to oon hundreth sex pound*is*
xiij^s. iiij^d.; the whiche he hathe promysed ⟨to pay / to my
hand*is* byfore the fest of Saynt Andrewe next cummyng.

Item Richard Lyster hath answered that he hathe payd
the prest, and for his discharge in that behalf hath the
Kyng*is* lettres vndre his prevy seall.

Item William Paulet hath made like answere.

Item James Worsley hathe answered that he hath be
assessed in the Kyng*is* courte at oon ⟨   / the
same, and there hathe made payment accordyngly.

Item Richard Norton, wrongly named in the said commyssion John Norton, hath answered ⟨that he hath / payd
the prest, and for his discharge hathe the Kyng*is* prevy seall.

Item William Vuedall hath made like answere.

Item John Wyntershull hath made like answere.

Item Thomas Well*is* hath made like answere.

Of all whiche premysses accordyng to the ⟨sayd late /
commyssioners I certyfy your grace by this my wrytyng
vndre my seall.

Dated at Wynchestre the   of Octobre a°. xv°.
H. viij.

* 80. TO WOLSEY

RO. S. P. 1: 29, f. 5.   Winchester.
Brewer iii. 3492.   October 1523.

My most syngular good lord,

In my right humble wyse I recommende ⟨me to your
grace. Pleas it the same tonderstand / that the iiiith day
of this moneth I receyved the Kyng*is* commyssion dated
⟨at Hampton Court vndre his great seall / the iiiith day
of Septembre last past. By the whiche his grace com-
maunde⟨d me that forasmuche as Sir Edward Darell, /
John Saymour, John Hungreford, John Danuers, Henry
Long and Anto⟨ny Hungreforde, Antony Styleman, /
Robart Kaleway, John Yorke and John Gawen, late
commyssioners ⟨within the counte of Wiltshire for the
practy/syng of a certaygne prest and loone, haue not yet

for there owne ⟨parties aduaunced to his grace any summe /
or summes of money by way of prest or loone, I shulde
therfor asw⟨ell call th⟩e say⟨d late commyssioners and euery /
of them byfore me to assesse them for a like loone; as also
soo to endeuer me for the levy⟨eng of the same, as it myght /
be payde to the Treasorer of the Kyng*is* Chambre in the
xv ᵐ. of Saynt Michaell then ⟨next folowyng. And over /
this that I shulde by my wrytyng certyfy your grace and
other of the Kyng*is* Counsell ⟨at West*minster crastino
Animarum*[1] then / next cummyng of my demeanour in
thexecution of the sayd commyssion: as more largely is
⟨conteyned in the same./

Accordyng whervnto by my seuerall lettres directed and
delyuered to the sayd late commyssioner⟨s, I by vertu of
the sayd / commyssion desyred and requyred them for the
causes aboue rehersed to come to me assoon⟨e as they
goodly myght / vppon the recept of my sayd lettres.
Whervnto euery of them, except Sir Edward Darell, w⟨hiche,
as I was certyfyed / by my messagier, was then owt of the
contree in the Cowrte attendyng vppon the Q⟨uene's grace,
and Sir / John Danuers, which, as I was in likewise certyfyed, dyed abowt*is* fyve yeres passed, a⟨nswerde as p*arty*-
cularly / foloweth:

Fyrst Sir John Saymour hath answered by his lettres
that he woll labour to the Kyng*is* h⟨ighnes to haue / a
remyssion of the sayd loone; and yf he can none suche
obteygne byfore thend of t⟨he term, he woll / then resort
to me and be contented to be assessed to the sayd prest.

Item Sir John Hungreford hath affirmyd that hys good*is*
be bettre in valour then the yerely valour ⟨of   /
and that the same good*is* excede not the valour of fowre
hundreth pownd*is*; after the whiche sum⟨me he is bownde /
to pay for his prest LIIJ*li*. vJˢ. vIIJᵈ.: the whiche he hathe
promysed to pay to my hand*is* byfore the fes⟨t of Saynt /
Nicholas next cummyng.

Item Sir Henry Long hath answered by his lettres that

¹ 3 Nov.

he is nowe and must be soo contynually occup⟨ied / in
thexecution of the King*is* commyssion concernyng the
temporall subsydy that he cannot come to me byfor the fest
of Saynt Martyne next cummyng: at whiche tyme, as he
saythe, he woll come to me and doo his du⟨e / concernyng
the sayd prest.

Item Sir Antony Hungreford hath answered by his
lettres that he hath payd the sayd prest, and for his discharge
in that byhalf hathe the King*is* lettres vndre his pryvy seall.

Item Antony Styleman hathe made like answere.

Item Robert Kaleway hath made like answere.

Item Thomas York, named wrongly in the sayd commyssion John Yorke, hath made like answere.

Item Thomas Gawen, in likewyse wrongly named in the
sayd commyssion John Gawen, hath made like ans⟨were./

Of all which premysses accordyng to the King*is* sayd
commyssion I certyfy your grace by this my wrytyng vndre
my seall.

Dated at Wynchestre the　　　　day of Octobre aᵒ. xvᵒ.
H. vɪɪj.

*81. TO WOLSEY

B.M. Cotton MS. Calig. B. vi, f. 287.　　　　Winchester.
Ellis, ser. 3, no. 114: Brewer iii. 2859.　　　　⟨1523?⟩

[Once again (cf. no. 57) Fox is asked to draw upon his memory. The Government has no 'wrytyng' about the events of 30 to 40 years ago. So Fox is
appealed to, to produce any record that he may have; and, if he has none,
to state what he can recollect.

There is no clear guidance as to date; but as Fox's signature is beginning
to fail, Brewer's conjecture seems likely to be correct.]

My most syngular good lord,

In my right humble wyse I recommend me to your grace.
Pleas it the same tondrestond that this evynnyng after vɪɪth
of the clock I receyved your lettre by this berer; by the
whiche your grace willeth and desyreth me to shewe you
the knowlege that I haue in twoo matiers.

Wherof the furst is whether the Kyng that dede is, whose

soule God pardone, made any entrepryse or ordynances for the subduyng of the Scott*is*, when the werre was bytwixt hym and theme. And yf he any suche made, and that I haue any wrytyng therof, I shuld then sende it to your grace; or yf I noone suche haue, that then I shuld shewe you yf I haue any knowlege of the said entreprise or ordynances, and what that shuld be.

My most syngular good lord, for myne answere in this byhalf, yt is of very trawthe that when the werre was bytwixt the Kyng that dede is and the said Scott*is*, I was duryng the said werre, that is to say byfore the begynnyng therof and at the begynnyng therof, and soo contynewally to thende therof was made by a treaty of peaxe, lyeng and abydyng in the bisshopriche of Durysne, Northumbreland, and Berwick; and some tyme with my lord of Northfolke in the castell of Alnewick, and for a great parte with my housolde in the castell of Norham. And thus, my lord, duryng the said werre I cam not nor was with the Kyng that dede is; and as towchyng the said entrepryse or ordynances, I neyther haue nor neuer see any wryting therof. But soo it is, that the said Kyng that dede is, dide ordeyn that my lord Dawbney,[1] which was then his chambrelayn, shulde haue comme with a great puyssance in to Northumbreland, and soo to haue invaded Scotland. And for the furnysshyng of the same hoste with vitale, the towne of Berwick was sufficiently providede with all thing*is* necessary in that byhalf; as William Pawne can more specially shewe you then I. And the said entreprise was broken by thinsurrexion[2] that began in Cornwell and Devonshire by reason of the Black Smyth; and of this entrepryse I doubt not my Lord Chambrelayn and Mr Lovell, and suche other as nowe be lyvyng and were then attendyng vppon the Kyng that dede is, can perfytly enforme your Grace. And this is all that I knowe towching the said entreprise, or any ordinances made for the same.

---

[1] Giles, baron Daubeney; lord chamberlain 1495; †1508.
[2] Suppressed in June 1497 at Blackheath.

The secunde matier wherof your grace desyreth me to put you in knowlege, concerneth indentures made for the keping of the marches of this realme in the tyme of werre ayenste Scotland.

My moste syngular good lord, as in this matier I knowe not that in the werre that was bytwixt the Kyng that dede is and Scotland, there were any suche indentures made, or that any person indented for the keping of the said marches for the said tyme of werre. And to my knowlege noo persone indented for this matier sens the deth of therle of Northumbreland,[3] father to therle of Northumbreland that now ys;[4] the which indented with the Kyng that dede is, in the furste yere of his reigne, byfore that I kept the Pryvye Seall.[5] And the said Erle indented not only for the kepyng of the said marches but also for the keping of the towne of Berwick at his hole cost*is* and chargies; and as I remembre he had for the supportacion of the said chargies three thowsand mark*is*,[6] or three thowsand pownd*is*, I remembre not well whether. Wherof the said Kyng being wery, toke Berwick in to his owne hand*is* and made Sir William Tyler capitaigne therof. And sens that tyme I trowe noo man indented for the keping of the said Borders for the tyme of werre.

I doubt not, my lord, it shalbe right necessary that the Kyng*is* grace make a warden for the este and mydle marches; for it shalbe to muche for any oon persone to bere the burdeyn of all three marches in the tyme of werre. And it shalbe right expedient that he be a very hable man that shalbe wardeyn of the said este and mydle marches in the tyme of werre; for vppon the este marches shalbe the moste busynesse of the werre. Savyng that if my lord Dacre wold leve his sone and his brother vppon the weste marches, wherby the Scott*is* haue not muche with a great army invaded those partyes, and lodge hym self in the este marches, in myne

3 Henry Percy, 1446–1489.
4 Henry Percy, 1478–1527, warden of the east marches 1503.
5 24 Feb. 1487.   6 £2000.

T

opynyon, for the great experyence, acquayntance, and
land*is* which he hath in Northumbreland, he shuld be right
meit to kepe the said este and mydle marches. And whoo
soo euer shalbe now warden of them, he owght not to looke
to haue the fees that the said Erle of Northumbreland had;
seyng that he had the said fees, as aboue is said, not only
for the kepyng of the said este and mydle marches but also
for the kepyng of the said towne of Berwick: which towne
is nowe in the Kyng*is* hand*is* and at his propre cost*is* and
chargies. And in my pouer opynyon the fees that the said
warden shall haue, owght, of reason, to be cessed much
aftur the nowmbre of the souldyers whiche he will bynde
hym to haue contynually attendante and serving in the
werre vppon the said borders.

And this is the knowelege that I haue of the said entrepryse and indentures, with my pouer opynyon concernyng
the fees for the said warden in the tyme of werre. Wherwith
I beseche your grace to be contented; assuryng the same
that yf I had any wryting concernyng the said entrepryse
or indentures for the werre, yf ye cowde noone otherwyse
haue them, I wold rather bryng you them vppon my fote
then ye shuld fayll of theme. As knowith our Lord: whoo
send your grace as good prosperitie and spede in all your
causes as your own good harte wold wisshe.

At Wynchestre this Thursday after ix^th of the clock in
the nyght.

Your humble preste and bedeman

Ri. Wynton.

To my most syngular good lord, my lord Cardinall of
Yorke, chauncellor of England and legate of the same.

* 82. TO WOLSEY

RO. S. P. 1: 31, f. 220.   Marwell.
Brewer iv. 518.   19 July ⟨1524?⟩

[No evidence is available to throw light on the dispute between Fox and his
episcopal neighbour, Robert Sherbourn; who held the see of Chichester
1508–1536. The failing signature requires a late year-date; but apart from
this Brewer only conjectures.]

My verey syngular good lorde,

In my right humble wyse I recommende me to your grace.
And yesterday in the overnone I receyved your honorable
lettres purportyng that my lorde of Chichestre, pretendyng
certayn duties to be owyng vnto hym by me, hathe hereto-
fore at sondry tymes, aswell by his lettres as otherwyse
(as he affermyth), demaunded the same; and that I haue
thereto made hym noo convenyent answere. By occasion
wherof he shulde be compelled for recouery of the said
duties to take suche ways, wherby shulde ensue to me
inquyetation and trowble; except that vppon your honorable request I doo shewe my self agreable to reason. In con-
syderation of whiche premysses your grace, as apperyth
by your lettres, ys right glad to interpone your self always to
remove and take away any suche matier as bytwene your
frend*is* and lovers (among*is* whome it pleaseth your grace of
your great goodnes by your said lettres to reken me as
oon) myght be cause or occasion of dissension and variance,
woll and desyre me to shewe me confirmable and tractable
in the premysses, and to make suche answere to the demaund*is* of the sayd Bisshop of Chichestre as he owght
of reason to stand contented. Wherby I shall not oonly
avoyd further sute and vexation, but also, for the faver
that it pleaseth your grace to bere toward*is* my sayd lorde
of Chichestre and me, doo the thyng to your sayd grace
contentation and pleasure.

My most syngular good lorde, in my most entier maner
and as hartyly as I can, I thanke your grace for your sayd
honorable lettres: whiche, by licence of your grace, that I may

soo say, I fynde full of all charytie, humanytie and humylytie, and like the lettres of a verey lovyng spirituall father and hede of the churche of this realme toward*is* his subiect*is* and obedyenciers. And veryly, my lorde, I am verey glad that my said lorde of Chichestre nowe maketh his resorte to your grace with his surmysed complaynt agaynst me. Albe yt he hathe in tyme passed sowght for his remydy; aswell at the hand*is* of my lorde of Cantrebury, byfore whome by my Chancellor[1] I made hym in effecte suche answere as I purpose vppon my pouer honesty and conscience to make byfore your grace, as also by consultations and advises that he hathe taken with lerned men in bothe the lawes: as your grace shall more largely vnderstand when the debatyng of this matier shall come byfore the same. And for answere makyng vppon my partye to the demaund*is* of my sayd lorde of Chichestre, yt may pleas your grace to assigne to eyther of vs some certain day of this next terme of Saint Michaell; and I shall then not oonly make answere to the surmysed complaynt*is* of my sayd lorde of Chichestre, but also beseche your grace to commaunde hym to make answere to suche complaynt*is* as I shall then by wrytyng lay agaynst hym. And after your grace haue harde the complaynt*is* of bothe parties, yf there shall then be matiers fownde contrary to honesty, conscience, lawe or reason, I haue great trust it shalbe fownde in hym and not in me. And where as by his vncharitable brutyng he hath byfore right great personagies noysed me to owe hym sex thowsande marck*is*,[2] I trust I shall then byfore your grace not only confownde hym in that partye, but also charge hym with matier inevitable: wherof I wolde not that he cowde lay the semblable to me, to wynne therby ten tymes tolde his sex thowsande marck*is*.

Fynally, my most syngular good lorde, by cause it becummeth me not to encombre your grace with long wrytyng, dayly and hourely occupyed with great and weyghty matiers, I must at this tyme omytt many moo matiers that were for me right necessary to be writen by

---

[1] John Incent: see no. 85.   [2] £4000.

thies my lettres in this matier bytwixt my lorde of Chichestre
and me; besechyng your grace thus to be pleased at this
tyme, and always to contynew my good lorde after your
accustomed maner: for the which I am and euer shalbe
your entier and harty seruitor and orator.

At my pouer house of Marwell the xixth day of July.

> your humble preste and dayly bedeman
>   Ri. Wynton.

To my most syngular good lorde, my lorde Cardynall of
Yorke, legate of Englond and chauncellor of the same.

‖83. FROM ST. JOHN'S COLLEGE, CAMBRIDGE

St. John's Register, f. 52.   Cambridge.
Hymers, p. 225.   26 September ⟨1524⟩.

[A contemporary copy in the Register at St. John's known as the Thin Red
Book. Dr. Scott, the present Master, has kindly informed us that it follows
in the Register a document of 19 Aug. 1524: so that the year-date is clear.
He suggests also that the College may have found its ground for appealing
to Fox for service-books or scholars, in the fact that he had been executor
to the Lady Margaret. The letter was first printed by J. Hymers, 1840, in
an edition of Fisher's *Funeral Sermon* upon her.]

REVERENDO IN CHRISTO PATRI AC DOMINO D. RICARDO
   WINTONIENSI EPISCOPO ORNATISSIMO, VIRTVTIS ET
   BONARVM LITTERARVM FAVTORI MAXIMO.

Quanquam maior sit tibi apud omnes iamdudum parta
gloria, Praesul ornatissime, quam que vlla temporis vetu-
state aboleri queat—extant enim semperque extabunt aeterna
tui nominis monumenta, quae te intermori sinent nunquam
—; tamen quum nihil dubitamus hunc animum quo tam
praeclare egeris, tibi a superis immortalibus eo datum quo
de omnibus quantum fieri potest benemeriaris, opere-
precium sane facturi videbamur si nostris litteris ampli-
tudinem tuam sollicitaremus ad preclari quidpiam apud
nos agendum: non quod te iam nunc aut ociosum putamus,
aut parta gloria indormiscere, verum quum quid cui facias
refert plurimum, et accipientium condicione commendantur

beneficia, existimauimus certe nihil maius ad tuae glorie cumulum accedere posse quam si, quod Oxoniae nuper feceras, Cantabrigiae quoque quasi trophaeum aliquod siue statuam erexeris magnitudinis tuae. Praeclara sunt, fatemur, quae Oxoniae feceris et immortalitate digna, quibus vel magni reges inuidere possunt. At cum te ipso indies maior euadis, et quam plurimis benefecisse prima laus sit; testetur, precamur, et Cantabrigia Wintoniensem Episcopum aliquando vixisse, neque vixisse modo sed virtutis etiam et bonarum litterarum fautorem fuisse munificentissimum.

Habes tu quidem, felicissime Praesul, hic magnam exercendae tuae virtutis materiam. Habes hic Collegium cui benefacias, non quodlibet sed Ioannis: quod si esset tam opibus suppellectileque instructum quam est litteris, vt speramus, et studiosa multitudine, non esset cur magnopere alienam peteremus opem. Verum vt vrbes et ciuitates a paruis olim initiis ortae ad summum tandem rerum euectae sunt fastigium, ita speramus et Collegium nostrum vna cum aetate auctius euasurum, quum bonorum hominum liberalitate, tum tua, Praesul optime, virtute et benignitate: quibus nos nunc maxime prosequaris oramus. Laboramus namque cum aliarum rerum inopia, tum librorum maxime quibus diuina officia cani solent, miro defectu; vt in numerosissimo quem superum fauore habemus choro, vix parti [1] terciae sufficiant codices.

Tua paternitas siue huic malo mederi velit, siue discipulos aliquot, quod dicimus, fundare, qui litteris et virtute per te inuigilent, seu quiduis aliud apud nos agere quod tibi gloriam pariat immortalem, nostris vero litteris vtilitatem afferat, libenter amplectemur munificentiam tuam, curabimusque sedulo ne te aliquando collati beneficii peniteat.

Iam vero non miraberis, amplissime Pater, quod te vnum prae caeteris libentius sollicitamus, quippe quum videmus nomen tuum, nostris omnibus libellis, codicibus schedisque inscriptum, nunquam non conspectui nostro occurrere, nunquam non oculis esse obuium. Existimauimus nullius

---

[1] parte *MS*.

opem nobis rectius inuocandam quam illius cuius iam diu
nostris auribus tam familiare ⟨nomen⟩ fuit. Quare quum
tantum apud omnes gloriae, apud Deum vero, cuius amore,
vt omnia, et istuc feceris, premii et mercedis tantillo bene-
ficio tibi lucraberis, aggredere ocius, colendissime Pater,
prouinciam nec grauem nec difficilem. Adde hoc tuis
virtutibus quasi colophonem, et quod apud Oxonienses
magnifice prestitisti, apud nos vtcunque presta. Celebrabitur in vtraque Academia tanti Presulis virtus tanta.
Florebit in omne aeuum tui nominis splendor atque gloria.
Denique quod maximum reputabis, viues apud homines,
viues et apud superos, clarus et immortalis. Bene valeat
dominatio tua diu felix atque fausta.

Cantabrig. e D. Ioannis Collegio 6°. Calendas Octobr.

Dabis veniam, ornatissime Pater, nobis magna rerum
mole laborantibus, qui illius ferme obliti sumus quod vel
primo loco dictum opportuit; nimirum vt dignetur dominatio tua nos reuerendo patri Norwicensi tuo suffragio
commendare. Nos vicissim nostris precibus te Christo
benignissimo commendabimus.

  Tuae dominationis scolastici deditissimi
    Magister et Socii collegii D. Ioannis Cantabrig.

*84. TO CLAYMOND

Corpus MS.   Marwell.
             1 March ⟨1526?⟩

[Fox granted the wardship and marriage of Peter Erneley to the College by
a deed dated 10 June 1523: in the College Archives, Bursary Transcripts xii.
239. This letter therefore cannot be earlier than 1524. As Wotton was
incorporated at Oxford on his Padua degree in March 1526, he may just
have returned at this time; so that Fox's message to him would be a sort of
greeting of welcome. There is mention of plague at Oxford in March and
April 1526, in the University Register H, ff. 151, 153, 155v°.]

Brother Mr President,

  After my hartiest recommendation, I haue vnderstande
by your last lettre that your childe Petre Erneley hathe taken
his leve of you, *et migrauit ad celum.* Wherfor ye shulde
gratulari illi et gaudere tibiipsi quod talem alumnum illuc tran-

misisti. His sister is professed in the monastery of Wharwell,[1] and therfor she cannot be his heyr; but the preste that is vicar in the churche of Saresbury, whiche was his vncle,[2] is his next heyr, and after hym my seruaunt Edwarde Erneley. And of eyther of theme ye haue, as ye well knowe, a seuerall release for the manor of Marwell; the whiche releases be a sufficient barre to the intaile, in myne opynyon. I haue this day sent Mr Stokley[3] to William Froste to knowe his mynde therin, and I advise you to take the counsaill therin of some well lerned men of those parties.

Also where I haue a leas of you of the lande that you haue inclosed within the parcke of Esshere, whiche lyeth within the parishe of Walton vppon Temmes, I intented to haue made by my wrytyng William Nutbeme[4] my deputye and assignye in the said leas for the termes that I haue of you therin. Yt apperyd by that parte of the indenture that I haue of you, that ye made me the sayd leas of suche land*is* as ye had within the parishe of Waltham: whiche is a great error, for they lye not within the parishe of Waltham, but in the paryshe of Walton *super Tamisiam.* And also it must be said *super Tamisiam,* by cause there is within the same shire of Surrey a nother towne called Walton vppon the hill. Wherfor yt shalbe right expedyent that when ye shall next come to me, ye bryng with you the other parte of the sayd indentures remanyng with you to thentent they may be reformed.

Yt shall in likewyse be expedyent that ye looke vppon the dede of the graunt that I made to you of the sayd land*is* vnder my seall; for if it be wryten in the said dede that the sayd land*is* lye within the paryshe of Waltham, the dede is vode and of noone effect. And soo it is also voyde, if it be sayd in the sayd ded*is* that the said land*is* lye within the pareshe of Walton, except it be exprestly specyfied that they

---

[1] See no. 65.

[2] William Erneley of New Sarum, clerk: his release is dated 22 March 1517.

[3] Fox's personal Treasurer.

[4] a 'gentleman' present at St. Cross when Fox gave his Statutes, 20 June 1517.

lye within the parishe of Walton vppon the Temmes within
the county of Surrey; by cause there is within the same
countye a nother towne called Walton vppon the hill. And
if ye fynde this errore within my sayd deede, it shalbe well
done that ye bryng it with you when ye shall next cum
hither, to thentent it may be reformed.

I intende to be at Woluesay[5] *in vigialia*[6] *Dominice in
Passione Domini*, and I shalbe right glad that ye be there the
same day. I shall in likewyse be glad that ye then bryng
with you Mr Ware: not as it were to abyde still with me,
but as it were to keepe you company for his recreation,
and then shall we farther speke to gyther for his interteygny-
ment. And with my harty recommendation makyng to
Mr Wotton,[7] I pray you shewe hym that my right syde
vnder my ribbs and my hede be excedyngly hote: wherin
I wolde knowe his advise. Commaunde me to your company; and if the dethe incresse, the sonner and the further[8]
that ye departe thens, the better shall it be for you. And
thus I pray God sende you all as well to fare as I wolde
wisshe my self to doo.

At Marwell the fyrst day of Marche.

Your brother

Ri. Wynton.

To my brother the President of Corpus Christi College in
Oxforde.

---

5 the Bishop's palace in Winchester, between the Cathedral and the School.

6 17 March 1526.

7 See no. 74.

8 It appears that 'the College' at Witney, to which Corpus later resorted
in time of plague, was not yet in existence.

*85. TO WOLSEY

RO. S. P. 1: 45, f. 52.   Marwell.
Brewer iv. 3583.   17 November ⟨1526⟩.

[Nos. 85–87 are placed by Brewer in 1527–8; but the death of Mr. Dowman shows that they must be put forward. He was an ecclesiastical official and lawyer, holding prebends in London and the archdeaconry of Suffolk. His will was signed on 8 Nov. 1526 (Brewer iv. 2694), and his death must have followed quickly; for one of his prebends was filled up on 11 Nov., and on 12 Nov. Wolsey's son, Thomas Winter, received the archdeaconry of Suffolk.]

My most syngular good lorde,

In my right humble wyse I recommende me to your grace. And where as my Chauncellor[1] nowe attendyng vppon the same hathe by his writing sygnyfied to me that partely by synyster information yeven to your grace, and partely for that he hathe accepted and made clame and title to a pareshe churche and a prebend that Mr Dowman had, your grace hathe taken soo great displeasure ayenst hym that ye haue yeven hym iniunctions vppon right great penalties that he be contynewally attendyng vppon your grace, and in noo wyse to departe withowt your especyall licence: Yt may pleas your grace that as towching the sayd information I beseche your grace as humbly and as entierly as I can or may, that after your accustomed maner in causes of justice, yt may like you to here to gether my sayd Chauncellor and them that gave you the sayd information. And soo doyng I doubt not but that ye shall fynde my sayd Chauncellor to haue be soo indifferent, vpright and equale in all matiers concernyng his office in my jurisdiction spirituall, that he shalbe fownde with owt any reproche or wrong doyng to any persone. I ascertayn your grace that he hathe sufficient lernyng and experience for thexercyse of the charge that he hathe vndre me; he is also wyse, discrete, sadde and circumspecte in jugement*is* yeving. He hathe also good will, diligence and boldenes to doo his office. And in my pouer

[1] John Incent. Fox made him one of his executors. Later he was vicar-general to Wolsey in the diocese of Winchester, and in 1540 dean of St. Paul's; †a. 12 Sept. 1545.

opynyon there be not twoo within this shire that woll complayn of hym for any wrong that he hathe done in his office.

And as towching thacceptation of any title or clame makyng to the sayd twoo benefices that were Mr Dowmans, I doubt not but that my sayd Chauncellor woll at your commaundement not oonly shewe you his sayd titles and clames, but also be ordred in the same as it shall pleas your grace to moderate and commaunde. And if his sayd titles and clames shalbe sene to your grace to stande with good right and lawe, I doubt not but that for your vpright justice shewed to euery man in euery cause ye woll semblably be good and graciouse lorde to hym in his right. And if they be of none effecte, he must, and I doubt not woll, renownce them and make amend*is* to the parties that he did wrong to: wherwith I doubt not your grace wolbe well contented.

My most syngular good lorde, I may in noo wyse spare the absence of my sayd Chauncellor for the dayly exercise of my jurisdiction; and specially for the keping of my consistories, wherof the next shalbe the Saterday immediatly aftre the feste of Saint Andrewe,[2] and also for a visitation whiche I haue appoynted for certayn speciall causes to be in the newe College called Saint Marie College bysyd*is* Winchestre, in the weke next aftre the sayd feste of Saint Andrewe. For thies causes and consyderations I beseche your grace in my most entier and humble wyse to licence my sayd Chauncellor to retorne to me, soo that he may be with me at the sayd fest of Saint Andrewe. And if it shall soo be your pleasure, he may appere agayn before your grace in the terme of Saint Hillary to stande and obey your pleasure and commaundement; for my mynde and speciall desyre is that he shall make answere before your grace to all suche matiers as can be layd to his charge. My lorde, he is very honest, vertues, sadde and circumspecte, and as liberall hospitalitie kepeth as in myne opynyon any man of his

[2] 30 Nov.

degree dothe within this realme. And if he had be your seruaunt as long as he hathe be myne, and that ye had taken as good prove of hym as I haue done, I thinke ye wolde esteme and repute hym amongis the best.

Wherfor I beseche your grace as entierly and humbly as I can, to be good and graciouse lorde to hym, and to yeve hym licence to retorne to me, after the maner and forme as aboue is sayd. And I shall aftre myne olde maner dayly pray for your long lyfe with good helth and perpetuall prosperitie.

At my pouer house of Marwell the xvij^{th} day of Nouembre.

Your right humble preste and dayly bedeman

Ri. Wynton.

To my most syngular good lorde, my lorde Cardynall of Yorke, legate of Englonde and chauncellor of the same.

* 86. TO WOLSEY

RO. S. P. 1: 45, f. 95.   Marwell.
Brewer iv. 3623.   1 December ⟨1526⟩.

My most syngular good lorde,

In my right humble wyse I recommende me to your grace. And where as by my other lettres delyuered to your grace by Mr Paulet, I for certayn true and vrgent consyderations, as affectuously as I cowde or myght, besowght your grace to haue licented my Chauncellor, then and nowe by your estrait commaundement attendyng vppon you, to haue retorned to me agaynst the feste of Saint Andrewe nowe past; I haue vnderstande by my sayd Chauncellor that it hathe not as yet pleased your grace to releas your said estrait commaundement, and that he dothe yet attende vppon your grace, and soo must contynewe duryng your pleasure: whiche is to the great hynderance of dyuers causes and matiers concernyng my jurisdiction.

And forasmuche as the tyme of the sessyng of the subsydy graunted to the Kyngis grace by the clergie for this yere present is nowe at hande, that is to say betwixt this and Christemas, wherwith my sayd Chauncellor is soo well experte by reason of thexercyse therof for the three yeres past, that he can and shall make more spede in that behalf by the tyme of xv days then any other can or shall doo by the space of oon hole moneth, I, as entierly as I can or may, beseche your grace that for the spedy sessyng of the sayd subsydy, and for thexpedition of dyuers other causes beyng in his charge and apperteynyng to his office, yt may like you to licence hym to retorne to me as spedyly as may stande with your good pleasure.

My lorde, I thanke the good Lorde, my wytt and body serveth me as it dyd when I spake last with your grace; but yet I trust, my lorde, ye woll not thynke nor mynde that I shulde in myne owne persone ryde or travaill the contree this wynter season[1] for the sessyng of the sayd subsydy. And if your grace knewe howe diligent and profitable my sayd Chauncellor hathe be, not oonly in and abowt*is* the sayd subsydies but also abowt*is* the prest*is* that the Kyng*is* grace hathe had of the clergie, I make me well assured ye wolde adiuge hym to haue done the Kyng*is* grace right good service. The subsydyes that he hathe medled with for thies three yeres past hathe yerely be sessed before Christemas, and soone after levied and holy paid before all other; and soo I trust shalbe this yere, yf it shall pleas your grace to licence my said Chauncellor spedyly to retorne to me. I trust there is noo persone that hathe or woll complayn vppon hym; and if any suche be, and that it shall soo pleas your grace, ye may commaunde hym to appere before you the next terme to make answere to the sayd complaynt or complaynt*is*, if any suche be: albe it, my lorde, I trust your grace shall fynally fynde hym the same man that I shewed hym to be by my last lettres. And thus eftsones and as affectuously and as entierly as I can, and as my specyall trust is in your grace, I beseche you to be his good and graciouse lorde, and for the consyderations aboue rehersed to licence

[1] Cf. no. 59 n.

hym at this tyme to retorne to me. And I shall dayly pray for the contynewance of your long good helth with per-petuall prosperitie.

At my pouer house of Marwell the fyrst day of Decembre.

your humble preste and dayly bedeman

Ri. Wynton.

To my most syngular good lorde, my lorde Cardynall of Yorke, legate of Englonde and chauncellar of the same.

* 87. TO WOLSEY

RO. S. P. 1: 46, f. 126.   Winchester.
Brewer iv. 3815.   18 January ⟨1527⟩.

My most syngular good lorde,

In my right humble wyse I recommende me to your grace. And where I haue vnderstande, aswell by Maister Paulet as by my Chauncellar this berer, that at my humble sute made to your grace by my other lettres the last terme, it pleased the same to be the more benygne and graciouse to my sayd Chauncellar: in my best maner and as hartily as I can, I thanke your grace for the same. And in likewise I benseche you, my most syngular good lorde, to be of semblable contynewance toward*is* hym in tyme to come.

And where it pleased your grace to shewe to hym at his last beyng with you certayn mysdemeanour*is*, partely by me and partely by hym done within my dioces in matiers concernyng my jurisdiction, as ye were in that partie informed, trawthe it is, my lorde, that the religiouse women of my dioces be restrayned of theyre goyng owt of theyre monasteries. And yet soo muche libertie appereth some tyme to muche. And if I had the auctoritie and powre that your grace hathe, I wolde indever me to mure and inclose theyre monasteries accordyng to thordynance of the lawe. For otherwyse can be noo surtie of thobservance of good religion. And in all other matiers concernyng theyre lyvyng or observance of theyre religion, I assure your grace they be as liberally and favorably delt with as be any religiouse women within this ream.

And as for the religiouse men, they haue be put to lesse cost*is* and chargies in my days then other be, aftre the common maner of other ordynaries in theyre dioces. I neuer toke procurations of any of theym for all the visitations of my tyme, by the space of xxvj^th yeres. And to many of theym I haue shewed right great beneficence, and our Lorde be thanked, they be in good condition bothe in theyre spiritualties and temporalties.

And as for the secular clerck*is*, I haue not be rigorouse vppon theym in poneshement*is*, except it were for manyfest fornycation or advowtrey. And yet for theme they neuer dyd open penance to theyre noys or infamy. And also I neuer pryved *person* in noo dyoces that I haue be in.

And except it be in Suthwarcke, whiche is vnder the jurisdiction of tharchedecon, I trowe there be as litle oponly knowen synne or enorme crymes, bothe in *person*es spirituall and temporall, as is within any dioces of this realme. And if your grace haue any information of the contrary, I beseche your grace in the way of cheritie to shewe the same to my said Chauncellar, and God willyng it shalbe spedyly reformed. And I shall dayly pray as hartyly for your good helthe and perpetuall prosperitie as any chapellayn or preste belongyng to your self.

At Wynchestre the xviij^th day of January.

Your right humble preste and dayly bedeman

Ri. Wynton.

To my most syngular good lorde, my lorde Cardynall of Yorke, legate of Englonde, and chauncellar of the same.

88. FROM FISHER

De veritate, 1527, fº. C.   Rochester.

1527.

[The preface to Fisher's *De veritate corporis et sanguinis Christi in eucharistia* . . .
aduersus Iohannem Oecolampadium, Cologne, P. Quentell, March 1527: composed in prosecution of his controversies with the German and Swiss Re-
formers. The dedication was ostensibly suggested by the name of Fox's
new College; but Fisher's wish perhaps was by this demonstration of affection
to cheer and solace one who seemed, in his old age and comparative retirement, to have become quite undeservedly an object of attack from many sides
(see nos. 66, 82, 85, 87).

Fisher's emphatic protestation that his own success was due to Fox rather
than to the great patroness for whom he had worked so much at Cambridge
is remarkable.]

PLVRIMVM REVERENDISSIMO PATRI AC DOMINO, DOMINO
RICHARDO WINTONIENSI EPISCOPO IOHANNES ROFFENSIS S.P.

Circumspicienti mihi, cui libellum[1] quem his diebus De
veritate corporis et sanguinis Christi in eucharistia scripsi,
quanquam occurrerint alii complures, quibus et plurimum
obnoxius sum, neminem tamen repperi cui accommodatius
id ipsum facerem quam dominationi tuae, atque id quum
ob alias, tum ob duas potissimum causas. Nam quum ipse
Collegium satis magnificum Oxoniis maximoque sumptu
nuper ad studiosorum, et imprimis theologorum, vtilitatem
extrui curaueris, in quo bonae literae cuiusque generis
docentur, Hebraeae, Graecae, Latinae, et quicquid ad veram
theologiae eruditionem conferre valeat, ibidem a prae-
ceptoribus ad hoc ipsum ingenti mercede conductis dili-
gentissime traditur; quumque libuit ob deuotionem animi
quam peculiariter ad eucharistiae sacrum habes, et habuisti
semper, insignire Collegium ipsum titulo nominis eiusdem
(vocatur enim Collegium Corporis Christi): consentaneum
vtique visum fuit vt liber qui veritatem eiusdem corporis
in eucharistia tuetur, inscriberetur paternitati tuae, ne
frustra titulum huiusmodi videreris indidisse, si nulla
prorsus ei subesset veritas.

Istud sane me mouit plurimum. Atqui nihilominus et

[1] *sc.* dicarem.

aliud me vaehementer impulit: nempe quod quum nemini
mortalium me magis agnoscam debere quam tibi, non aliter
officio meo satisfacere videbar nisi munusculo quopiam,
licet tuis erga me meritis impari, testarer saltem me tuae
dominationis immemorem haudquaquam fuisse. Nam sic
a prima noticia dominatio tua me complexa fuerat, vt aura
tui fauoris non solum ad bonarum studia literarum verumetiam ad vitae probitatem ardentius amplectendum vaehementer accendebar. Adde quod Regi Henrico septimo, qui
tunc habenas regni summa prudentia moderabatur, principi
certe seculis omnibus atque id multis nominibus, vt alibi
diximus, admirando, meam paruitatem commendasti; vt
sola existimatione quam te[2] toties inculcante de me concepit,
et mero motu, quod aiunt, citra quoduis aliud obsequium,
citra cuiusquam preces, quod et mihi non semel affirmabat,
episcopatum Roffensem, cui iam indignus praesum, vltro
donauerit.[3]

Non desunt forte complures quibus creditum est geni-
tricem illius, nempe Comitem Richemondiae Derbiaeque,
foeminam eximiam et plane incomparabilem, haeramque
mihi multis rationibus charissimam, suis precibus a filio
dictum episcopatum impetrasse mihi. Verum longe aliter
sese res habet. Quod et tuae dominationi compertissimum
est, qui a secretissimis conciliis ipsi Regi fueras: quemadmodum et te, quamdiu per valetudinem aulam frequentare
licuit, vsus est et illustrissimus atque florentissimus rex
Henricus octauus, qui iam solium patris iustissima succes-
sione tenet.

Neque istud dixerim vt merita quibus me sibi iure
deuinctissimum egregia illa virago reddidit, imminuam
quouis pacto: nam erant sane maxima. Quod si nihil aliud
esset quam amor ille summus et syncerus, quo me prae
caeteris et sine fuco, quod et certissimum habeo, proseque-
batur: si nihil, inquam, aliud quam istud esset, quid tanto
et tam non vulgari amori tam spectatissimae principis inter
mortalia munera par existimari queat? Sed et praeter

---

[2] vt *cod.*   [3] in 1504.

X

amorem fuit etiam in me sane munificentissima. Nam etsi beneficium, quod vocant, ecclesiasticum nullum contulerit, non defuit ei studium, si quo modo rem nostram augere potuisset. Quod et non verbis solum verumetiam re ipsa comprobauit, quum alias, tum quando fuerat ab hac luce ad Christum migratura. Caeterum quum huius praestantissimae foeminae laudes oratione quadam funebri satis abunde prosecutus sim, licet nunquam satis de tam eximia singularique principe dici a quoquam poterit, hic tantum adiiciam, quod quum ipsa confessionis auricularis audiendae, pariter et instruendae vitae gratia, me sibi commonitorem asciuisset, ingenue fateor me plus ab eius egregiis virtutibus, quod ad probe viuendi institutum conducat, didicisse, quam vicissim illi communicarim vnquam.

Sed ad dominationem tuam redeo; cui, vt dixi, post Regem prudentissimum defunctum, omnia commoda quae mihi meisque suppetunt, ex hoc episcopatu me debere confiteor. Habeant licet alii prouentus pinguiores, ego tamen interim pauciorum animarum curam gero; adeo vt quum vtrorumque ratio reddenda fuerit, quod et propediem haud dubie futurum est, nec pilo meam sortem optarim vberiorem. Quare vel huius beneficii causa, vt de reliquis sileam (quae nec pauca sunt), aliquo xenio testari debueram quam essem tuae dominationi obstrictissimus.

Et ista sane me permouerunt vt librum hunc quem nuper aedidi, tuae reuerendae paternitati nuncuparim. Complectitur enim solidissimas et easdem, si me iudicium non fallat, ineuertibiles demonstrationes pro asserenda veritate corporis et sanguinis Christi. Quam veritatem Oecolampadius, licet alioqui literis clarus et ad nauseam vsque, quod aiunt, plenus, acriter et pluribus oppugnauit. Sed hoc vehementer imposuit homini, quod fidei tantum tribuat, vt eam vel solam cuique suffecturam asserat. Qua priscos etiam Iudaeos qui fideles erant, ita nobis aequat vt eosdem insertos Christo nihilominus arbitretur quam iam Christiani sint, neque nos verius edere carnem et sanguinem Christi quam fecerint illi; quum dicat Paulus, omnes eandem escam spiritalem manducasse, tam nos quam illos. Caeterum palam est eum non recte capere mentem Pauli; quum Paulus ibi tantum de spirituali manducatione loquutus fuerit, quae et fide fit; quemadmodum et hodie Christi corpus a multis editur, nempe spiritualiter solum, credentes in eucharistia verum Christum adesse, non autem sumentes corporaliter.

Ad illum modum haud dubie prisci fideles, priusquam Christus fuisset incarnatus, carnem Christi spiritualiter edebant in manna figuratam. Sed is esus non praestitit eis vt essent membra corporis Christi ex carne eius et ex ossibus eius, quod de nobis affirmat et testatur Paulus; neque enim tunc extiterant caro et ossa Christi, quum nondum esset Christus incarnatus. Quocirca nec adhuc erant ipsi prisci Iudaei membra corporis Christi ex carne eius et ex ossibus eius. Erant membra, fateor, corporis eius mystici per veram fidem. Nam hoc vera fides illis contulit, sicut et perfidia perfidis tribuit, vt membra fiant Satanae. Est enim et ipse caput impiorum omnium, sicut et piorum Christus. At vt impii non ita sunt ipsius Satanae membra vt sint ex carne eius et ex ossibus eius, quum nihil eiusmodi Satan habeat, ita nec prisci illi fideles ante Christi incarnationem erant membra corporis eius ex carne eius et ex ossibus eius, qualia nondum susceperat Dei verbum. Per esum ergo corporeum carnis et sanguinis Christi, nobis Christianis praestatur vt simus membra corporis eius ex carne eius et ex ossibus eius.

Quare falsum est quod sola fides ad hanc incorporationem sufficiat. Nectimur enimuero, non inficior, corpori Christi mystico per solam fidem. At nihilominus per esum corporis et sanguinis Christi multo altius et solidius incorporamur Christo quam fide sola. Quam rem nos abunde monstrauimus, non solum Irenaei, Chrysostomi, Damasceni, Cyrilli, Hilarii, caeterorumque priscorum theologorum assertionibus clarissimis, verumetiam apertissimis Scripturarum testimoniis. Quare plurimum interest inter Christianos, qui carne Christi tam spiritualiter quam corporaliter vescuntur, et priscos illos fideles qui Christi incarnationem praecesserant, qui spiritualiter duntaxat manducabant: id quod ex subsequentibus quoque nostris responsionibus clarius intelligere licebit.

Bene valebis, amantissime Pater, studiumque hoc erga te nostrum, quo libellum hunc nostrum nomini tuo nuncupamus, boni consules.

Ex Roffa M.D.XXVII.

*89. TO HENRY VIII

RO. S.P. 1: 47, f. 180.   Winchester.
Brewer iv. 4149.   7 April ⟨1527⟩.

[When the Legatine Court sat in July 1529 to examine the question of the Divorce, a statement was put in about an examination of Fox at Wolvesey on 5–6 April 1527 by Dr. Wolman, a cleric learned in the law, acting on the King's behalf. Fox had been closely attached to Henry VII since 1485, and had promoted the Spanish marriage. In 1527 he was one of the few survivors of those who had welcomed the young Princess in 1501. To the best of his ability he testified of what he had seen and known, though his memory did not always serve him. About his own age, he declared that he was then 79; and that he had known Henry VII for more than 41 years.

Fox's counsellors were excluded from the examination, and his statements were recorded by a single notary. At the end he was presented with a written paper containing his deposition and was asked to sign it. At first he declined on the ground of his blindness; but on learning that Wolman was instructed to sign it, if he himself would not, he gave way: see Brewer iv. 5791.

Next day, Sunday, he addressed this letter to the King; protesting that he had done his best, with his 'dull memory', to answer the questions put to him. His signature here bears out the statement of his blindness.]

Pleas it your grace, Syr. I haue by thand*is* of your right trusty counsailar Mr doctor Wolman receyved your most graciouse lettres, and also harde suche credence as it pleasede your highnes to commytte to hym concernyng the matier comprised in your said lettres. And accordyng to the commaundement of your said lettres and the said credence, I haue vppon the faithe and trawthe that I owe to your grace, and as farre as my poore wytte, my dull memory and my conscience, whiche shalbe my juge before God, faithfully and truly done and performed all that your grace commaunded by your said letteres, or that was requyred of me by vertue of the said credence: as dothe appere by the wrytyng*is* thervppon devysed, and at your commaundement with my hande subscribed; and as I doubt not the said Mr doctor shall more largely shewe to your grace. Besechyng the same always to contynewe my good and graciouse lorde, and in this cause and all other to haue graciouse consyderacion of my great age, blyndenes and lacke of good heryng. And I shall as faithfully and hartily dayly pray the good Lorde to sende your highnes as good lyfe and long, and as muche honour and prosperitie as euer had noble prynce reignyng vppon this royalme or any other.

　At Wynchestre the vii^th day of Aprile.

Your most humble subiecte
Ri. Wynton.

To the King*is* grace.

*90. TO THE DUKE OF NORFOLK

RO. S.P. 1: 47, f. 243.　　　　　　　　⟨Winchester?⟩
Brewer iv. 4200.　　　　　　　　　　　?

[The MS. has suffered much, on both sides and at the foot. The last line has only a few letters left, in the middle, which are not shown here; and the signature has disappeared. In addition to the secretary's address on the verso, there is a direction by another writer, perhaps an official of the Treasury: 'Too Thomas Stokys of the Receyte'.

　Brewer places this letter with one of the Lord Chamberlain to Wolsey, 25 April 1528, about a summons to Fox and 40 others to furnish footmen to accompany Wolsey to Guines; but the ground for connecting the two seems slight.]

Honorabyll and my moste speciall gode lorde,

　After humble recommendacion vnto your lordeshyp, please yt the same, I late / receyuyd fro owre souerayne lorde the Kynge hys honorabill letter to me directe for a prest of a hundred markes vn to / . . . . . ynday: the whyche by the credence of the same I shulde delyuer to your gode lordeshyp by owre ladyday of Assumpcion [1] / . . . .
. . . . there is no man within thys hys royalme of

<hr>

[1] 15 Aug.

my pore degre that ys of better wyll nor fayuer / . . . . . .
. . . . olde, yf yt myght lye in my power so
to do. My lorde, yt ys evidently and notary knowyn / I
haue hadde gre⟨te char⟩ges and costys now late in Suthwerk
in byldyng and repayreng of my ruynose howses and /
lyvelode there, ⟨that⟩ myght no lenger haue ben differryd:
whiche ys nott yet fully fynysshyd ne remade. Also I haue /
now in honde meche gretter charge in bildyng and kepyng
vpp of my churche of Hyde,[2] and haue hadde thys ɪj yerys /
paste and more, and so dayly yett moste haue, I can nott
sey how long: the whyche and yt shulde be defferyde now,
ys / of lykelyhode to fall. The whyche Almyghty Godde
defende; for and yt dude, yt were to me, my couent and
succe⟨ssors / to moche ⟨and grete ch⟩arge, and neuer in
owre powers to performe and bere the charges thereof, and
many othere gre⟨te and extra / ordinary ⟨cost*is* whiche I⟩
haue also dayly.

    Wherefor I humbly and with all my herte beseche and
pray your gode ⟨lordeshyp / to consider these premysses,
and to be speciall gode lorde and means to the Kyngis gode
gra⟨ce . . . . / peraduenture ⟨on the⟩se
behalfe, that yt may please hys sayde gode grace to amytte
and accept ⟨this prest of xʟ marcs . . . . / of . . . . .
. . . . now to me g⟨eue⟩ grete charge, Godde knowytht.
Whyche xʟ marcs I se⟨nde vn to your gode lordeshyp /
by m⟨y Chauncellar, to wh⟩om I pray it may please your
gode lordeshyp to geve full ⟨credence.

    / And ⟨. . . . . I shall⟩ pray to allmyghtye
Godde for your gode prosperite and lenge li⟨fe.

    To my right honorabill and m⟨oste / speciall gode lorde,
my lorde Tresorer of Englonde.

   [2] A Benedictine house founded c. 900 as New Minster, ɴ. of the Cathedral:
removed c. 1110 to Hyde, in the ɴ. part of the city.

‡91. FROM WILLIAM HAWLES AND
THOMAS COKE

Corpus MS.   Lincoln's Inn, London.
                                            7 November ?

[This letter was found, since we began, by Dr. and Mrs. Milne among some
papers about Temple Guiting (no. 62), in a mass of miscellaneous documents
nearly filling a great oak chest, which till recently was in the Clerk's office,
now the Junior Common Room. In spite of three locks the chest had been
standing open, perhaps for centuries; but it seemed as though the documents
had not been disturbed for a long time.

We have not been able to trace the lands concerned nor to assign a year-
date. Richard Lee was clerk of the Council in 1516 (Brewer ii. 1857).
Hawles was in the commission for Hampshire in Oct. 1523, being then
resident in Lincoln's Inn (no. 79). The Wayte family of Hampshire appears
in no. 78.

The letter is only a draft; from which a fair copy was no doubt made for
dispatch. The handwriting is the same throughout, apparently that of Coke;
except that each writer signs his own name, in an unusual arrangement. At
the foot of the page is the following distich, perhaps in Claymond's hand:

Hunc ludum hasque aedes erexit Wintoniensis

Foxus pro pueris: $\begin{cases} \text{gratia sit Domino} \\ \text{gloria sit superis} \end{cases}$.

On the verso a contemporary hand has written 'A lettre writing to Bishop
Foxe'.]

Pleasith it your good lordship that this last Fryday Mr Lee,
clerke of the Councell, and we gaue attendance for William
Wayte, and he apperid not. Whefore this Saturday, if he
appere not, we entend with your councell to call for a
atachement ayenst hyme.

And apon Thursday last past the Priour of Henton,
Mr Norwiche and Mr Shelley and we assembled at the
Blake Freres in London: wher apon the sight of the seid
Priour's euydenc*is* it is thought by the seid Norwyche and
Shelley for the suertie of the lond to be hadd to your good
lordshipp, that Thomas Snygge shall by indenture bargayn
and sell the lond to your good lordshipp and your heires,
and then the seid Snygge to make a feoffement to such
persons as your lordshipp will name, and then the old
feoffees and the seid Priour vnder his couent seale to relese

to the new feoffees, and the seid new feoffees to recouer ayenst the seid Snygge, and then they to graunte an annuite accordyng to the endenture.

From Lyncolnes Inne the vij day of Nouember

by your seruauntis in hast

William   Thomas
Haweles,   Coke.

APPENDIX I
LETTERS NOT INCLUDED HERE

1. From the Lady Margaret	March 1488	(Batten p. 21).
2. To Innocent VIII	12 Nov. 1488, London	(SP. Venice i. 542).
3. From Claymond	⟨1510–11, Oxford⟩	
4. To Claymond	⟨1511–12⟩	Corpus MS. 280:
5. From Balliol College	⟨c. 1511, Oxford⟩	see below.
6. From John Newland	⟨a. 1515, Bristol⟩	
7–12. From Leo X	4 Jan., 8 Feb., 19 Feb., 20 April, 26 Sept., 31 Oct. 1514, Rome	(Brewer i. 2559 etc.).

The Corpus MS. 280 contains a number of miscellaneous extracts in the handwriting of the well-known antiquary Brian Twine, Scholar 1594, Fellow 1605, † 1644. On f. 201 v⁰ begin some 'Excerpta ex Reiectaneis Coll. Corp. Christi in Vniuersitate Oxon., scilicet in capsula Reiectaneorum &c. in Archiuis': evidently notes of personal letters 'rejected', as 'trash papers' from the legal documents and letters about the landed property, which were then regarded as the only important part of the College Archives.

The first letter which is of interest here is one from Bryan Higdon to Claymond, 21 April ⟨1511⟩, Rome, which mentions at the end 'that Mr Stokesley ⟨no. 69 n⟩ is at Rome and studieth Greeke effectually'. Then follow letters 3 to 6 of this appendix; and further on Twine copies extracts from nos. 61, 23, 33, 22, 69.

3. FROM CLAYMOND

f. 201 v⁰.   ⟨Magdalen College, Oxford⟩
                                              ⟨1510–11⟩

[Carter was Vice-president of Magdalen in 1510–11. It seems likely that 'another letter' is no. 23; and that that year-date must therefore be corrected.]

Jo. Claymond, then president of Magdalen College, his letter to the Founder, for a decision of a great styrre that was then amongest them: and it seemes to haue byn this, *An aliquis possit eligere seipsum*. It appeares by Mr Bryan Higdon's letter written from Rome to Mr Claymond, that Mr Claymond had written to him to Rome to knowe the

Y

opinion of the court of Rome about that question; to whom
amonge other thinges the sayd Bryan Higdon returneth this
answer from Rome, that if a man shoulde but aske such
a question of learned men in that court, they would repute
him at *fatuum*, to doubt of it &c. Romae 26 August.

The question was betwixt one Mr Carter, vice-president,
and the President. By another letter it appeareth that the
President had the better.

4. TO CLAYMOND

f. 202.   ?

1511–12.

[Ant. Wilkyns was Fellow of New College in 1510, †1514. For Barnacke
see no. 36.]

The Founder's letter to Mr Claymond in the behalfe
of one Antony Wilkyns, a scholler of Newe College, whom
the Founder maynetayned there &c. In his letters to him,
beinge then President of Magdalen College, and afterwardes
when he was President of Corpus Christi, he still greeteth
him by the name of 'Brother Mr President'; and so he
doth the Warden of Newe College. This was about aᵒ.
Henr. 8ⁱ. 3ᵒ, as it appeareth there by an acquittance. Radᵘˢ.
Barnacke, socius coll. B. Marie Wynton, was his Tutor.

5. FROM BALLIOL COLLEGE

f. 202.   Oxford.

⟨c. 1511⟩

[L. Huchynson of Balliol inc. 30 June 1511.]

A letter from the Mr and Fellowes of Baylioll College
in Oxon to Rich. Foxe, bishop of Wynton, that whereas
it had pleased him to allowe to Mr Rich. Stubbys and
Inceptor Hutchenson 4ₗₗ by the yiere for the erudition of his
poore schollers there, they might receaue it: with request
to knowe his lordship's minde for the further continuance
thereof &c.

6. FROM JOHN NEWLAND

f. 202.   ⟨Bristol⟩
                                                    ⟨a. 12 June 1515⟩
[For Abbot Newland see no. 50 introd.]

A letter of John, abbat of St. Austyns, to the Founder for the c^{ll}. which he promised to lend him for the vse of their poore monastery &c. In dorso it appeareth that the money was paid by Jo. Claymond and deliured to my lord of Wynton's chaplaine, Mr Stokesley.

APPENDIX II

BOOKS AT AUCKLAND, 1499

[A list of books transferred at Fox's order, possibly his gift, to the new Dean of the collegiate church of Bishop Auckland: copied into Fox's Durham register, f. 26 v⁰. Theology and Law are preponderant. The Classics are represented by Cicero (with a quite modern commentary, no. 11, by Petrus Marsus, c. 1430–1509), Silius Italicus and Boethius. Three of the books, nos. 15, 17, 42, are printed. The words '2⁰. fo.', which occur in almost every case before the 'probatory words', are omitted here after the first entry.

The list is printed by J. Raine, *Wills and Inventories of the Northern Counties* (Surtees Society), 1835, pp. 101–3.]

Hec indentura facta xx^{mo}. die mensis Iulii anno domini millesimo cccc^{mo}. nonagesimo nono et anno translationis domini Ricardi Dunolmensis episcopi quinto, inter venerabilem virum magistrum Willelmum Thomeson in sacra theologia bacallarium, decanum ecclesie siue capelle collegiate infra manerium de Auckeland Episcopi situate ex vna parte, et Robertum Dykar clericum siue custodem registri dicti domini Ricardi Dunolmensis episcopi ex altera parte, testatur quod idem venerabilis vir magister Willelmus Thomeson, decanus predictus, recepit et habuit die confectionis presentium de dicto Roberto Dykar, de et ex mandato dicti domini Ricardi Dunolmensis episcopi, omnes et singulos libros subscriptos pro vsu, commodo et vtilitate dicte ecclesie siue capelle collegiate predicte ac in libraria eiusdem perpetuis futuris temporibus remanendos et saluum custodiendos. In quorum omnium et singulorum fidem et

testimonium partes predicte alternatim sigilla sua hiis inden-
turis apposuerunt. Dat*um* mense die et anno predict*is*.

In primis T*extus* Biblie cum exposicione   2°. fo.
     domini Nicholai de Lira in quatuor   *Nolui*
     voluminibus

Secundum volumen   *erit sacerdos*

Volumen tercium in quo cont*inentur* libri
     prophet*arum*, Isaie, Iheremie, Treno-
     rum, Baruch, Ezechiel*is*, Danyell*is*,
     Osie, Ioelis, Amos, Abdie, Ione, etc.

iiij^tum volumen iiii^or Euangelistarum,
     Mathei, Marci etc.

Liber Sentenc*iarum* cum tabula secundum
     ordinem librorum   *quare pater*

Vocabular*ius* communis super Bibli.
     vocat*us* Num tre   *mediam et super sacram*

Scripture in vniuersali ecclesia vsitate
Distinctiones cum ceter*is* content*is*
     theologie   *distinct' in terr'*

5 Sermones discipuli de tempore et de
     sanctis et Promptuar*ium* eiusdem cum
     tabul*a* conuenien*ti*   *corpus Philippi de Pergamo*

Speculum regiminis anime.

Catho morolo.   *a veritate*

Sermones dominicales per annum et de
     sanctis   *est de propriis*

Boicius de consolatione cum comment*o*
     et tabul*a* in pergameno   *Relatione*

10 Tabula ex*empl*orum   *laborare*

Petri Marci interpretacio in Offic*ia* Cice-
     ronis   *Sed eciam*

Epistole Ciceronis cum commento   *qui cum imperio*
et Cilius Ytalicus super bella Punica in
     eodem libro   *orare fatali*

Sermones de Litio de laudibus sanctorum   *de nobilitate*

15 Item Boicius impressus de consolacione
     philosophie cum commentar*io*

Sanctus Thomas   *vera securitas*
Item Boicius de disciplina scolarium.   *quare*
   Opus est cum commento et est im-
   press*um*
Tractatus fratris Egidii de peccato origi-
   nali   *secundum hec*
Epistole Lilij quas Correcto*rias* vocant   *hiis epistolis*
20 Concordancie Bibl*ie* et Canonum et tocius
   iuris canonici   *orilegium sapientie*
De vilitate condicionis humane   *parabolice*
Liber pergameni ligatus in asseribus, di-
   uersos libros continens:
  in primis Kalendar*ium*
  secundo Manuale   *dominical' et c.*
Exposicio beati Augustini de Sermone
   in Monte   *diligatis*
Decreta cum glosa Bartholomei Brexensis   *naturalem*
25 Decretales Gregorian*e* cum glosa Ber*nardi*   *60*
Liber sextus cum glosa Iohannis A*ndree*   *extollit*
Liber Clement*is* cum glosa Io. An.   *vt fertur*
Alius liber Clement*is* cum glosa Iohannis
   An. et cum glosa Willelmi de Monte
   Haudino[1]   *clement'*
Item in eodem libro, Constituciones
   dominorum Othon*is* et Otobon*i* cum
   glosa Iohannis de Atona   *glose qui c*
30 Item dominus Innocencius super quinto
   libro Decretalium   *in medico*
Item Willelmus in speculo in tribus
   voluminibus:
  prima pars domini Willelmi Durant in
   Speculo   *accessor'*
  secunda pars domini Willelmi Durant in
   Speculo   *nunt*
  tercia et quarta pars domini Willelmi
   sub vno volumine   *possum*

       [1] *sc.* Lauduno.

Item Reportorium vtriusque iuris reuerendi patris domini Petri Brixensis
episcopi: *scriberes part*
secunda pars et vltima Reportorii vtrius-
que iuris reuerendi patris domini Petri
Brixensis episcopi   *temporalibus*
Item Constituciones secundum vsum
Cantuariensis prouincie cum glosa
Willelmi Sherwode in pergameno   *sub specie sacri*
Summarium textuale et Conclusiones
super Clementinas in eodem libro
cum tabula titulorum   *in dei*
35 Domini Panormitani Practica de modo
procedendi in iudicio
Ars inueniendi themata
Vocabularius vtriusque iuris   *vt in iuribus*
Dominus Willelmus Durant speculator
super Reportorium aureum cum casibus tocius iuris, in quibus casibus
aliquis est ipso facto suspensus   *sciendum quoque*
Exposiciones siue Declarationes vtrius-
que iuris titulorum   *in nomine*
40 Item liber Belial et Constituciones Cant'
in pergameno   *cum tant' veloci"*
Domini Digni super regulas iuris   *cum ad regulam*
Ortus sanitatis impressus et ligatus:
primus tractatus eiusdem de herbis   *effundere aquam*
secundus tractatus de animalibus   *confert palpita*
tercius tractatus de auibus   *Achant'*
quartus tractatus de piscibus   *aque elimento*
quintus de lapidibus   *alabandina*
sextus de vrinis   *corol' primum*
43 Liber Iuniani Maii vocabulorum secun-
dum ordinem alphabeticum   *abigere*

APPENDIX III

*FOX'S WILL

Corpus MS.

Marwell.

15 February 152⅞.

[This document is in the handwriting of the notary who attests it, William Browne; signed by Fox and witnessed by five persons, who also subscribe. For the last four letters of his signature Fox's wandering pen appears to have been guided by a firmer hand: the same feature appears later in the foundation-deed of Grantham, which he signed three days before his death. As Dr. Fowler points out, this document disposes only of Fox's residuary property: much having already been given to his various foundations and his friends.

Two days earlier than this, on 13 Feb., Fox had signed, more firmly, the final draft of his Statutes; copied out by Robert Warmyngton, admitted 9 Aug. 1517, Fellow 1522, whose hand, entering admissions, appears also in the *Liber Admissorum* i, ff. 10–17, 1528–34. The Statutes, which are still in the possession of the College, were also attested by Browne; with Incent, Coren, Stokley, and Burton present, but not subscribing.

Fox died at Wolvesey on 5 Oct., and was buried in his cathedral the same day.]

Quoniam vanum fragile et transitorium est huius vite curriculum, neque (vt ait Apostolus) habemus hic ciuitatem manentem, sed aliam inquirimus celestem, ego igitur Ricardus, Winton*iensis* ecclesie (licet indignus) episcopus et minister, ad dictam ciuitatem festinans atque ex Dei gratia, non meis meritis, in eam ingredi sperans, manifeste perspiciens quod paucitas dierum meorum finietur breui, sequutus consilium prophete ad Ezechiam dicentis, 'Dispone domui tue, quia morieris': In nomine sancte et indiuidue Trinitatis, Patris et Filii et Spiritus Sancti, vnius Dei, decreui tam pro sepultura putidi cadaueris mei quam de bonis a Deo mihi donatis ordinare et disponere in modum qui sequitur.

In primis, si contingat me mori in palacio de Woluesay vel in Hospitali sancte Crucis citra meridiem alicuius diei, tunc volo quod corpus meum aliqua hora eiusdem diei pomeridiana sepeliatur in capella quam adhoc ordinaui intra ecclesiam sancti Swithuni. Si vero contingat me mori in predicto palacio seu hospitali post meridiem alicuius diei, tunc volo quod corpus meum, si ita fieri possit, eodem die deferatur ad ecclesiam predictam et deponatur in choro eiusdem, ibidemque remaneat vsque in crastinum, et tunc sepeliatur in loco antedicto: alioquin in crastino deferatur ad ecclesiam predictam, et ibidem sepeliatur ante meridiem eiusdem diei.

Et quoad luminaria, volo quod de centum torchetis que modo habeo prompta et parata, quinquaginta sint accendenda et expendenda circa delationem corporis mei ad ecclesiam predictam et ad exequias illo die faciendas: reliqua vero quinquaginta ad missam et alia officia sequentis diei facienda. Voloque quod reliquie dictorum torchetorum remaneant sacriste sancti Swithuni. Volo insuper quod vnusquisque eorum qui portabit aliquod ex dictis torchetis, habeat duos solidos per manus executorum meorum; ita quod seruientes mei domestici preferantur. Item volo quod quilibet sacerdos secularis illo die occurrens et celebrans missam in ecclesia cathedrali sancti Swithuni, die quo celebrabitur principalis missa pro anima mea, habeat per manus executorum meorum duodecim denarios.

Si vero contingat me mori in aliquo alio loco extra dictum palacium de Wolvesay et Hospitale sancte Crucis, tunc volo quod corpus meum deferatur ad ecclesiam cathedralem predictam, et modo antedicto sepeliatur, quamprimum commode possit; ita tamen quod non remaneat inhumatum vltra duos dies. Et in illo casu augeantur torcheta et alie expense funerales secundum discretionem dictorum executorum meorum. Et volo quod quilibet sacerdos adueniens ad locum vbi continget me sic mori, et ibidem celebrans missam antequam corpus meum ad dictam cathedralem deferatur ecclesiam, habeat duodecim denarios per manus executorum meorum.

Item quanquam arbitror me sufficienter reparasse et in bono statu reliquisse omnia mea, ecclesias, castra, maneria, et alias domos et loca illis pertinentia, attamen si contingat reuerendissimum dominum Cardinalem Eboracensem, legatum Anglie, immediate mihi in hoc episcopatu Winton*iensi* succedere, tunc volo quod predictus reuerendissimus Cardinalis habeat sub condicione sequenti quingentas marcas in pecunia numerata per manus executorum meorum; preter et vltra nonnulla aulea specificata in primis duabus separatis particulis inuentarii bonorum meorum de dato presentium et manu mea subscript*i*, et futuro successori meo per idem inuentarium, videlicet in finibus dictarum duarum particularum, expresse relicta; et preter et vltra certas particulares pecias vasorum argenteorum, quorum quedam sunt in toto deaurata, quedam vero in parte deaurata, et quedam omnino alba, in predicto etiam inuentario apertius specificata et ad quingentas marcas per me estimata, et similiter futuro successori meo per idem inuentarium relicta. Quorum quidem vasorum nonnulla ad vsum hospitii mei remanent in manibus officiariorum cellarie mee, quedam in manibus officiariorum aquarie, quedam vero in manibus officiariorum panetrie ⟨et⟩ clericorum coquine; prout magis no⟨minatim / et specifice apparet per quasdam indenturas inter ipsos officiarios et magistrum Rogerum Stokley, thesaurarium camere mee, respec⟨tiue / factas.

Que quidem omnia et singula predicta idem reuerendissimus dominus Cardinalis habeat sub ea condicione, et non aliter ⟨neque / alio modo, quod gratiosus sit et beneuolus meis executoribus, et vt priusquam predictam summam quingentarum marcarum vel a⟨liquam / partem eiusdem, aut dicta aulea vel aliquam partem eorundem, aut dicta vasa argentea vel aliquod eorundem, recipiat, generalem acqu⟨ie/tantiam faciat et tradat dictis executoribus meis pro omnibus et omnimodis actionibus, querelis et demandis, quas contra eos vel eor⟨um / aliquem ratione administrationis bonorum meorum tunc habeat vel quoquo modo habere possit.

Sin vero aliquem alium quam reuerendissimum dominum Cardinalem et legatum antedictum mihi immediate in dicto episcopatu succedere contingat, tunc volo quod idem talis success⟨or / habeat aulea et vasa argentea predicta et nihil amplius: sub ea tamen condicione, et non aliter neque alio

z

modo, quod sit beneuolus exec⟨u/toribus meis, et vt priusquam predicta aulea aut vasa argentea seu aliquam partem
eorundem recipiat, generalem acquietantiam faciat et
trad⟨at/ executoribus meis pro omnibus et omnimodis
actionibus, querelis et demandis, quas contra eos vel eorum
aliquem ratione ad⟨minis/trationis bonorum meorum tunc
habeat vel quoquo modo habere possit.

Et quoniam, vt predixi, testante conscientia mea nullam
scio vel intelligo esse dilapidationem aut ruinam notabilem
in ecclesiis, castris, maneriis, aliisue edificiis ad dictum
meum episcopatum pertinentibus, in visceribus Iesu Christi
obsecro obtestorque successorem meum, quicunque futurus
sit, vt sola antedicta mea legatione sit contentus, nihil
amplius a meis executoribus exigens, sed eosdem ab omni
molestia et vexatione liberos et immunes esse permittat;
sicut mihi in illo die ire, calamitatis et miserie coram summo
Iudice et eodem equissimo respondere voluerit. Ad quem
nu⟨n⟩c pro iniuria, si qua postea contra hoc meum testamentum et voluntatem vltimam et eiusdem executionem per
successorem meum inferatur, prouoco et appello, de eius
iusta et seuera sententia nullo modo dubitans.

Preterea lego illustrissimo viro Henrico Courteneye,[1]
marchioni Exon*iensi*, aulea mea vocata 'Le Hercules', continentia nouem pecias, prout planius exprimuntur in dicto
inuentario bonorum meorum, preter et vltra vnum salinum
aureum cum coopertorio in antedicto inuentario specifica-
tum et etiam legatum eidem.

Item lego nobilissimo viro Willelmo Sand*is*, domino de
Sand*is*, camerario regio, aulea mea Anglice vocata 'Le
Vyneyerd*is*', continentia decem pecias, prout planius exprimuntur et specificantur in inuentario predicto, preter et
vltra quendam lectum cum apparatu eiusdem, vt in predicto
manifestatur inuentario.

Item lego predilecto mihi Willelmo Paulett, militi, aulea
mea Anglice vocata 'Le Grisell', continentia quatuor pecias,
vna cum duabus peciis de sancto Iob, prout in dicto

[1] See no. 44 n.

inuentario apertius exprimuntur et specificantur. Cui etiam
donaui quendam lectum cum apparatu eiusdem, vt in predicto manifestatur inuentario.

Item do et lego cuilibet executorum meorum summam
viginti librarum. Nonnulla autem alia bona mea per me
data legata vel aliter disposita clare et aperte exprimuntur
in dicto inuentario bonorum meorum remanentium in
custodia magistri Rogeri Stokley, thesaurarii camere mee.
Que quidem sic per me data, legata vel disposita et in dicto
inuentario expressa eandem virtutem et vigorem in iure
habere volo quam haberent si essent per presens testamentum meum data, legata vel disposita; reliqua vero bona mea
neque per presens testamentum meum neque in dicto inuentario neque aliquo alio modo per me data legata vel
aliter disposita, siue in dicto inuentario contineantur siue
non, vendantur per executores meos; et pecunie prouenientes
de precio eorundem distribuantur per executores meos pre-
dictos intra vnum annum obitum meum proximo sequentem,
inter tales qui temporibus vite mee fuerunt tenentes mei
in aliquo dominiorum episcopatus mei Winton*iensis* infra
comitatum Sowth*ampton* et balliuatum de Dounton in
comitatu Wilts; illos videlicet tenentes qui secundum discretionem executorum meorum temporibus huiusmodi dis-
tributionum inueniantur maxi⟨m⟩e pauperes et egentes.

Executores autem huius mei testamenti constituo et
ordino dominum Willelmum Paulett, militem, magistrum
Ioannem Claimond, presidentem Collegii Corporis Christi in
Vniuersitate Oxon*iensi*, magistrum Iohannem Incent,[1] custodem Hospitalis sancte Crucis, cancellarium meum, magistros
Willelmum Disney et Leonellum Norris, armigeros, et
magistrum Rogerum Stokley, thesau⟨ra/rium camere mee.

Superuisores vero huius mei testamenti facio et constituo
prefatum dominum Merchionem Exon*iensem* et dominum
de San⟨dis,/ camerarium regium; eosdem intime obsecrans
obtestansque pro mutua dilectione que inter nos longo
tempore est habita, vti dictis executoribus meis assistant,

[1] See no. 85 n.

quatenus hoc testamentum meum in singulis particulis
inuiolabiliter obseruetur, ⟨et/ impedientibus summopere
obsistant. In quorum omnium et singulorum premissorum
fidem et testimonium, quoniam ob cecitatem oculorum
meorum pre⟨sens / testamentum meum legere non potui,
idem presens testamentum meum scribendum et postea
coram me (etiam audiente) legendum magistro Will⟨elmo /
Browne, notario publico, demandaui; nomenque meum
propria manu subscripsi et sigillo meo consignaui, in presentia dicti notarii, et mag⟨istri / Oliueri Coren, sacre
theologie professoris, confessoris mei, Nicholai Harpisfeld,[1]
decretorum doctoris, commissarii mei, magistri Gilberti
Burto⟨n, in / decretis baccalaurei, secretarii mei, domini
Iohannis Lambert, capellani, et Ioannis Rufford, generosi,
ad hoc specialiter vocatorum, rogatorum at⟨que / sub-
scriben*tium*, in cubiculo manerii mei de Marwell decimo
quinto die mensis Februarii anno domini millesimo q⟨uin-
gen/tesimo vicesimo septimo, indictione prima, pontificatus
sanctissimi in Christo patris et domini nostri domini Cle-
mentis, diuina prouidentia illius nominis Pape septimi, anno
quinto, et translationis mee anno vicesimo septimo, et anno
regni regis Henrici octaui decimo nono.

Ri. Wynton.

per me Oliuerum Coren suprascriptum
per me Nicolaum Harpisfeld predictum
per me Gilbertum Burton suprascriptum
per me Iohannem Lambert supranomina⟨tum
per me Iohannem Rufford prescript⟨um

Et ego Willelmus Browne, Couen. et Lich. dioc. publicus sacra auctoritate
apostolica notarius, quia suprascripti testamenti factioni, lectioni, publica-

[1] No doubt an elder kinsman of the author of the *Historia Anglicana
ecclesiastica*. The younger Nicholas records in the *Historia*, Douay, 1622,
p. 644, that as a Winchester schoolboy he was present at Fox's burying.

tioni, et voluntatis sue declaracioni, atque suorum et eiusdem testamenti executorum nominationi et constitucioni, ceterisque premissis, dum sic, vt prescribitur, dictis die et anno per prefatum reuerendum in Christo patrem ac dominum, dominum Ricardum permissione diuina Winton*iensem* episcopum, agebantur et fiebant, vnacum prenominatis testibus presens personaliter interfui, eaque omnia et singula sic fieri vidi et audiui. Et ideo hoc presens testamentum, manu mea propria de mandato dicti reuerendi patris scriptum, sigillo et subscriptione dicti reuerendi patris de visu meo signatum subscriptum et munitum, subscripsi, publicaui et in hanc publicam formam redegi, signoque et nomine meis solitis et consuetis vna cum subscriptione testium supranominatorum signaui, rogatus et requisitus, in fidem et testimonium omnium et singulorum premissorum.

INDEX OF CORRESPONDENTS

GENERAL INDEX

[For places from which letters are written see the Table of Letters, pp. 1–3. Documents which appear in Brewer are not fully indexed here.]

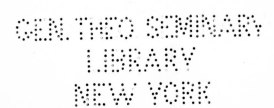

INDEX OF WORDS

PRINTED IN GREAT BRITAIN AT THE UNIVERSITY PRESS, OXFORD
BY JOHN JOHNSON, PRINTER TO THE UNIVERSITY

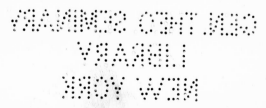